VOLUM

ALIGNING
WITH THE
APOSTOLIC

AN ANTHOLOGY OF APOSTLESHIP

APOSTLES AND APOSTOLIC MOVEMENT
IN THE SEVEN MOUNTAINS OF CULTURE

DR. BRUCE COOK
GENERAL EDITOR

Cover Design: Wendy K. Walters with James L. Nesbit

Interior Formatting: Wendy K. Walters

Published By KINGDOM HOUSE PUBLISHING | LAKEBAY, WASHINGTON, USA

Scripture quotations marked (AMP) are taken from the Amplified® Bible, Copyright © 1954, 1958, 1962, 1964, 1965, 1987 by The Lockman Foundation, La Habra, CA. Used by permission. All rights reserved.

Scripture quotations marked (KJV) are taken from the King James Version of the Bible ®, Copyright © 1982 by Broadman & Holman Publishers, Nashville, TN. Used by permission. All rights reserved.

Scripture quotations marked (MSG) are taken from The Message ®. Copyright © 1993, 1994, 1995, 1996, 2000, 2001, 2002. Used by permission of NavPress Publishing Group. Colorado Springs, CO. All rights reserved.

Scripture quotations marked (NIV) are taken from the HOLY BIBLE, NEW INTERNATIONAL VERSION®, NIV®. Copyright © 1973, 1978, 1984, 2011 Biblica, Inc™. Grand Rapids, MI. Used by permission of Zondervan. All rights reserved worldwide. www.zondervan.com The "NIV" and "New International Version" are trademarks registered in the United States Patent and Trademark Office by Biblica, Inc™.

Scripture quotations marked (NKJV) are taken from the New King James Version (NKJV) of the Bible. Copyright © 1982 by Thomas Nelson, Inc., Nashville, Tenn. Used by permission. All rights reserved.

Scripture quotations marked (JBP) are taken from the J.B. Phillips Version of the New Testament. Copyright © 1958, 1972 by G. Bles, London, England (UK). Used by permission. All rights reserved.

Scripture quotations marked (ESV) are from The Holy Bible, English Standard Version® (ESV®), copyright © 2001 by Crossway, a publishing ministry of Good News Publishers. Used by permission. All rights reserved.

Scripture quotations marked (CSB) are taken from the Holy Bible: Holman Christian Standard Bible. Nashville, TN: Holman Bible Publishers, 2004. Revised in 2009. Used by permission. All rights reserved.

Scripture quotations marked (NASB) are taken from the NEW AMERICAN STANDARD BIBLE®, Copyright © 1960,1962,1963,1968,1971,1972,1973,1975,1977,1995 by The Lockman Foundation. Used by permission. All rights reserved.

Scripture quotations marked (NLT) are taken from the Holy Bible, New Living Translation, copyright © 1996, 2004, 2007 by Tyndale House Foundation. Used by permission of Tyndale House Publishers, Inc., Carol Stream, IL 60188. All rights reserved.

To contact the Publisher or General Editor, call 253-858-8929 or text 512-845-3070, or email kingdomhousepublishing@gmail.com, or Skype: wbcook1, or visit:

www.KingdomHouse.net | www.KEYSnetwork.org
www.GloryRealm.net | www.VentureAdvisers.com

DEDICATION

TO THE CHIEF APOSTLE: JESUS, THE ONLY-BEGOTTEN SON OF GOD

(John 3:16-18, John 14:6, Rom. 8:32,
Rom. 10:9-13, 1 John 4:9-15)

*"Therefore, holy brothers, who share in the heavenly calling,
fix your thoughts on Jesus, the apostle and high
priest whom we confess."*
(Heb. 3:1, NIV)

AND TO THE NEXT GENERATION OF APOSTLES –

We Invite You to Stand Upon Our Shoulders

ACKNOWLEDGMENTS

Thanks to all those who helped to make this book series possible, especially all of the Contributing Authors who wrote and submitted chapters. I was constantly encouraged and amazed by your grace, wisdom, humility and Christlikeness throughout this lengthy process, and by your willingness to allow the Holy Spirit to use you without asking to see a list of other contributors or my chapter titles, or without having an assigned topic, or without any thought of compensation. This show of unity and solidarity and oneness in spirit by the apostolic community is both remarkable and commendable, and in some ways, unprecedented. Thanks for trusting your stories, articles, essays and chapters to my care, and for trusting the Jesus in me. This book series, and the world, will be better because of each of you courageous 70 Kingdom leaders.

I would also like to thank my prayer teams and intercession leaders for covering me and this project in prayer for the past nine months while the research, writing, editing, formatting and design were underway. They include Michelle Seidler and the Samuel Company team of prophetic intercessors, and Jon Grieser and the K.E.Y.S. team of apostolic-prophetic intercessors. I also thank my wife, Caroline, for her support and intercession during this lengthy process. Next, I want to thank my spiritual covering, Apostle Mark Henderson, and his wife, Prophet Susan (Suzi) Henderson for their friendship, support, example, prayers and prophecies over the last 11 years. Thanks for seeing the gold in me that needed to be refined, and looking past the dross. Thanks also for inviting me into spiritual leadership on the local church level, for imparting and activating spiritual gifting, and for investing yourselves into my wife and me and our callings, and helping us to birth K.E.Y.S., along with so many others in the body of Christ like Apostles Vance and Debbie Russell, Bishop and Mrs. Kenneth Phillips, and Pastors Charlie and Caren Lujan.

Next, I wish to thank all of those who have influenced, impacted and inspired me and taught me about the workplace and the apostolic and the five-fold and the Seven Mountains, including Dr. C. Peter Wagner, John P. Kelly, Dr. Bill Hamon, Bill Johnson, Naomi Dowdy, Lance Wallnau, Johnny Enlow, Os Hillman, Rick Joyner, Dr. Mark Kauffman, Dr. John Muratori, Dennis Peacocke, Linda Rios Brook, Mike and Cindy Jacobs, Morris Ruddick, Ed Silvoso, Bob Fraser, Dr. Pat Francis, Roberta Hromas, Dr. Myles Munroe, Mike Rovner, Jim Barthel, Laurie Boyd, Sylvia Monique Reed, JoAn Risdon, Walt Pilcher, Carolita Oliveros, Michael Oswald, Robert and Cheryl-Ann Needham, Rich Marshall, Kent Humphreys, Patricia King, Ed Turose, Ken Eldred, John and Mary Anderson, Charlie and Lisa Fisher, Jess Bielby, Dennis Wiedrick, Christopher and Debbie James, Doug and Therese Wall, Dr. Ron Jenson, Dr. A. L. Gill, Stephanie Klinzing, Steven Butlin, Russell Naisbitt, Dr. James Boswell Sr., Robert Henderson, Lloyd Phillips, David Regnier, Bill Fowler, Dr. David Andrade, David Tai, Dr. Shaun Wang, Dr. Che Ahn, Dr. Ray Chen, Dr. Chuck Pierce, Jim Lillard, David Roth, Rob Moss, David Wood, Ray and Kayla Walter, Jim Lang, Roger Wurtele, Jim Dismore, Peggy Cole, Dr. Carr Bettis IV, Teri Werner, Paul Cuny, Brett and Lyn Johnson, Mike and Amy Macari, and Graham Power.

Also, Max and Sherry Greiner Jr., Dr. Tony Dale, Mauro and JoAnn Alvarez, Arthur Burk, James Nesbit, Mike and Sharon Molnar, David and Becky Van Koevering, Kim and Dr. Lee Laney, Ras and Bev Robinson, Dr. Doug Atha, Carla Campos, Bill and Sue Hart, Charles and Liz Robinson, David and Petie Newsome, Dr. Joseph Umidi, Dr. Joseph Mattera, Dr. Sharon Stone, Dr. Paula Price, Duncan and Wendy Campbell, Bill and Diane Collins, Dr. Tommi Femrite, Alice Patterson, Dr. Richard and Paula Eberiga, William Fury, Tim Taylor, Berin and Lisa Gilfillan, Stacey Campbell, Sharnael Wolverton, James Goll, Graham Cooke, Beth Alves, Ray Nelson, Georgian Banov, John and Carol Arnott, Rob Robinson, Sharyn Dacbert, Matthew Fleming, Debbie Alexander, Dr. Michelle Morrison, Marcy Rivera, David Yarnes, John Boneck, Benjamin Anyacho, Joann McEachern, James Brewton, Curtis Gillespie, Dr. Carl White Jr., Dr. Tim Hamon, Bill Thomas, Paula Lubrano, Tim and Kathy Rushing, Jim Ballew, Linus and Karen Vaughn.

Also, Dr. Richard Blackaby, John Bibee, Archie and Bess Binnie, Keith and Jane Hinsz, Mary Hargraves, Bruce Lindley, Lindsay Smith, Marc Brisebois, Kari Browning, Mark Pfeiffer, Lorne Tebbutt, Daniel Geraci, Irvin Perry, Ashley Wolfe, Patrick Kucera, John Robb, Michael and Jill O'Brien, Tudor Bismark, Paul Wilbur, Joe Dobrota, Jean Steffenson, Amy Everette, Kluane Spake, Wesley Tullis, Doug Spada, Jerry Jones, Marty and Lyn McClendon, Axel Sippach, Maryal Boumann, Joe Knight, Bobby Orange, Loran and Tanya Swanberg, Jay Swallow, Negiel Bigpond, Kenny and Louise Blacksmith, Jim and Faith Chosa, Art and Lori Oujay, John David and Gaylene Gomez, Louis and Diana Barragan, Dutch Sheets, Mickey and Sandie Freed, Doug Stringer, Jeff Ahern, Charlie and Fran Lewis, Bob Long, Tim Price, Anne Tate, Brian Kooiman, Jonathan Shibley, Mark Sterns, Joe Poore, Dale and Barbara Wentroble, Dr. Jim and

Jean Hodges, Shawn Bolz, Jason Sobel, Cheryl Allen, Karen Covell, Brad Fieldhouse, Lani Netter, Dr. Larry Poland, Dr. Timothy Byler, Jack Taylor, Bob Jones, Rich Jordan, Dr. Jack Hayford, Rob and Fran Parker, Don Lisle, Dr. Tom Schlueter and many others that are too numerous to list here.

I give a "shout out" to the members of our pioneering Apostolic Alignment tribe, better known as the "A Team," which includes Gary Beaton, Jackie Seeno, Wende Jones, Matt Beard, Kyle Newton, Cristian Voaides, Dr. Gordon E. Bradshaw, Deborah McMillan, Dr. John Saba, Russel Stauffer, Alex McCaskill, Sharon Billins, Margaret Sammis, and Dr. Stan Jeffery. A special thanks to Cristian Voaides for creating the two graphics used in my chapters in Section I, and also thanks to Nathanael White for helping me to organize and edit some of the chapters and sections and format the footnotes.

I want to recognize and acknowledge our design team led by Wendy and Todd Walters and their staff at Palm Tree Productions. You are called and chosen by God and pros at what you do. More than that, who you are on the inside shines through brightly and speaks loudly on every project you undertake for others on behalf of the Kingdom. It is an honor to know you and call you friends. Also, thank you to Dr. Philip Byler for research and special services assistance. Special thanks also to Mark Gurley, who prophesied this apostolic anthology into existence on April 9, 2011.

Finally, I honor my mother, Lottie Mae Cook, who instilled in and imparted to me a love for writing and a passion for books at an early age, and to the Father of lights, who gave me the gift of writing, a love for words and language and people, and the calling of an apostle and prophet.

CONTRIBUTING AUTHORS

In Alphabetical Order

LaRue Adkinson

John Anderson, M.B.A.

David Andrade, Ph.D.

Doug Atha, D.S.L.

Ted Baehr, J.D., Hh.D.

Gary Beaton, B.A.

Ken Beaudry

Sharon Billins, B.S., Hh.D.

Laurie Boyd

Gordon Bradshaw, Ph.D., D.D.

Kari Browning

John Burpee, D.Min.

Philip Byler, D.R.E.

Duncan Campbell

Al Caperna, B.S.B.A.

Nick Castellano, Ph.D.

Bob Cathers, Hh.D.

Bruce Cook, Ph.D., Th.D.

Paul Cuny, B.A.

Tony Dale, M.D.

Stan DeKoven, Ph.D., D.Min.

Henry Falany

Tommi Femrite, D.P.M.

Charlie Fisher

Daniel Geraci

Berin Gilfillan, D.Min.

A.L. ("Papa") Gill, Ph.D.

Curtis Gillespie, B.S.B.A.

Max Greiner Jr., B.E.D.

Jon Grieser

Fernando Guillen, M.B.A.

Tim Hamon, Ph.D.

Mark Henderson

Robert Henderson, Hh.D.

Ray Hughes, D.D.

Kent Humphreys, B.A.

Christopher James

Stan Jeffery, M.B.A., D.Tech.

Bill Johnson, Hh.D.

Wende Jones, B.S.B.A.

Rick Joyner, Th.D.

Mark Kauffman, Ph.D.

Stephanie Klinzing

Erik Kudlis, Ph.D.

Candace Long, M.B.A.

Lee Ann Marino, Ph.D., D.D.

Joseph Mattera, D.Min.

Michelle Morrison, J.D.

CONTRIBUTING AUTHORS CONTINUED

John Muratori, D.C.L.

James Nesbit

Alice Patterson

Mark Pfeifer, B.A.

Lloyd Phillips, B.A.

Cal Pierce, B.S.B.A.

Walt Pilcher, M.B.A.

Paula Price, D.Min., Ph.D.

Gayle Rogers, Ph.D.

Morris Ruddick, B.S., M.S.

Michael Scantlebury, D.D.

Axel Sippach, Hh.D.

Kluane Spake, D.Min.

Tim Taylor, B.S.B.A.

Lorne Tebbutt

Ed Turose, B.S.B.A.

Larry Tyler, M.B.A.

Joseph Umidi, D.Min.

Thomas Webb, B.A., B.Th.

Arleen Westerhof, Ph.D.

Dick Westerhof, M.Eng.

Carl White Jr., D.D.

Dennis Wiedrick, B.A.

In addition to the General Editor, this multi-volume anthology was contributed to by 70 authors—almost all apostles and a few apostolic leaders; these are 70 spiritual elders in the body of Christ. Their contribution adds a depth of experience and authority to this historic work.

ENDORSEMENTS

There has been a lot of attention lately to 1 Chronicles 12:32. The men of Issachar, they knew the times and knew what to do. I believe Dr Cook's new book, *Aligning with the Apostolic,* represents that kind of knowledge and wisdom. We are in a season where God's gaze is upon the marketplace. He is raising up people who are stepping into their God-given authority and being received by church and market leaders alike. I encourage you not only to read this book but to embrace its timely message.

Al Caperna

Director, Call2Business | President, Affirm Global
www.c2bevents.com | www.affirmglobal.com

Aligning with the Apostolic is very timely. There is such a need for unity in the Kingdom and five volumes of wisdom, knowledge and understanding from so many apostolic leaders will help meet that need. These volumes will bring greater clarity, demonstration and establishment of the Kingdom of God.

Dr. John G.L.Burpee

President, John Burpee Ministries
www.johnburpee.com | www.thebridgelincoln.com

When I think about of the "new order" of Apostolic Kings in the marketplace, Dr. Bruce Cook is at the top of my list. In this apostolic anthology you will catch the heart of what God is saying in this new move of God's Spirit through the contributions of seventy authors, who together with Dr. Cook are on the "cutting edge" of apostolic advancement of God's Kingdom on earth. If you want to be in the middle of what God is saying and doing today, I highly recommend this extensive, five-volume book, *Aligning with the Apostolic.*

Dr. A.L. ("Papa") Gill

President, Gill Ministries | www.gillministries.com

What a tremendous and important assignment. I am overwhelmed with the excellent spirit in which the book has been written, (not that there was any doubt) the tremendous research that has gone into it along with the Kingdom-minded and professional caliber of contributing authors; and yet the simplicity in which one with no understanding of the apostolic can grasp in reading just a few pages to give them a paradigm shift. Phenomenal! I love that you included your "research methodology."

Thank you Bruce for not only taking on this Holy Spirit-led endeavor, but for thinking enough of me to solicit my contribution. I am thrilled to be part of such an historically monumental work of creativity.

Dr. Gayle Rogers

President and Founder | Forever Free, Inc. | www.doctorgayle.com

This is not just a book; it is a reference manual for the church in the days to come. You have personally helped me in my walk with God and this manual has given me revelation and clarity on where I fit in the Body of Christ.

This is truly a five-fold ministry project and you have built a bridge in the Body of Christ. The five-fold ministry unfolds with each author-apostle and is a demonstration of how the Body of Christ should work together in advancing God's kingdom.

An orphaned army lays dormant waiting for a Davidic leadership to rise up and lead. As Dr. Mark Kauffman points out, "we are moving from the church age into the Apostolic Father-Son Kingdom Age." When spiritual fathers take their place and lead, the sleeping generational army will be unstoppable.

Bruce, you have created a living legacy for such a time. Can the bones of this orphaned army arise and live?

"O Lord, you know."

Jane Twohey
President, Beth Ministries

Dr. Bruce Cook is one of the most brilliant Kingdom-minded men I know. His insights into apostolic alignment are profound and yet foundational. He has truly received "insight from above" that he has so generously shared with us in this work. Thank you for this gift Dr. Bruce Cook!

Patricia King
Founder, XPministries and XPmedia | www.XPmedia.com

Wow, what a tremendous book this is going to be! Bruce, I commend your vision, faithfulness and diligence in completing this important assignment ... it is the completion of things which sets you up for an even bigger assignment! I smiled when I read that Holy Spirit downloaded the entire format in one hour; yes, that has happened to me many times. It's part of the scribe's anointing, I believe, and such experiences are so precious. Kudos, blessings and favor on this book!

Candace Long
President, Creativity Training Institute | www.candacelong.com

Thank you, Bruce, for all this work and for the research and diligence with which you performed this monumental task compiling *Aligning with the Apostolic*. As I have prayed over this the last few weeks, I am constantly hearing the phrase "seminal work." I can't tell you how many times the Lord has said that, but it is dozens of times.

From the Merriam Webster Dictionary:

Seminal:

1. formal : having a strong influence on ideas, works, events, etc., that come later : very important and influential - a seminal book/work/writer of, relating to, or consisting of seed or semen

2. containing or contributing the seeds of later development : creative, original <a seminal book>

Thank you for your labors and thank you for giving me the privilege of participating.

Paul L. Cuny
President, Marketplace Leadership | www.marketplaceleadership.com

Aligning With The Apostolic is an anointed compass that will accurately guide the reader into the apostolic-kingdom movement of our day. Dr. Bruce Cook is to be commended for pioneering this masterpiece, five-volume series that will prepare the church to reclaim the earth for King Jesus.

Dr. Cook sounds a clarion call that will spoil you for every day religion and cloak you with a mantle that will empower you to transform the spiritual landscape of your world. This anthology will take you beyond the syndrome of visitations of God so you can become His holy habitation in the present movings of the Spirit. Thank you, Dr. Bruce, for your gracious gift to this generation and generations to come! I highly recommend this life-changing series. ENJOY!

Dr. Mark Kauffman

CEO, Kingdom Regency Alliance | Founder, Jubilee Ministries International
www.kingdomregencyalliance.org | www.jubileeministriesint.com

Dr. Bruce Cook has done an outstanding job in bringing together notable Apostolic leaders to write related to their areas of expertise. Christians from all stripes and denominations who are curious about the roots, beliefs, activity and trends of the global apostolic movement will benefit from reading this work. I highly recommend it!

Dr. Joseph Mattera

Overseeing Bishop of Christ Covenant Coalition and City Action
Coalition International | www.josephmattera.org

I am very honored that you have allowed me to preview your incredible anthology of apostleship. This work is the climax of apostolic acuteness from the Spirit-mind of pioneering kingdom leaders. What a read—brilliant and superbly written! It is filled with explanations, case studies, and tactical applications of the office of the apostle, along with the mandate of apostolic leaders to propell the church to its proper unification for the advancement of The Kingdom. This is a global manual -

the best to date. Can't wait to purchase my copy and refer it to other kingdom leaders. Blessings!

Apostle James Brewton

President, Community Empowerment Ministries, Inc.

www.community-empowerment-ministries.org

Standing with Dr. Bruce Cook in intercession from the inception of this endeavor, I have witnessed firsthand the depth of commitment, diligence, and love sown into this anthology. The results are nothing short of incredible. This compilation provides a blueprint for apostolic Kingdom structure and operations. Within these pages rest the strategic revelation and wisdom to, teamed with the other five-fold ministry offices, conquer each of the seven mountains of culture and "occupy until He comes" (Luke 19:13).

Jon Grieser

Intercession Coordinator, Kingdom Economic Yearly Summit (KEYS)

I highly recommend *Aligning with the Apostolic* as an excellent resource of information not only for those who are new to the apostolic, but also those who are seasoned. Having the opportunity to witness the Lord working with Dr. Bruce Cook as an elder and as the senior prophet in our local church setting for many years, I have not seen anyone who more eagerly desires for all of the 5-fold ministry gifts (as referenced in Eph. 4:11 and 1 Cor. 14:1) to come forth and to mature than Bruce. Dr. Cook shares his valuable insights from many years of experience in learning how the apostolic giftings and offices successfully operate in many settings— not just in the local church, but also in the marketplace, etc.

Mark Henderson

Senior Leader | Glory House Christian Center | www.gloryhouse.net

CONTENTS

SECTION I—INTRODUCTION & OVERVIEW
Dr. Bruce Cook

xviii | ALIGNING WITH THE APOSTOLIC—VOLUME I

"With stakes this high, there is nothing more important than the book you have in your hands right now. The dialogue surrounding this subject is so desperately needed that I can only applaud Dr. Bruce Cook for the labor he has put into advancing this game-changing conversation."

Dr. Lance Wallnau
President, Lance Learning Group

"I think this is an unprecedented compilation of apostolic writings ... I believe this book to be an important foundation for all future discussions on the apostolic. ... I believe it begins to serve as an apostolic symphony of truth and foundation for advancement with that which is undeniably a Biblical priority."

Johnny Enlow
Author and Speaker

RESEARCH METHODOLOGY

I thought it would potentially be helpful to readers in general and the academic and apostolic communities in particular to include a brief description of the research methodology for this book, even though the collection of data was informal. I initially envisioned this book as being something that I would write myself under the guidance, direction and unction of the Holy Spirit as one volume. I have endeavored to read and review as much of the extant literature and body of knowledge on this topic as possible, and have read extensively in this area for the past several years, and more intensively the last nine months.

As I began outlining the book, I sensed a leading of the Spirit to invite a few apostolic leaders with whom I am in covenant to each write and submit a chapter for the book. The first such email invitation was sent July 10, 2012 and immediately accepted by several. Then as the work continued, the Holy Spirit kept highlighting others for me to invite into the sample group, and so the process of inviting and receiving guest chapters from other apostles and/or apostolic leaders continued through Dec. 9, 2012.

In all, 300 apostolic leaders from around the globe were contacted during this roughly five-month period and invited to submit a guest chapter on a topic of their choice. They were contacted in a progressive manner chronologically as they came to mind, or were brought to my attention. Similar to the Parable of the Vineyard in Matt. 20:1-16, some were invited in the first hour of the project, some at the last hour, and most somewhere in between. In other words, some people were inadvertently given more time than others to write their respective chapter as a function of when they were invited. This group of 300 represents a broad cross-section of apostles and apostolic leaders globally in terms of gender, ethnicity, education, socioeconomic status, nationality, theology, sphere(s), and other factors.

This sample group was weighted heavily toward the United States, where the majority of my apostolic contacts and relationships are based (243 of the 300, or 81.0%) – although leaders from six of the seven continents were invited, representing 25 nations – and was biased toward people for whom I had personal contact information, a personal relationship or personal knowledge of the individual, or a personal referral, or specific spiritual discernment. This group is by no means a complete list of apostles or apostolic leaders in the earth today, and in fact, far from it, nor is it a true random sample.

Having said that, the vast majority of marketplace network leaders globally were contacted and invited to participate in this project, as were the major apostolic network leaders worldwide – at least the ones of whom I am aware. A number of other apostolic individuals were also invited, who are influential and in some cases keep a lower profile and are not part of public groups.

The results and response rate from this sample group were somewhat more than expected, as I targeted a 10.0% positive response rate, which is 30.0 guest contributors, and the actual results were more than double that number – 23.0%, or 69.0 guest contributors. Since married couples were counted as one contributor in the sample, and one couple co-wrote a chapter, there were 70 contributing authors. A number of those invited said they were too busy to write a chapter and did not have the time to participate, while others were unable or unwilling to be publicly identified as apostles or apostolic leaders for various reasons—some for security or political or business/financial reasons, and others for personal or theological reasons of not being comfortable with or understanding the term "apostle." Of these latter, some were not open to or accepting of the idea that they were an apostle or apostolic leader, despite abundant evidence to the contrary, while a few others were unsure of whether apostles still exist today, and declined.

As the first major study of its type, compiled and edited by a "witness from the workplace" – along with considerable and substantial support from a "crowd of witnesses" – rather than by a professional theologian or fulltime paid ministry leader, it is unclear whether the results and conclusions from this study would be similar or replicable in future studies on apostles and apostolic leaders in the seven spheres of society using different sample groups and/ or methodologies.

However, because well over half of the sample group was made up of recognized, high profile network leaders, many of whom have global influence, including 57 from outside of the U.S. (19.0% of the sample group) representing 25 nations, it is probable that future studies targeting such global and national apostolic leaders would have similar outcomes in some cases and under certain conditions, although there would possibly be a cultural bias difference if the sample group were largely from outside the U.S., or exclusively made up of ecclesiastical apostles or any other subset such as female apostles or First Nations apostles.

Having said that, many of the U.S. leaders have extensive international experience and networks, and some are expatriates or have dual citizenships. So, the cultural bias potential for future studies would be more likely if a future sample group was composed primarily of developing nations apostles versus industrialized nations apostles, or of nations with no historical context or reference to, or understanding of, apostles and apostolic function.

Gender bias is another possibility that might cause future studies to have different outcomes, as 54 female apostles were invited, or 18.0% of the total sample. Of these, 11 were co-invited with their apostolic husbands jointly as a unit. Since 13 females in the sample group submitted chapters (one wrote two chapters), that is a 24.07% response rate among women, compared to 246 males invited, or 82.0% of the sample, and 56 men who submitted chapters (two wrote two chapters), for a 22.76% response rate. Ten First Nations apostles and/or apostolic leaders were also invited to participate, but none did, for a 0.0% response rate.

Despite the inherent difficulty in trying to accurately determine or assess whether someone is a workplace or ecclesiastical apostle, and my own personal distaste for these terms, I finally decided to try and quantify this breakdown among contributing authors for the benefit of history, our readers, and the academic and apostolic community. My experience, observation and understanding is that sometimes apostles are both, and it is more a question of season and timing than function, since many or most apostles have functioned in both arenas or spheres at some point in their walk with the Lord, careers, and lives.

So, in terms of assessing or measuring this distinction for quantitative analysis, it seemed to me that one obvious way to approach this would be primarily as a matter of 1) percentage and amount of time spent on ministry, and 2) percentage and amount of income received from ministry, compared with other activities and income streams, if any. However, this is not as simple as it sounds, since Wagner has well stated that the Biblical Greek word *"diakonia"* is translated about equally as both "ministry" and "services" in the New Testament. "This means that if you are serving people on your job, then you are ministering," he noted (*Apostles Today*, p. 112). I agree with him on that point. Our differences as apostles are in assignment and sphere, character and maturity, and not our calling.

I also do not find this distinction particularly useful in terms of ministry practice or effectiveness, and as I mention in Chapter One in some detail, such a distinction is not found in scripture among the early church or first apostles, or even in later writings by church fathers and historians from the second and third century A.D.; these officers of the kingdom of God who birthed the church were each simply called "apostle." In fact, such artificial, man-made distinctions help perpetuate the clergy-laity divide in the church in my opinion. However, I realize and acknowledge that some view this as a present truth revelation, so time will tell.

Having said that, one of my goals in compiling and editing this book, was to include a balanced representation and perspective from the global apostolic community in these chapters, and amazingly, with no prior, formal planning or design on my part, the results ended up that way. Those who submitted chapters were evenly split between workplace apostles (31) and ecclesiastical apostles (31), with seven (7) other apostles categorized as "both," since they are business owners or active professionals but also function as the senior spiritual leader of a local church or network. I based these designations on the full-time status and primary focus of activity and time for each individual contributing author, and not on their income, since I did not have access to any of their financial records, nor did I request such or deem that information necessary or important for purposes of this book and study. In terms of the total sample group, the split was as follows, using the same criteria: workplace apostles (144), ecclesiastical apostles (128), and both (28).

Finally, this study and book was self-funded, and chapter contributions from others were voluntary and nonpaid. The invitations to the sample group were open-ended in terms of possible chapter topics, and leaders were invited to write on any subject which they deemed or sensed to be appropriate and relevant to the title of this book, and of interest, importance and/or timeliness to the Church and Kingdom of God. That is why a few of the chapters have similar titles, although the content is different. In other words, the content is Spirit-led and author-selected.

In closing, I depended heavily on the Holy Spirit and my intercession teams to cover this process and project in prayer, and for the outcomes and results to be pleasing and useful to the Lord and the body and bride of Christ. By way of mutual disclaimer, the views expressed by me do not necessarily reflect those of the other authors, and vice versa, the views expressed by other authors do not necessarily reflect my own or each other's. May the Lord bless you as you read.

FOREWORD BY
C. PETER WAGNER

Never before has this quantity of material written by so many authors been compiled on the subject of apostles and the apostolic movement. I commend my friend, Bruce Cook, for the vision, the dedication, and the persistence that has gone into this work. As much as anything I have known, this anthology validates the widespread affirmation that the New Apostolic Reformation is truly recognized as an important component of contemporary Christendom.

As I read through chapter after chapter of this work, I kept praying that God would show me how best to fulfill Bruce Cook's assignment to me to write a foreword to it. It is obvious that there is scarcely any piece of new information on the subject that could possibly be added. So with that in mind, I thought it best to attempt to give an overview of the historical and current form of the apostolic movement. I have now been studying the New Apostolic Reformation (NAR), working as a participant observer, and writing on it for 20 years. Some authors of Internet articles and blogs have erroneously labeled me the *leader* of the NAR. I say "erroneously" because there is not, nor has there ever been, any one leader of the movement. I will admit to coining the term "New Apostolic Reformation" in the early 1990s, but that came only through researching this new wineskin that at the time was already around 100 years old!

Some who become aware of this anthology on apostleship will undoubtedly regard it offhand as spurious because their belief system tells them that, while there might have been apostles in New Testament times, that gift and office of apostle ceased once the canon of Scripture was determined. It is true that across maybe 1800 years of church history little can be found affirming the activity of apostles in the churches. Why? Because the original apostolic government of the church had largely been laid aside in favor of a more bureaucratic, administrative, and legal structure among both Catholics and Protestants. But no longer. My studies lead me to believe that the New Apostolic Reformation itself began around 1900 and that here in North America the Second Apostolic Age began in 2001.

Let's look back in history. The first component of the NAR, as I see it, was the African Independent Church movement which began around 1900. It emerged from the traditional mission churches and was led by Africans, not foreign missionaries, in an attempt to more thoroughly contextualize or Africanize Christianity. The second component was the Chinese rural house church movement which started when the Cultural Revolution came to a close in 1976. Over the following 30 years, this movement sparked the greatest national harvest of souls ever recorded throughout history. The third large component of the NAR was the explosive grassroots church movement beginning in the 1970s in Latin America. Megachurches and their related apostolic networks began blossoming in almost every large Latin American metropolitan area. There was no central, unifying organizational structure to the NAR even though its various churches and forms of church leadership had a great deal in common. The government was an apostolic form of government, distinguished from a pastoral form of government in the old wineskin.

God attempted to introduce the apostolic movement into North America in the years following World War II. Many apostles and apostolic networks emerged, but for the most part they were not sustained. They were pioneers, and like most pioneers, they made their share of mistakes. A number of these "World War II" apostles, some of whom accepted the title "apostle" and some of whom didn't, became household names. Although their structures, by and large, faded, much of their fruit is sustained today, especially in the person of some of today's "Microsoft apostles," who have profited from their predecessors' mistakes.

For a period of 30 years or so, the apostolic movement faded into the background in North America. It was sustained only by the independent charismatic church movement which began around 1970 and has increased ever since. Leaders of these independent churches had to weather sharp criticisms of "sheep stealing," "church splitting," "name-it-and-claim-it," "manipulation," and "autocratic empire-builders," but they courageously helped prepare the way for the Second Apostolic Age.

Simultaneously, God began to open the body of Christ on a wider scale to recognize apostolic government. One of the more prominent weaknesses of the "World War II apostles" was that they were not properly aligned with intercessors and prophets. In order to help correct this, God used the decade of the 1970s to initiate the great worldwide prayer movement including the recognition of the gift and office of intercessor. Following that, the 1980s witnessed the activation of the gift and office of prophet. There were, of xxviii | ALIGNING WITH THE APOSTOLIC—VOLUME I

course, prophets through the whole history of the church, but they did not begin to receive general affirmation until the 1980s. The 1990s marked the reemergence of the gift and office of apostle, this time characterized by "Microsoft apostles," who, unlike their predecessors, began to align with intercessors and prophets.

Parenthetically, the historical sequence of intercessor-prophet-apostle merits comment. Why would God have done it in this order? I believe it was because the main function of the gift of intercessor is the ability to open the pathway between heaven and earth so that, among other things, the voice of God can be heard more clearly. While all believers should be tuned into the voice of God, the members of the body of Christ with most specialization in hearing directly from God are the prophets. This means that prophets will be better prophets if the intercessors are doing their job, and it is one reason why many intercessors also have the gift of prophecy and vice-versa.

While there are exceptions to this rule, generally speaking, prophets can accurately receive and communicate the word from the Lord, but they have no concept of what to do with it. Here is where apostles come into the picture. Apostles can hear from God, both through prophets and directly themselves, and strategize its appropriate application to real life. The three together form an unbeatable team for advancing the kingdom of God.

Some who come across this anthology might be wondering where the New Apostolic Reformation is positioned within worldwide Christianity. David Barrett, widely recognized through his two editions of *World Christian Encyclopedia* as the outstanding Christian researcher of our generation, divides Christianity into six "megablocks." The Roman

Catholic megablock is the largest.[1] However, among the other five, the "Independent/Postdenominational/Neo-Apostolic" megablock (NAR) is the largest , and among all six the only one growing faster than the world population and faster than Islam. This may not be evident to North Americans or Europeans because the most explosive growth of the New Apostolic Reformation is actually taking place in the Global South.

Churches and associations of churches in the NAR constitute a new wineskin within Christianity. The old wineskin, among Protestants, is the denominational structure. Most apostolic leaders strongly respect the denominational community because (1) they have their spiritual roots there and (2) denominations at one point in history were God's new wineskins. However, they want God's new wine today, and they know from the Bible that God pours His new wine only into new wineskins (see Matthew 9:17).

So, what are some of the differences between the old wineskin and the new wineskin? The NAR represents the most radical change in the way of doing church since the Protestant Reformation. Notice that this is not a change in *doctrine*, but rather in *practice*. Of all the changes in the new wineskin, the most radical of all relates to *the amount of spiritual authority delegated by the Holy Spirit to individuals.* I highlighted this statement in italics to help give it the merit it deserves. In the old wineskin, the individual (such as an apostle) was never entrusted with making the final decisions. Authority was delegated to *groups*, not to *individuals.* That is where we get familiar ecclesiastical terminology such as board of deacons or session or church council or vestry or congregation or presbytery or synod or state convention or quarterly meeting or diocese xxx | ALIGNING WITH THE APOSTOLIC—VOLUME I

or general council or denominational assembly—all describing *groups* of people entrusted with authoritative decisions on various levels.

On the other hand, the apostolic movement looks to individual men or women as the final authority. This plays out on the local level with the pastor as the *leader* of the church, not as an employee of the church which is characteristic of the old wineskin. On the translocal level, the apostle has the final word over associations of churches, called apostolic networks, or over whatever ministries might be formed for various aspects of the work of the kingdom.

Does this new wineskin leadership design lend itself to possible abuse? It obviously does. As I have mentioned, "World War II apostles" did tend to succumb to many of the possible abuses. Prominent among them was a legalistic type of control or manipulation of subordinates. Some of it developed into the now discredited "discipleship movement" or "shepherding movement." A number of the apostles developed an exaggerated sense of ownership over their followers. They required those aligned with them to tithe their income "up" to the apostle. This made them very protective and they typically demanded full loyalty. Any thought of aligning with another apostle would be considered disloyal at best or traitorous at worst. On the other hand, "Microsoft apostles" are open to dual or multiple alignment. Financial bonding is required, but the amount is optional. The new generation of apostles are fulfilled not by their own success but by the success of those following them.

What I have said will raise questions as to how apostles are recognized and selected. Many of the chapters of this work address those questions directly and attempt to answer them from different perspectives. A good many of the authors focus on the quality of apostleship. They deal with the character and functionality of true apostles. They analyze who apostles are and what apostles do. They suggest that not only do apostles minister in the church, but also in the workplace. As part of their analysis they expound on the Seven Mountains that shape every culture: religion, family, education, media, government, arts & entertainment, and business, and they look at how apostles might function in every one of those spheres. Some go so far as to argue (and I happen to agree with them) that the future expansion of the kingdom of God here on earth will stand or fall on the activation of workplace apostles.

We are positioned today toward the beginning of what Bishop Bill Hamon calls "The Third and Final Reformation." It is one of the most exciting times in history to be alive. There is much to do before we can expect the Lord's return. Jesus taught us to pray "Your will be done here on earth as it is in heaven." Now that biblical government has come back into place, such an objective becomes more possible than ever. As you read on, you will see that this work provides us a handbook for action in extending the kingdom of God!

C. Peter Wagner
Presiding Apostle Emeritus, International Coalition of Apostles

ENDNOTE

1.   David B. Barrett and Todd M. Johnson, eds., *World Christian Trends AD30-AD 2200* (Pasadena CA: William Carey Library, 2001) p. 543.

"Our previous understanding of the Apostolic has been like a beginning blueprint—flat and 2-dimensional. The scope and information offered by Aligning with the Apostolic takes our flat pictures and transforms them into a sculpted 3-D model. This added dimension gives new weight, form, and depth to our understanding of apostles, apostleship, and the apostolic church."

Lynn Wilford Scaborough
Talk Like Jesus and *Spiritual Moms*

"No longer will the apostleship be relegated only to religious circles, but will be seen as the valuable kingdom asset that God intended it to be, shaping and changing the world around us with great effect. This book, Aligning with the Apostolic, serves as a spiritual parallel to the 'Library of Congress,' a provision of important literary works that are forever archived to serve as a reference for how we function and flow as the human race."

Dr. Gordon Bradshaw
GEMS Network

FOREWORD BY
KENT HUMPHREYS

The Spirit of God has always been at work in the marketplace, but in recent days this work has been more apparent and increasing. The book that you are preparing to read, reveals what God has been doing in recent years, bringing leaders from various spheres of influence together to bring transformation to marketplaces, cities, and nations. Many books have been written by workplace leaders over the last decade, but this book is unique in its focus. It gives key insights into what apostolic leaders are doing to tear down the walls that have existed for nearly 2,000 years between workplace leaders and religious leaders, and how they are building bridges of co-operation between the two groups. Communication between the various spheres is now commonplace in key cities across our nation and around the world.

Dr. Bruce Cook has given us a wealth of scriptural background for those who, like me, love to see how God has woven His sovereign will through time. It gives historical summaries of centuries for those of us who want just the bottom line. Yet, for the academic mind with years of theological study, Dr. Cook writes with all of the desired detail. Just the definition of terms is worth the price of the book for those who are new to this arena of thought.

Some of you are a little intimidated by the term "apostle." It is not in your normal vocabulary, and seems to only relate to the immediate followers of Jesus 2,000 years ago. You will be provided great understanding how God has been sending His leaders around the globe for all of these years, while many of these "sent ones" have been called by other names. And even those of you long-time apostles will be informed by the multitude of details that the author has provided for us on the history and varieties of the term. You will hear from various apostles who are leading the body of Christ in all different kinds of ministries. Their unique viewpoints, experiences, and backgrounds will remind you again how God works in the life of each leader.

Recently, I was asked to address a conference at a large evangelical seminary. Attendees included key leaders of one of the largest mission organizations, along with other seminary, church, and workplace leaders. At 2 a.m. on the day of my scheduled talk, God woke me up and gave me a word for that group of leaders. God showed me the problems of dualism, the sacred/secular divide, the lack of understanding of the "priesthood of the believer" (that is, equipping ALL of the saints for the work of the ministry), spiritual pride, and the presence of a religious spirit. I then asked the Holy Spirit to show me the solution. He answered that it was simply to understand "the apostle with a small a". Each of us has been commissioned by God. We have been sent. And God has set up leaders and Apostles with a large A in specific positions from various parts of the Body of Christ to lead His Church and establish His Kingdom. This book will take you on a journey of understanding of the various ways that God is doing His work through those leaders.

I must say that I have had the unique privilege of working with Dr. Bruce Cook as a business leader, a conference speaker, the leader of a ministry to CEO's and business owners, and an author. In every case he has exhibited the qualities of a tireless servant worker and a man of integrity. Even in some very difficult circumstances, he has modeled to me the things of which he has spoken and written. I know that God has prepared him to give us this tremendous overview of the Apostolic Movement. God has given him a platform of respect, which he has used to bring this large group of apostles from around the world to contribute to this series from their various viewpoints.

I know that you will enjoy seeing God at work in new and fresh ways, because, for the first time, leaders from totally different backgrounds are coming together to see His Kingdom being brought to our cities. I am so thankful that you and I get to join Dr. Cook in this marvelous journey of God's grace to our generation.

Kent Humphreys, Ambassador
Fellowship of Companies for Christ, Christ@Work

Editor's Note: Kent Humphreys graduated from this life on Jan. 30, 2013 as this book was going to press after a three-year battle with a rare lung disease. His was a life well lived and he will be greatly missed, deeply mourned and joyfully celebrated by all who knew him. Kent leaves a lasting and powerful legacy, and was a personal support, example and encouragement to me in many ways during this project and over the years.

"Dr. Cook has managed to produce for the body of Christ a compendium of doctrine, history, and practicality that brings the church full circle, back to where it began, with apostles."

Dr. Paula A. Price
President, Paula Price Ministries

"Bruce Cook has blessed the Body of Christ by presenting an in-depth study of the ascension gift ministry of the Apostle...His works will bless the Church for years to come. God bless you Bruce, for your vision and work to establish the Apostle more freely within Christ's Church."

Bishop Dr. Bill Hamon
Christian International

PREFACE

A modern-day restoration is occurring in the church and in the kingdom of God that has been underway for the past several decades or longer, and that is the restoration of the apostles and apostolic calling, ministry, vision and function to the body of Christ for the transformation of culture and society. In fact, God is restoring the church to His original pattern, blueprint, intent and design so that it becomes His Spirit-filled and Spirit-led bride and not a rules-led, religion-filled bureaucracy.

To be properly understood and implemented, this must be seen as part of a larger movement of the Spirit of restoring and implementing kingdom government on the earth, which also includes restoration of the prophet and prophetic ministry, as I have written about in a previous book, *Partnering with the Prophetic*, and which many others also have addressed. Along with current events in general, and the Middle East and Israel in particular, this restoration sets the stage for a continued fulfillment of more of the end-time prophecies from scripture.

There have been many excellent books and articles written on the role and function of New Testament apostles, from scholars and practitioners such as Dr. Peter Wagner, Dr. Bill Hamon, Dr. Paula Price, Dr. Gordon Bradshaw, Dr.

xxxviii | ALIGNING WITH THE APOSTOLIC—VOLUME I

John Tetsola, Dr. Joseph Mattera, Dr. Jonathan David, Dr. John Polis, Dr. James Boswell Sr., Dr. Ron Cottle, Dr. Philip Byler, Dr. Kluane Spake, Dr. Alan Pateman, Dr. Timothy Early, Dr. David Cannistraci, Dr. Michael Scantlebury, Dr. Rick Joyner, Dr. Elizabeth Hairston, Dr. Jeff Van Wyk, Derek Prince, Ernest Gentile, Gordon Lindsay, Dick Iverson, John Eckhardt, Bill Johnson, Glenn Shaffer, Robert Henderson, Roger Sapp, Hector Torres, Ben Gray, Jonas Clark, Peter Lyne, Barney Coombs, Bill Scheidler, David Cartledge, Tudor Bismark, Naomi Dowdy, Mark Pfeiffer, Bill Vincent, Roderick Evans, Ed Delph, Ulf Ekman, Ed Nelson, Tim Catchim, Alan Hirsch, Mike Breen and many others too numerous to list. Included are various typologies of apostleship, primarily related to and based on roles and function, with many of the same ones appearing on multiple lists, so there appears to be a fairly strong consensus and agreement among the apostolic community on this.

Now the fulfillment, discharge and execution of the apostleship is quite another matter, and there appears to be a wider range of viewpoints on that. Wagner has written extensively in several books on a taxonomy of apostles, and Tetsola has written on the stages and levels of maturity of apostles. Several others have touched briefly on the apostolic in a chapter or as part of a book on five-fold or team ministry, including Graham Cooke, Danny Silk, Kenneth E. Hagin, Ben Peters, Ron Meyer, G. Marie Carroll, Lee Stoneking, Terry W. Stephens, Philip Mohabir, Matthew D. Green, Don and Sharon Duke, Dr. Paula Price, Dr. Stefan Sos, Dr. Sam Matthews, and Dr. Mark Virkler.

All of these books were written from and focused on – either primarily, or in most cases, exclusively – a Religion mountain or sphere paradigm and framework. Much valuable knowledge, insights, research and revelation have been released and made available to the body of Christ through this growing body of literature. However, the vast majority of these authors and their books frame their discussion and theories of the New Testament apostle from a church planter, theologian or Religion mountain perspective, with few exceptions.

Some of them, such as Wagner, Hairston, Hamon, Price, Bradshaw, Henderson, Byler, Dowdy, Lyne, Marino, Early and Spake, do acknowledge and teach that there are apostles in all seven societal spheres, and a few of these issue clarion calls for these other apostles to come forth, be accepted and recognized and commissioned, and take their place in church government. This book is a direct response to those calls, and similar ones made through other writers and leaders approaching this discussion from more of a workplace and kingdom focus and context, most notably Rich Marshall, Ed Silvoso, Richard Fleming, Kent Humphreys, Morris Ruddick, Bob Fraser, Os Hillman, Johnny Enlow, Aaron Evans, and Dr. Marcus Hester.

Humphreys compares Christian businessmen to horses in his excellent book, *Shepherding Horses, Vols. I & II*, written to pastors and church leaders from a business perspective on the dynamics between pastors and business leaders in a local church setting. In Vol. I, Humphreys described a vision he had in 2004 about a divine bridge connecting the church and the workplace, with a leader(s) from each sphere meeting in the middle of the bridge and kneeling to pray in unity over their respective cities, and the potential result being transformation. That prophetic vision is also relevant to this book.

Rich Marshall stopped short of referring to Christian workplace leaders as apostles in his first book, *God @*

Work; however, in his second book of that same title (Vol. II) five years later, that had changed, and in his public ministry, Marshall has commissioned many business people as marketplace apostles over the last 25 years. Ed Silvoso, Gunnar Olson, Bob Fraser, Morris Ruddick, Richard Fleming and Dr. Marcus Hester also prophetically discerned and apostolically decreed around the same time as Marshall and Humphreys, much of what is happening now in the body of Christ in regard to a growing awareness and acceptance of the five-fold ministry gifts and offices in existence and operation in the workplace and Seven Mountains of Culture.

Bob Buford, Laurie Beth Jones, Linda Rios Brook, Os Hillman, Dennis Peacocke, Dr. Laura Nash, John Beckett, Bill McCartney, Larry Julian, Ken Eldred and many others have also helped to fuel the current marketplace movement with their writing and teachings, seminars, workshops, cultural immersion events and specialized conferences and institutes, which we will discuss in greater depth in Chapter 7.

Dr. Myles Munroe has also helped to educate and teach the body of Christ over the last decade through his writing and speaking on the kingdom of God and the Holy Spirit, to help shift the body of Christ from a church-centric to a kingdom-centric mindset and worldview. Similarly, Johnny Enlow and Lance Wallnau, through their writing, teaching and speaking on the Seven Mountains of Culture in recent years, have also struck a chord and helped to shift, reposition and impact the church globally. Others have pioneered models and written books on strategic warfare and workplace and governmental intercession, while still others have done this in the areas of inner healing and deliverance.

The combined effect of this growing body of literature and Spirit-led revelation, both from the theological and ecclesiological realm, and the workplace arena on the integration of faith and work, has now reached a convergence, critical mass, tipping point, and fullness of time, in my opinion, with intertwined threads from which God is weaving a global, generational, kingdom tapestry. I will attempt to tie some of these streams and threads together in my opening chapters, to help frame the discussion that follows and establish the focus and direction, but the cumulative, synergistic effect of these five volumes and the messages of the contributing authors also help to accomplish this as well in considerable measure, certainly much better than I could do by myself.

It has been said that some things are better caught than taught, and such is the case here, although both approaches are employed and utilized. As a five-volume anthology of apostleship—the first such collection on record, to my knowledge—written by a representative sampling of around 70 apostles and apostolic leaders globally, the range and diversity of expression, thought, function and practice of the apostolic calling, gifting, and office of apostle are communicated, demonstrated and illustrated. This approach allows their key principles, fresh revelation, case studies and testimonies to be caught as well as taught. The fact that there are 70 apostles and apostolic leaders collaborating in unity in writing this anthology is prophetically significant and adds spiritual weight to what the Spirit is saying. (See Ernest Gentile on LXX, *Why Apostles Now?*, pp. 264-266; and Dr. Gordon E. Bradshaw on the transfer from Moses to the 70 elders, *The Technology of Apostolic Succession*, pp. 262-264).

There is a vibrant, growing, dynamic, community of apostles alive today. At this critical point in history, what is needed in the apostolic community, the Church, the kingdom of God, and society is revelation, application, demonstration, activation and impartation rather than more theory, sermons and platitudes. We need modern-day prototypes, models, incubators, centers, networks, pioneers, reformers, visionaries, strategists, and true apostolic fathers and mothers who are walking in both the kingly and priestly dimensions and graces. There are untold millions in the kingdom of God who are actively "doing the stuff." It's time to join them, and to learn from them.

My hope and prayer is that this book will not be seen as the work of a man, or a group of men and women, but as a work of the Spirit, that speaks with one heart and voice through many leaders from different backgrounds, different streams and different nations. My declaration and decree is that this collaborative effort from a broad cross-section of the global apostolic community—representing both the ecclesiastical and workplace spheres—will yield much fruit for the kingdom, summon and engage those in the caves, cellars, courts, colleges, corporations, counting houses and castles to link arms, lock shields, align apostolically by tribe and sphere, form ranks, join the fight and engage the enemy, and reawaken interest in, redirect attention to, and reposition how we conceive of the Eph. 4:11 five-fold model and mandate in general, and the apostolic and apostles in particular (Acts 2:42-32; Eph. 2:19-22, 3:4-5; 1 Cor. 12:27-28; 1 Cor. 4:1-2; Luke 11:49; 1 Tim. 4:16; Rev. 18:20). This will yeild increased relevance to the cultures and systems of this

> **Rather than religious leaders and elite scholars, Jesus chose to impart the DNA of His Kingdom to "unschooled, ordinary" men.**

world, advancement and furtherance of the kingdom of God, and the mission and governance of the Church.

Jesus had a blank slate to write on in selecting his core team and inner circle and the first generation of church leaders, and yet he chose "unschooled, ordinary men" to impart the DNA of His kingdom to rather than the religious leaders and elite scholars of His day; their primary claim to fame was that "they had been with Jesus" (Acts 4:13). From this humble beginning the church was birthed, the kingdom was established, the Holy Spirit was imparted to the 120 disciples in the Upper Room in Jerusalem on the Day of Pentecost (Acts 2:1-4), and these "turned the world upside down" (Acts 17:6) in one generation.

Apparently all 120 of the disciples in the Upper Room in Acts 1-2 were also from the marketplace. This simple collection of fishermen, tax collectors, physicians, tentmakers, teachers, etc. became Jesus' "mighty men" in the same way that the malcontents, misfits, outcasts, supporters, and army of the giant-killer and future king David became his "mighty men." God is still looking for mighty men and women today, and Dan. 11:32 says that "those who know their God shall do mighty exploits [deeds]." That is where you and I come in.

WORKPLACE APOSTLES ABOUND

I contend and will present the case here that rather than there being only thousands or tens of thousands of apostles and apostolic leaders on the earth today, as some believe, there are far more likely to be millions of them in existence currently, largely unknown except perhaps locally and to the Holy Spirit, including some who are unaware and even a few who are unwilling. Most of these are found in the workplace rather than behind a pulpit, where risk and reward is an ever-present reality and a daily discipline, and where they have been positioned and trained to solve complex problems, make executive decisions, lead multi-cultural and multi-disciplinary teams, research underlying trends and conditions, assess threats and opportunities, establish and implement protocols, produce new products and services, devise and plan strategies and campaigns, define objectives and measure outcomes, change or enforce organizational culture, discover and harness new technologies.

They are also trained to generate revenues and profits, prepare and balance budgets, increase market share, innovate and pioneer new ways of conceptualizing and implementing things, build and promote brands, instill and maintain order, eliminate or minimize chaos, bring clarity and dispel confusion, motivate and inspire subordinates, meet or exceed accepted standards of excellence or quality, create systems and processes for maximum efficiency and optimization, recognize and acknowledge exemplary performance, administer bureaucracies, negotiate contracts and agreements, and effect damage control in crisis situations.

It is fairly self-evident to anyone with an open mind and pure heart that the workplace is a great "training ground" for apostles and other five-fold leaders, despite the presence and influence of the Babylonian spirit and world economic system. The workplace is also intended and designed by God to be a "reigning ground," where God's glory and wisdom and power emanate and shine through us to affect culture and dispossess darkness, establish dominion, and transfer and manage resources for His kingdom as wise stewards. This is not to say that all Christian workplace leaders are apostles, though many are apostolic; that is absolutely not the case. But, some percentage of them doubtless are, just as other Christian workplace executives, professionals and entrepreneurs are prophets, pastors, teachers or evangelists, as the Lord has determined and assigned in His sovereignty, grace and wisdom (Eph. 4:7-13, 1 Cor. 12:11).

Walt Pilcher has written an excellent book on this topic, titled *The Five-fold Effect: Unlocking Power Leadership and Results for Your Organization*, which I recommend and encourage you to read. Apostles are not just defenders of the faith and interpreters of doctrine, but also interpreters of culture and defenders of the weak, helpless, oppressed, overlooked, neglected and innocent. As we will discover and discuss more fully later in this book, apostleship is not primarily a title, a brand, a license, a franchise, a club, a promotion, or a benevolent dictatorship. Instead, it is a divine grace, a five-fold ascension gift and personal calling from the Lord, a royal ambassadorship, a multi-purpose function, and an appointed office. It is also the foundation (along with prophets) upon which God builds and establishes both His kingdom and His church (note in Eph. 2:19-20 the terms "fellow citizens" and "members of God's household" to denote respective spheres).

Of these millions of apostles and apostolic leaders in the earth today—located primarily in the workplace—they encompass a wide spectrum of spiritual maturity, ranging from young, immature, inexperienced, novice apostles to emerging apostles, unaware apostles (those who don't know yet who Christ is in them in terms of their spiritual identity and calling), to apostles in hiding, apostles in waiting, apostles in training, those with apostolic gifting or an apostolic calling, to seasoned, mature leaders who are active in their local churches and/or in other city-wide, regional, state-wide, national or international spheres, ministries or parachurch ministries, or who are leading their own ministries. Many of them are probably serving faithfully in other ministry roles currently such as teacher, prophet, pastor, evangelist, elder, intercessor, worship team member, counselor, or administrator and being trained for other gifts and callings to be added later.

Apostleship is often an increase in responsibility after being faithful in another area of calling and gifting or five-fold office.

This service and preparation can be, and most often is, expressed in the context of both a local church body as well as the workplace.

That has been the pattern with all of the apostles I know, including me, as well as the apostle Paul, and seems to be the general norm for this position. Tetsola, in his classic book, *Understanding Apostolic Culture and Patterns*, set forth a typology of apostolic stages of maturity and functioning, which supports my own experience and understanding of apostleship, such that it is often an increase in responsibility after being faithful in another area of calling and gifting or five-fold office, which God in His sovereignty and divine wisdom, chooses to add to the body.

Some, like the original 12 "Apostles of the Lamb," were called by God directly into apostleship, as part of an intensive and immersive discipleship process, so there is no universal formula that fits or applies to all apostles, though certainly there are biblical, generally-accepted, and widely-recognized criteria for these officers. But even then, they were selected and entrusted with this increased responsibility and authority only after intensive prayer and after already being called by God and becoming disciples, and serving faithfully for some period of time, short though it may have been.

So, we have to be aware of and factor in the special circumstances and start-up environment involved with birthing the 1st century church. Jesus needed a hand-picked, specially-trained group of leaders for this task who were confirmed by God personally through all-night prayer, and who were "all in" and willing to lay their lives down for the cause of Christ and His kingdom, as all but one of them did. Guess what? That is still a requirement today. Apostles must count the cost of responding to their calls.

I invite you to begin this journey and look further into the pages of this anthology and the revelation that is contained herein concerning this proton officer of heaven: the apostle. May the Lord bless you as you read this and may the eyes of your heart and the understanding of your mind be opened and enlightened to see and comprehend what God is doing and saying to the church in this day and hour as His kingdom is established, advanced, expanded and/or strengthened and territories and spheres occupied through a global network of "living stones," with Jesus Christ being the Chief Cornerstone (1 Pet. 2:4-6), as the Bride of Christ prepares herself and makes ready for the return of the Bridegroom.

May the Lord use this collaborative and apostolic anthology for His purposes and glory, to advance His kingdom, strengthen His church, remove the barriers and break down walls of division and misunderstanding between the leaders of the workplace church and the ecclesiastical church. In a growing number of cases, leaders are learning to integrate and differentiate between the Church and the kingdom, and to use one of Ken Eldred's book titles to make a summary point, we need to grow and mature as the body and bride of Christ, from living **"the integrated life"** (a healthy and necessary starting point), to living **"the integrated community"** and from there to **"the integrated government"** of that community, the *ecclesia*, in both its local, translocal and universal forms. Finally, we must live as **"the integrated kingdom"** to exercise influence and authority in the Seven Mountains of Culture.

Respected spiritual fathers and mothers have now been telling us by the Spirit to do this for at least a decade, and in a few cases maybe longer, so at some point, the Church must decide to be obedient to its apostolic elders and to the Holy Spirit. And, in a growing number of cases, that is happening. Apostolic centers, apostolic teams, apostolic networks, and apostolic churches are springing up across the globe in response to this new move of the Spirit, as Wagner and many others have reported and documented.

However, the Church in general, and many denominations in particular, are still holding back, either ignorant of or resistant to the Spirit and seemingly frozen in time, culture, structure and the traditions and teachings of men, "having a form of godliness but denying its power," and being influenced by "deceiving spirits and doctrines of demons" (1 Tim. 4:1, 2 Tim. 3:5). God will work with "whosoever wills" in each generation, and He can save and bring victory and change, whether by few or by many.

Just ask Joan of Arc, Martin Luther, William Wilberforce, William Wallace, George Washington, Winston Churchill, Susan B. Anthony, Booker T. Washington, Rosa Parks, Graham Power, Angus Buchan, Loren Cunningham, Vonette Bright Billy Graham, Bill Hybels, Rick Warren, Pat and Dede Robertson, Paul and Jan Crouch, Marcus and Joni

Lamb, David and Barbara Cerullo, Rory and Wendy Alec, … or perhaps ask Noah, Abraham, Moses, David, Esther, Daniel, Gideon, or Joseph. Ask anyone who defied the odds and overcame the impossible, and saw God move and change the status quo and their own reality.

After more than 1700-1800 years of the Church not acknowledging apostles and prophets and workplace leaders (who in many cases are one and the same), I believe that an important first step in this process is recognizing, affirming, receiving, respecting and honoring the true, legitimate, and authentic five-fold ministers, officers and stewards of the grace of our Lord and Savior, Jesus, the Christ, the Risen and Coming King, the Messiah, the Lamb of God, the Anointed and Exalted One. This includes those in the Seven Mountains of Culture. Quite frankly, **this is much more a matter of maturity and obedience than a matter of doctrine**, in my opinion.

MUTUAL SUBMISSION IS THE MODEL

I would like to suggest and submit for consideration that the standard presented in scripture for five-fold, kingdom leaders working together is **"mutual submission,"** not just recognizing and respecting each other's titles or giftings or functions or spheres of authority or rank or position or seniority, or whatever other measure or method someone may be using by which to relate. Eph. 5:21 says, "Submit to one another out of reverence for Christ." That can only happen when we trust and love and honor one another, not just tolerate each other.

I have experienced that personally in spiritual leadership as an elder, prophet and apostle from my own apostolic leader and senior pastor of the last 11 years, and it has been freeing, healing, and empowering for me, after having served in leadership at several prior churches where the pastors or senior leaders were less accessible, less transparent, less humble, less personable, less accountable, and less accepting and affirming of workplace and other five-fold leaders.

From that place of mutual affirmation, acceptance, honor and respect as spiritual equals in the work of Christ in our local church and extended ministry, God has released me to model and express that to other leaders, both in the workplace and the ecclesiastical realm. In fact, just as I have submitted myself to another man's authority and leadership in our local church and ministry, and served faithfully in several different capacities over the years, he voluntarily approached me several years ago and asked to submit himself to my leadership in the areas of prophetic ministry and the workplace, because he said he recognized the authority and favor God has given me in those areas.

Now that is real humility, security and honor in action! It is certainly something that I would have never thought of, or requested if I had, but I suggest this as a model to follow for other apostolic kings and priests. And, rather than this harming our relationship, it has actually improved it and grown us closer in understanding, honor, love and respect.

While this level of king-priest dynamics and relationship between apostolic leaders working together may be hard for some ecclesiastical leaders to accept, it is neither a new nor isolated phenomenon. A few out of many, many examples which could be cited of local apostolic leadership teams are Dr. Mark and Jill Kauffman and their church Jubilee Ministries Intl., and two of their elders and fellow apostles Tony Flowers and Ed Turose; and Dr. Gordon and Angela Bradshaw and their church Voice of God Ministries, and two of their elders and fellow apostles Alex McCaskill and

Curtis Gillespie. Both Dr. Kauffman and Dr. Bradshaw lead separate apostolic networks, function in both the ecclesiastical and workplace spheres, and have a balanced and healthy approach to apostolic authority, leadership and governance, family life and spiritual fathering. Another such apostolic center is IHOP, which Mike and Diane Bickle founded and lead, and where numerous "apostolic kings" such as Bob Fraser, Bob Hartley and Walt Meyer have been serving in leadership capacities for many years, along with their equally-anointed and gifted wives.

Other examples of apostolic centers which have their own networks are Bethel Church, Redding, Calif. overseen by Bill and Beni Johnson, and supported by leaders such as Kris and Kathy Vallotton, Steve and Dawna DaSilva, Paul and Sue Manwaring, Danny and Sheri Silk, Brian and Jen Johnson, Eric and Candace Johnson, Banning and SeaJay Liebscher, Charlie and Julie Harper, Dann and Christie Farrelly. Harvest Rock Church and the HIM Network led by Dr. Che and Sue Ahn and their team in Pasadena, Calif. is another example of an apostolic hub, with leaders including Gabe Ahn, Mark Tubbs, Angela De Forrest, Greg Wallace, and Andy Geerken, as is Glory of Zion and Global Spheres in Corinth, Texas led by Dr. Chuck and Pam Pierce, with a strong supporting team including Dr. Robert and Linda Heidler, Joseph Pierce, John Dickson, Lee Ann Squier, Lisa Bailey, Ted and Margie Leigh, etc.

MorningStar Ministries, Fort Mill, S.C. is led by Dr. Rick and Julie Joyner; Robert Henderson leads Global Reformers network in Colorado Springs; John Eckhardt and Axel Sippach lead Impact Network in Chicago; and in Santa Rosa Beach, Fla., Christian International Ministries Network is led by Dr. and Mrs. Bill Hamon and their eldest son, Dr. Tim Hamon. Tom and Jane Hamon are also in senior leadership.

In New York City, Dr. Joseph Mattera and his team lead a thriving apostolic center encompassing Christ Covenant Coalition and City Action Coalition International.

In the Toronto, Ontario area in Canada, Catch the Fire Ministries is led by John and Carol Arnott and Kingdom Covenant Ministries and Kingdom Leaders Network are led by Dr. Pat Francis. Mel and Heather Mullen lead Word of Life Centre Church and Life Church network in Red Deer, Alberta and Dr. Michael and Sandra Scantlebury lead the Dominion-Life International Ministries church and network in Vancouver, BC, and Drs. David and Ruth Demian lead Church of Zion and Watchmen for the Nations network there.

In Amsterdam, Dick Westerhof leads an apostolic network, Coalition for Apostolic Reformation, as does Naomi Dowdy in the U.S. and Asia and Dr. Sharon Stone and Greg Black in the U.K. and Europe. Many other apostolic networks also exist globally, and more are being formed all the time, especially in Asia, India, South and Central America, and Australia.

As the body of Christ in general, and spiritual leaders in particular, learn to work and relate together in apostolic teams at the local level and apostolic networks at the translocal or national level, the synergy and compounding and exponential effect inherent in the five-fold gifts and offices are unlocked and unleashed, and spiritual reproduction and multiplication will occur naturally, spontaneously and organically.

A BETTER WAY

Over the last five years, as my wife and I and our speakers, sponsors, volunteers and local hosts have served the body of Christ through the various K.E.Y.S. events in the U.S. and internationally, God has given me favor with other leaders and brought around me mighty women and men of God who are looking for a different way of relating with other leaders and experiencing the kingdom with a like-minded and like-Spirited tribe with the same spiritual DNA that is more entrepreneurial, covenantal and governmental in nature (i.e., apostolic-prophetic). Several of these are also network leaders, and so I now have another layer of mutual submission with them as a safeguard and protection and additional source of counsel, wisdom and covenantal blessing.

Jesus said that the greatest among us must become servant of all. That is still the standard and measure of Kingdom leadership and authority. Fortunately, there are a growing number of mature apostles who are true spiritual fathers and mothers who are leading kingdom apostolic networks that represent new wineskins for the body of Christ. Some of them have written chapters for this book, but there are many others globally who are strategically positioned in all Seven Mountains of Culture and spheres of society. I can assure you they are praying for you and waiting for you to join them, so next generation leaders, keep looking for them until you find ones that God confirms to you. They are certainly looking for you (Mal. 4:6).

Let us choose to forgive, love and honor one other as apostles of Jesus, model servant leadership to the other five-fold leaders specifically and the body of Christ generally, rise up and build together, and set an example for others to follow by living lives "worthy of the calling" we have received, "redeeming the time," and being "wise as serpents but harmless as doves." As someone has wisely said, "If you want to travel fast, go alone; if you want to travel far, go with others" (as a team or delegation or army or generation).

As followers of Christ, we are never alone, since we have the indwelling Holy Spirit to comfort, guide, and "teach us all things." So, in that sense, we are able to travel fast in terms of the Spirit dimension, whenever necessary. In this season, however, we have the opportunity to travel both fast and far, by joining together and coming to a new place of maturity and obedience in Him, both individually, but more importantly, collectively and corporately. When that happens, we will look and think and act more like the beautiful, ravishing, strong, wise, healthy and discerning bride that Jesus is waiting for and will one day return for. Until then, let us "be about our Father's business" and "occupy until He comes."

Today marks the beginning of a new era. What the Mayans could not foresee, and so ended their calendar on this date, the Spirit of God foreknew and planned for you and me and many others, since Jesus is "the Alpha and the Omega, the First and the Last, the Beginning and the End" (Rev. 22:13, NIV). The Mayflower pilgrims landed at Plymouth Rock on this date in 1620, almost 400 years ago. A month earlier they had drafted the Mayflower Compact, the first form of government in the New World, based upon God. Today God is re-establishing and restoring His government in the kingdoms of the earth and the Seven Mountains of Culture as well as the Church. Apostolic reformers are again leading the way.

Dr. Bruce Cook
Dec. 21, 2012

GLOSSARY

- **Ambassadorial Apostle** – An apostle who represents a network, church or other group, body, association, federation or organization as an ambassador sent forth by the governing leader.

- ***Apostasy** – A renunciation or abandonment of a former loyalty (as to a religion). (Webster). This speaks to the opposing demonic counsel and attitude that directly contrasts the work of an apostle, attempting to revert previously-submitted kingdoms and kingdom citizens back to allegiance with demonic cultures. False teaching in the church has been called "doctrines of demons" by Paul the Apostle in 1 Tim. 4:1.

- ***Apostle (s)** – *"Apostolos"* (Greek) A sent one, an ambassador; a reformer. The apostle is the five-fold ministry gift which also functions as a foundation within the New Testament church structure and the Kingdom of God (Eph. 2:19-21), just as the 12 Apostles of the Lamb are part of the foundation of the gates and walls of heaven (Rev. 21:14). God has installed this office to institute Time, Place, Order and Importance in the Body of Christ.

- **Apostle (s)** – The Five-fold ascension gift officer in the Body of Christ assigned to project proper Timing, Placement, Order and Importance of issues, strategies, revelation, and relationships in the advancement of God's kingdom and the building of the Church and maturing of the saints. (1 Cor. 12:28, Eph. 4:11)

- ***Apostle** – A person who initiates or advocates great reform. (Webster)

- **Apostleship** – The assignments, attitudes, attributes and actions of one who functions as an apostle. The governmental nature or state of being of such calling, position or office is implied, as in kingship or rulership or ambassadorship.

- **Apostles of the Lamb** – The original 12 apostles that Jesus appointed and commissioned while He was on the earth, before His resurrection and ascension. Their names are listed several places in scripture (Matt. 10-1-4, Mark 3:13-19, Luke 6:12-16, Matt. 19:28, Rev. 21:14).

- **Apostle's Rod** – A rod symbolizing authority and typically given to a leader by God, such as the staff of Moses. Such a rod may be literal (physical) or seen or felt or sensed in the spiritual realm and dimension. Sometimes this can be used as an offensive weapon in spiritual warfare.

- **Apostolate** – The sphere of activity that expresses apostolic design, authority, culture and functions. The dignity or office of an apostle.

- **Apostolicity** – The degree of expression relating to apostolic design, culture and functions.

- **Apostolic** – The expression of the nature and/ or function of an apostle and of matters related to apostleship and the apostolate. The whole Church, or body of Christ, is designed and called to be apostolic in nature and mission and character (but not function), just as Paul and Moses respectively exhorted the New Testament churches and the Israelites to all be prophetic people. The five-fold gifting or calling is very different, however, than the office or function of such, as I discuss in detail in Chapters 2, 3 and 4 of this volume, and in Chapter 11 of *Partnering with the Prophetic.*

- **Apostolic Accountability** – This usually refers to a group of individuals who are spiritual and/or business or financial leaders and serve as accountability partners for an apostle or apostolic leader. Such a group may be formal or informal in nature and function and typically is comprised of peer-level apostles or apostolic leaders. See my discussion of this in Chapter 4 of this volume. See also the definitions of Apostolic Covering and Apostolic Alignment, which are related terms.

- ***Apostolic Agency** – The instrumentation, or administering vehicle of apostolic movements and mannerisms.

- ***Apostolic Agriculture** – The process of properly planting, establishing and sending forth apostolic offspring into their assignments. It is the act of harvesting the fruit of an apostolic relationship with spiritual sons and daughters.

- **Apostolic Alignment** – The coming into alignment of an apostle (s) with other like-minded and like-spirited apostles and/or apostolic networks, councils, associations, coalitions, tribes, etc. Such alignment can be either horizontal or vertical, and can also be between churches, ministries and networks, and not just individuals. Such alignment can either be covenantal or noncovenantal, depending on the terms, conditions and/or requirements for alignment, but in any case, true alignment is more relational than missional or doctrinal, although each plays a part. Similar core values, spiritual DNA, callings, motives, maturity and effective communication and leadership are the bonds and glue that make alignment work and create "stickiness."

- **Apostolic Assignment** – An assignment that is apostolic in nature, purpose, design or intent. This can also refer to an assignment for an individual apostle or group of apostles.

- **Apostolic Authority** – The governmental mantle of authority given to bring apostolic designs and purposes to fulfillment. It derives from Christ, "The apostle and high priest of our profession" (Heb. 3:1). See also Chapter 4 in this volume for a detailed discussion of the 12 dimensions of spiritual authority, with particular application to and focus on apostolic authority.

- **Apostolic Center** – A city or regional governmental church or parachurch ministry fulfilling, modeling or representing an apostolic purpose or mission, and typically offering a variety of programs and classes and activities and led or overseen by an apostle or apostles.

- **Apostolic Ceremony** – A ceremony officiated or overseen by an apostle or group of apostles or apostolic leaders. This may also refer to a ceremony whose purpose or focus is apostles, such as a procession, commissioning, or ordination.

- **Apostolic Company** – A group of believers dedicated to the application of apostolic principles and purposes. They share core values, beliefs and vision for kingdom design and are able to institute change in their assigned spheres.

- **Apostolic Correction** – This refers to corrective words and/or actions of an apostle or a group, body, council, association, coalition or alliance of apostles for the purpose of order, maturity, restoration, reformation, or renewal in doctrine, teaching, leadership, direction, practice, attitude, behavior, conduct, worship, church government, administration, or other matters.

- **Apostolic Council** – A group of apostles and (or) apostolic believers who provide godly counsel through the office, gifting, authority and anointing of an apostle. Its purpose originates from the supernatural wisdom and counsel of God. The Jerusalem Council in Acts 15 is one such example.

- **Apostolic Covering** – This term refers and relates to spiritual covering, and generally refers to an individual who serves or acts as an overseer or resource apostle to whom another apostle has voluntarily submitted for spiritual oversight or covering. These type of relationships can be short-term or long-term, and covenantal or denominational. Such a relationship works best when it is based upon mutual honor and respect and hopefully love rather than simply authority or position. See Bart Pierce's book, *Cover Me in the Day of Battle*, for a more in-depth discussion of this topic. God is the ultimate source of covering for all believers as numerous scriptures make clear. However, due to the complexity of life and the need for wisdom and guidance, safety and protection, most spiritual leaders recognize the benefits and safeguards of being under a human covering also. Sometimes this covering is a small group of leaders rather than an individual. A more recent trend that has emerged is Apostolic Alignment, which also is beneficial, but not necessarily the same as apostolic covering. See also the definition of Apostolic Accountability.

- **Apostolic Culture** – The beliefs, attitudes, core values, spiritual DNA, best practices, historic traditions and influences brought about through association with apostles and apostolic people.

- **Apostolic Delegation** – One or typically a group of apostles or apostolic leaders chosen and sent forth to represent a king, ruler, noble, dignitary, potentate, nation, organization or other entity or individual in an official capacity as a plenipotentiary and ambassador.

- **Apostolic Discipline** – see Apostolic Correction. In this book I use these terms interchangeably.

- ***Apostolic DNA** – The supernatural seed by which God creates a pattern for reproduction in people, places and things.

- **Apostolic Education** – Education that is apostolic in nature, content, form, scope, substance, organization or purpose. This can also refer to a curriculum, course of study or degree program focused on apostles, apostleship, apostolicity and /or the apostolate.

- **Apostolic Embassy** – A mission headed by an ambassador apostle, the headquarters of an ambassador apostle, or a body of persons entrusted with a mission to a sovereign or government, especially an ambassador and his or her staff.

- ***Apostolic Estate** – The assets, abilities and assignments of an apostolic tribe or network. It includes every aspect of their heritage and inheritance as given by their spiritual parents.

- **Apostolic Foundations** – Foundations that are rooted and grounded in Christ Jesus and His nature, personage, teachings, doctrine, eternal ministry and Kingdom.

- **Apostolic Function** – The application of apostolic principles that bring Kingdom of God design, order and activity to people, places and things.

- **Apostolic Gift** – The various supernatural gifts and enhanced natural attributes that empower apostles to function in their office effectively. Apostles also release their gifting in the form of impartations to others.

- **Apostolic Government** – The structure, function, systems, processes, application and administration of governance by one or more apostles, or a team led or overseen by an apostle.

- **Apostolic Grace** – The special anointing, authority and ability to empower and enable people, places and things with the sovereign purposes of God.

- ***Apostolic Industry** – The viable and powerful resource of supernatural energy that gives birth to new supernatural technologies. It creates an on-going supply of resources and references that help build and energize the Kingdom of God.

- **Apostolic Influence** – The power and spiritual equity of apostolic authority and culture and personal example; also, the results and fruit that are effected and manifested through placement and demonstration, and through godly leadership, relationships, wisdom, love, honor, respect, reputation, counsel and humility.

- **Apostolic Intercession** – Intercession that is focused on decreeing and legislating the will and heart of God in the heavenlies and on earth, protecting, advancing and upholding His duly-appointed representatives of the kingdom and their divine assignments and destinies.

- **Apostolic Leader** – An individual with apostolic calling, gifting, grace, mantles, anointing and/or authority for a specific assignment, territory, group of people, situation or sphere; also, someone who is part of an apostolic team or delegation.

- **Apostolic Leadership** – Leadership that is apostolic in nature, and characterized by wisdom, humility, love, honor, relationship, selflessness, influence, authority, strategy, and partnership.

- **Apostolic Mantle** – The supernatural and God-given source of an apostle's governmental authority, assignment and abilities for functioning in the kingdom of God.

- **Apostolic Mission** – A mission led, directed, authorized and/or overseen by one or more apostles or apostolic leaders.

- **Apostolic Movement** – A change of existing cultures, conditions, atmospheres, attitudes, beliefs, kingdoms, governments, norms, strategies, values and/or results and outcomes brought about, precipitated or caused by apostles and/or apostolic people.

- **Apostolic Network** – A network of apostles and/or apostolic leaders. Sometimes prophets and other five-fold officers are invited and included as affiliate members on a case by case basis. The best of these have strong leadership, core values and spiritual DNA that create a distinctive tribal culture and identity (see Apostolic Tribe).

- **Apostolic Office** – The ascension gift position of apostle and its various sources of executive authority and power in the natural and spiritual dimensions. It is the manifestation of Christ the apostle in earthly vessels. It should be noted that this refers to God-appointed office rather than man-appointed or -elected office (see Matt. 10:1-5 and Luke 10: 1).

- **Apostolic Order** – One of the primary purposes of an apostle is to bring, create and/or restore order in situations, organizations, relationships, families, churches, ministries, cities, regions, nations, territories, governments and economies, to name just a few. This can also refer to specific religious orders of apostles in certain denominations, and/or to the fact that Jesus established apostles as a new and eternal order in His kingdom.

- **Apostolic Protocol** – The set or canon of written or unwritten rules, laws, regulations, customs, norms, procedures, standards, guidelines, principles, rituals, and behaviors related to and/or associated with apostleship, the apostolate, or apostolicity. Protocol is typically associated with kings, rulers, ambassadors and diplomats and has to do with authority and position. Jesus stepped out of accepted protocol to wash the disciples' feet and to speak with the Smaritan woman at the well. See Dr. Theresa Phillips' book on *Ministerial Protocol,* Dr. Philip Byler's book, *Profiles in Protocol,* and Natasha Vermaak Grbich's book, *The Protocol of the Kingdom* for a deeper discussion of this.

- **Apostolic Spirit** – The Spirit of apostleship, the apostolate or an apostolic tribe or company.

- **Apostolic Succession** – The process of leadership transfer among apostles or apostolic leaders in a group, organization, church, business, government agency, denomination or network. See Dr. Gordon E. Bradshaw's book, *The Technology of Apostolic Succession,* for a more detailed discussion of this subject.

- **Apostolic Teaching** – Teaching that is apostolic in nature, form, substance, content, organization or purpose. Generally this will involve revelation.

- **Apostolic Team** – A team of disciples, usually led by an apostle, who apply apostolic principles and vision to their assignments. They bring the kingdom order, power, authority, wisdom and the government of God to people, places and things.

- **Apostolic Tribe** – A group of disciples who have chosen to align themselves in vertical or horizontal relationships with an apostolic leader, a set of core values, vision, a common mission and purpose for a shared destiny and spiritual DNA (see Apostolic Network).

- **Apostolic Weapons** – (See 2 Cor. 10:3-5). Such weapons are in the spiritual realm or dimension and can only be seen by or through the eyes of faith. These include signet rings, crowns, scepters, thrones, mantles, gavels, apostles' rods, keys, quill pens, scrolls, plumb lines, white horses, chariots, etc. These are typically available to spiritual leaders of a certain rank and maturity, usually those in the office of apostle. Other spiritual weapons are available to all believers, such as worship, prayer, the sword of the Spirit (word of God), decrees and declarations, binding and loosing, wisdom, faith, forgiveness, love, joy, peace, patience, kindness, mercy, longsuffering, holiness, purity, righteousness, etc. See chapter 4 for a more detailed discussion of this topic.

- **Apostolic Worship** – Worship that ascends into the heavenlies and ministers to the Lord, and attracts His attention, presence and glory, and shifts atmospheres.

- **Bilateral Apostle** – An apostle whose influence, assignment or metron of authority encompasses two spheres or mountains of culture.

- **Bishop** – An overseer of a local church or local group of churches. This term is sometimes used to refer to an elder or pastor, and is derived from the Greek words *presbuteros* (presbyter) and *Episkopos* (superintendent, overseer). (See Chapter 6 for a discussion of the history of bishops, and how many denominations have chosen without scriptural precedent or basis to use this term and man-elected office to refer to the apostolic function and office of apostle).

- **Convening Apostle** – An apostle who convenes, invites, facilitates or gathers others for special meetings, events or occasions.

- **Ecclesiastical Apostle** – A Religion Mountain or Church apostle.

- **Elder** – A ruling officer of local church government appointed by an apostle or group of apostles historically, as in the example of Paul and Timothy. Apostles may also function as elders in some churches and can hold both offices or positions concurrently or simultaneously on a case by case basis as elders are local officials and local situations vary from church to church. In modern times, elders have also been appointed or elected by pastors or other five-fold ministers, bishops, or by vote of a local church membership or a ruling council of lay leaders. Such methods and procedures are without biblical precedent.

- **Eldership** – The state or position or rank of being an elder, or in some cases, this can refer to a plurality or body of elders of a local church.

- **Evangelist** – A minister called and gifted by God to evangelize and win souls and disciple individuals, people groups, cities and/or nations.

- **Five-fold** – The ascension gifts, callings, functions and/or offices of apostle, prophet, teacher, evangelist and pastor. This term is used to refer to Eph. 4:11 and can be applied collectively or individually to describe these five ministries.

- **Governing Apostle** – An apostle who governs or leads an apostolic network, coalition or association of apostles or other venture, enterprise, endeavor or initiative that is apostolic.

- **Horizontal Apostle** – A peer-level apostle who has special gifts, callings, functions or assignments but does not lead or govern other apostles.

- **Marketplace** – A term used to refer to a place for buying and selling goods or services, or more generally, to the collective activities, entities, institutions, and sectors therein, such as business, finance, commerce, economics, banking, technology, trading, science, education, training, healthcare, media, arts, entertainment, sports, lodging, travel, tourism, publishing, agriculture, manufacturing, distribution, wholesaling, retailing, warehousing, research, exchange, etc.

- **Marketplace Apostle** – An apostle whose influence, assignment or metron of authority involves the marketplace generally, and specifically business, finance, commerce, economics, banking, technology, trading, science, education, training, healthcare, media, arts, entertainment, sports, lodging, travel, tourism, publishing, agriculture, manufacturing, distribution, wholesaling, retailing, warehousing, research, exchange, etc.

- **Multilateral Apostle** – An apostle whose influence, assignment and/or metron of authority encompasses more than three spheres or mountains of culture.

- **Pastor** – A minister called and gifted by God to shepherd and tend the flock, comfort, counsel and disciple individuals, people groups, cities and/or nations.

- **Prelate** – an ecclesiastic of a high order, as an archbishop, bishop, etc.; a church dignitary.

- **Present Truth** – Current revelation given by the Holy Spirit to an apostle or apostles for a local church or group of churches, an apostolic network, the apostolic community, and/or the entire body of Christ. This phrase is taken from 2 Peter 1:12 (KJV, NKJV).

- **Presiding Apostle** – An apostle who presides over meetings, functions, gatherings, forums, conferences, and/or events.

- **Prophet** – A minister called and gifted by God to see, hear, discern, decree, declare and prophesy the voice, will, counsel and heart of God, and to disciple individuals, people groups, cities and/or nations.

- **Seven Mountains** – A term describing and meaning gateways of culture or cultural influencers or mind-molders or spheres of influence. These include Family, Education, Business, Government, Media, Arts & Entertainment, and Religion.

- **Seven Spheres** – see Seven Mountains definition. In this book I use these terms interchangeably.

- **Teacher** – A minister called and gifted by God to exegete and expound on Scriptures, books, curricula and Christian living and to teach, train, equip and disciple individuals, people groups, cities and/or nations.

- **Territorial Apostle** – Geographic area apostle assigned to territories such as city, region, state, nation.

- **Trilateral Apostle** – An apostle whose influence, assignment and/or metron of authority encompasses three spheres or mountains of culture.

- **Unilateral Apostle** – An apostle whose influence, assignment and/or metron of authority encompasses one sphere or mountain of culture.

- **Vertical Apostle** – Leads and covers other people including apostles in a group, church, tribe, company, association, denomination or network. He or she leads by being the chief servant apostle.

- **Workplace** – A collective term for the marketplace and government spheres combined; i.e., any area of employment, profession, occupation, industry, commerce, administration, legislation, taxation, justice, enforcement, exchange, etc.

- **Workplace Apostle** – An apostle whose influence, assignment or metron of authority involves the workplace generally, and specifically business, finance, economics, banking, technology, trading, science, education, government, etc.

*Designates use by permission from Dr. G. E. Bradshaw and excerpted from *The Technology of Apostolic Succession*.

SECTION I:

INTRODUCTION & OVERVIEW

CHAPTER ONE

COMING INTO APOSTOLIC ALIGNMENT

OVERVIEW OF RECENT HISTORY AND MOVEMENTS IN THE CHURCH: RETURN OF THE APOSTLES

The whole of the 20th century and the first 13 years of the 21st have been accompanied by dramatic changes within Christianity. The history of those changes has been well documented through numerous books and articles, has been widely preached and taught from pulpits and in classrooms, has been dramatized in motion picture and television productions, and broadcast across every form of media available to Christian communications.

The modern Charismatic movement, which became recognized and accepted in the mid-1960s after tracing its origins to 1901 in Topeka, Kansas and then to Azusa Street in Los Angeles a few years later and from there to the world, marked the most significant and far-reaching change in Christianity since the Protestant Reformation. In amazing numbers, people embraced the baptism of the Holy Spirit and the restoration of the "charismata"—the supernatural gifts of the Spirit. That movement sparked a tremendous flow of evangelism and a subsequent outpouring of dynamic teaching ministries which eventually stretched around the world. Tremendous revivals were unleashed in

South America and later in sub-Saharan Africa and Asia whereby millions of people were saved and drawn into the kingdom of God.

By the late 1990s, a significant prophetic movement had gained serious traction, precipitating a restoration of the apostolic and a cry for a return to a more foundationally-connected understanding of the kingdom of God, of the purpose of the Church, and of the nature of the connection between the workplace and the organized Church. The rise of a contemporary apostolic movement has proven to be more than the mere passing interest of a few forward-thinking individuals; it has become a ground-swell of change, reaching deep into the Church and becoming intrinsically engaged with the marketplace as well.

The primary catalyst for these changes has been the restoration of a present reality of the kingdom of God, the realization that the Church is a smaller construct and subset of God's much larger kingdom, and an understanding that the Gospel of the Kingdom was the primary gospel message Jesus taught while on earth, with salvation and discipleship fitting within the larger message. This is in direct contrast and contradistinction to the familiar and popular but theologically false message and view of God's kingdom merely being an ultimate reward after the rapture or return of Christ.

The message Jesus preached was God's present, active kingdom. Wherever He went, he healed the sick, dispelled demonic forces, offered forgiveness, and demanded repentance, declaring "the kingdom of God is at hand." He gathered a band of followers around him whom he taught and prepared for the establishment of the Church, choosing 12 of them from among his disciples to become apostles of

His message, sent from Him to preach and establish His kingdom on earth. Once trained and fully committed, He bestowed on them the presence, power, and authority of his Holy Spirit, empowering them and subsequent generations with supernatural resources that would release the influence and demonstrate the reality of His kingdom.

This initial group of apostles was the core leadership for the founding of the Church. No other offices, officers, officials, administrators, representatives, managers, or directors were mentioned prior to Acts 6. The entirety of the leadership team was the 11 hand-picked apostles, plus Mathias, whom they appointed after the death of Judas Iscariot. Their message and ministry quickly spread throughout the known world as the Church, that is the body of believers, became the conduit for the expansion of God's kingdom. For them, church never meant buildings or institutions. Their sense of organization was based on a functionally-strong leadership who knew God's purpose and were dedicated to establishing His order. They followed the direction of those delegated leaders, embraced the responsibility of personal, effective ministry, and endured the personal suffering and social isolation which accompanied their faith.

The organization of the early Church was based on a functionally-strong leadership who knew God's purpose and were dedicated to establishing His order.

What generally escapes the understanding of 21st century Christians is how little the early Church resembles the way we function as the Church today. Everything they did, they did in the context of their daily living. In other words, they were utterly and completely marketplace Christians. Their leaders were men and women of business, labor, and industry, a fact we will explore in more detail in another chapter. Their gatherings were usually conducted in secretive settings with the purpose of encouraging, empowering, and building their strength to endure the daily struggles of Christian experience. They would never have been content with the carefully-choreographed presentations we define as worship. They were eager to live their faith in the midst of every struggle and trial.

Through the centuries, men and women have always embraced such an attitude of faith, but the emphasis on spirituality has long since shifted away from the marketplace toward the organized structure of the Church. Spiritual life has largely been separated from secular life in the minds of most people, Christians and non-Christians alike. What must be understood, however, is that in parallel with the restoration of the apostolic to the Church, there has come a far more extensive, if less recognized, rise of the apostolic in particular and five-fold in general, beyond the confines of modern church organization and practice.

THE RISE OF THE APOSTOLIC IN THE WORKPLACE

This rise of the apostolic in the workplace has rather conspicuously been identified as the Marketplace Movement, marketplace ministry, or workplace ministry. In reality, it extends far beyond the economic marketplace into the inner workings of every sphere of cultural influence. Millions of apostles and apostolic leaders are strategically positioned, equipped and engaged; some must remain in stealth mode below the radar screen and in the background and behind the scenes due to the sensitive nature of their assignments or positions, while others have risen up more publically with their faith, and/or are rising up to exercise their influence in godliness and integrity and justice and righteousness across the globe. In far too many cases, they are an unsung multitude, unrecognized or under-recognized, or even misjudged or misunderstood at times by the Church.

Fortunately, that has been changing rapidly over the last several decades as the Holy Spirit is restoring apostles and prophets, and ecclesiastical leaders have increased their understanding of the strategic importance and mission-critical nature of both workplace leaders and the workplace itself to the prime directive of the Church. Increasingly, workplace apostles are extending their reach far beyond the confines of traditional church organization and practice, embracing levels of responsibility, authority, and culturally-impacting or transforming activity in unprecedented ways.

The leading-edge of this movement is being populated by apostolic leaders, often called "marketplace apostles," especially by those within the ranks of the ecclesiastical community. However, that is changing as well. As the understanding and perspective of the apostolic expands, more and more ecclesiastically-oriented leaders are recognizing the significance of this powerful, viable, marketplace component. It is there that the influencing structures of the world can most effectively be encountered and ultimately transformed from darkness to light.

People do not live primarily within the boundaries of the Church, its organizations, and its institutions. The influences which dominate their mindsets reach far beyond their spiritual perspectives or their religious persuasions. While spirituality dominates the mindsets of multitudes in one fashion or another, that spirituality is not necessarily a consequence of God's light or God's truth, and has often been compromised, polluted, perverted, or watered down by worldly or carnal or demonic influences and sources.

More often, it is a spirituality guided by dark forces intent on mental, emotional, financial and physical domination. Of this, most readers are likely aware, and many of us have confronted darkness to the extent we are confident that we walk in the light. We know the redemption of Jesus, know the peace which came through His forgiveness, know the power which comes from His Holy Spirit, and know the security of being in a personal, life-giving relationship with Him. Still, many of us... perhaps to some degree all of us... are influenced or affected in some measure or on some level by the forces which dominate our culture and mold our mind-sets.

CONFRONTING CULTURAL PERSPECTIVES

Some years ago, seven specific cultural structures or spheres were identified as the major influential forces which shape a society's overall way of thinking. They have been called the mind-molders of culture, the influence shapers of social order, or more recently characterized as the Seven Mountains of Cultural Influence. It has been reasoned, and well-defined as spiritual revelation by several globally-recognized and -respected Christian leaders, that to the degree that individuals control or influence these structures, and the "high ground" associated with them, they impact the mind-set and life conclusions of a culture and generations. In the case of Hollywood, this influence or impact can be even across global cultures. These seven structures are government and law, education, business and finance, the arts and entertainment, the media, the family, and religion, with religion not necessarily being specified as the Church or Christianity.

By and large, the Church has operated from the pinnacle of the Religion mountain for a very, very long time, and continues to do so. In so doing, the functional mindset of the Church has been for many centuries that other cultural stimuli in Western society must do so and are irredeemable unless they come under its influence. This way of thinking relegates redemption and reconciliation into a course of action approved by the Church structure. That parallels the perspective of Jewish leadership during Jesus' day, making the Church the locus of spiritual transformation rather than the kingdom of God. Rather than this approach and attitude bridging the gap between the Church and the remainder of social order, it has created a barrier which people must cross in order to be accepted as brethren.

Such thinking is myopic and out of harmony with scripture, and God is now changing the paradigm there. This dichotomy has been described in detail by Nash and McLennan, in their book, *Church on Sunday, Work on Monday*, in which they document and describe different values, different cultures, different language and different rules and rulebooks for the Church and the workplace. What the Church has failed to realize is that perhaps their most valuable asset and weapon is their workplace leaders. Those Christians in the workplace understand both sets of rulebooks, and are equipped, designed and called to operate effectively from within rather than from without, to be the salt, light and leaven referred to in Matt. 13. They also understand the kingdom as well as the Church.

JESUS CAME TO REDEEM AND RECONCILE ALL THINGS

From scripture, we see a very different perspective, approach and emphasis on how the Church is to relate to the broader culture and society, and to its own members. *"There is [now no distinction] neither Jew nor Greek, there is neither slave nor free, there is not male and female; for you are all one in Christ Jesus"* (Gal. 3:28, AMP, author's emphasis). One chapter earlier, the writer echoes this: *"...God is not impressed with the positions that men hold and He is not partial and recognizes no external distinctions..."* (Gal. 2:6, AMP, author's emphasis).

The apostle Paul adds to this as follows:

"[In this new creation all distinctions vanish.] There is no room for and there can be neither Greek nor Jew, circumcised nor uncircumcised, [nor difference between nations whether alien] barbarians or Scythians [who are the most savage of all], nor slave or free man; but Christ is all and in all [everything and everywhere, to all men, without distinction of person]" (Col. 3:11, AMP, author's emphasis).

In these familiar verses, we see that Jesus came to break down the walls and barriers of division between all parts of society and culture, helping us to find our unity, purpose, strength and identity in and through Him. Included in the work and fruit of Christ referenced here, although not named in these two lists, is removing the barrier between priests and kings. This statement introduces a whole new theme which has not been identified or addressed. That has already been done through Jesus, but although we still hear sermons occasionally on race, gender, slavery, and Jew-Gentile relations, we rarely, if ever, hear sermons on king-priest relations. Jesus filled both offices and positions.

He was both a King and a Priest, the only priest in the Bible to do so officially other than the mysterious Melchizedek referred to in Gen. 14, Ps. 110, and Heb. 7, who was listed as "King of Salem and Priest of God Most High" (Heb. 7:1-2).[1] That's one reason that scripture says Jesus is "in the Order of Melchizedek" (Heb. 6:20, NIV), and that it is an eternal order, with Jesus serving as High Priest forever in the heavenly tabernacle. According to Aaron Evans:

> "As the royal priesthood, we have been given access to His divine presence and the awesome privilege of interacting and communing with the Living God.
>
> "A priestly seer company needs to be trained, equipped, and taught concerning the order of Melchizedek (Hebrews 7:17, 24-25). Melchizedek was both a king and a priest. This order will produce a priesthood of believers who minister according to the power of an indestructible life, administered by the Holy Spirit. The priestly order of Melchizedek is the highest priestly order that the Lord has established for His people. It affects the priesthood of the believer in the church and the marketplace. The eternal priestly order empowers spiritual leaders to be involved in a profitable business and a church or ministry, just as Paul was, as we see in Acts 18:1-4.
>
> "Under the order of Melchizedek, every believer is in full-time ministry. Ministering unto the Lord will give us access to the wisdom, influence, and favor we need to affect the seven mountains."[2]

Guess what: Jesus is also serving as King of Kings and Lord of Lords forever, too. By serving and occupying both positions and offices, Jesus reconciled or made peace between the two, just as he did with all the other types of human relationships prone to enmity, abuse and misunderstanding.

In the Old Testament, there was a direct prophecy about this. That story is recorded in Zech. 6:13 (AMP, author's emphasis): *"Yes, [you are building a temple of the Lord, but] it is He Who shall build the [true] temple of the Lord, and He shall bear the honor and glory [as of the only begotten of the Father] and shall sit and rule upon His throne. And He shall be a [a]Priest upon His throne, and **the counsel of peace shall be between the two [offices—Priest and King]**."* This same passage translated elsewhere says: *"A Message from God-of-the-Angel-Armies. Be alert. We have a man here whose name is Branch. He will branch out from where he is and build the Temple of God. Yes, he's the one. He'll build the Temple of God. **Then he'll assume the role of royalty, take his place on the throne and rule—a priest sitting on the throne!—showing that king and priest can coexist in harmony"*** (Zech. 6:12-13, AMP, author's emphasis).

News flash! Now well over 2000 years later (more like 2500 years), Jesus came to make peace between kings and priests as well as other key types of human relationships. So as apostles of Jesus, and/or five-fold officers of His church and kingdom, we all need to learn and put into practice how to "coexist in harmony." That's just for starters. We're also commanded to "build each other up in love," until we all attain or reach "maturity in Christ." This is not an option, as some in the church and the five-fold seem to think. As I stated earlier in the Preface, we do that through "mutual submission" (Eph. 5:21), which first requires mutual humility, love, acceptance, affirmation, respect and honor.

In fact, Peter the Apostle says that the whole church is now "a holy priesthood" and "a royal priesthood" (1 Pet. 2: 5, 9). Rev. 1:6 refers to the Church as "kings and priests" and Rev. 5:9-10 adds (MSG, author's emphasis): *"And they sang a new song: 'Worthy! Take the scroll, open its seals. Slain! Paying in blood, you bought men and women, Bought them back from all over the earth, Bought them back for God. Then you made them a Kingdom, Priests for our God, **Priest-kings to rule over the earth.'"***

The King James translation of this passage says, *"And they sung a new song, saying, 'Thou art worthy to take the book, and to open the seals thereof: for thou wast slain, and hast redeemed us to God by thy blood out of every kindred, and tongue, and people, and nation; And hast made us unto our God **kings and priests: and we shall reign on the earth.'"*** In other words, through Jesus, the King-Priest, we who are joint heirs of salvation with Him and members of God's royal family and household by adoption and through faith (see Rom. 8, 10), and have available to us the "full rights of sons" (Gal. 4:4), are empowered, positioned, called, equipped and authorized to serve as both kings and priests on the earth and to "coexist in harmony" — first, within ourselves, and secondly, with other five-fold officers and ministers.

Therefore, as leaders of the Church and kingdom of God, we need to stop making "distinction of persons" among the five-fold officers of Jesus, based simply on title, position, calling, gifting, office, or sphere of authority, and instead, submit one to another in love, humility and honor.[3] Ed Silvoso agreed, stating, **"This unbiblical classification of believers results in first- and second-class statuses within the Church. Such distinctions should not exist** because Jesus Himself was not an elitist."[4]

Dr. Bill Hamon also concurred, stating:

"Jesus chose twelve men from the business world and ordained them as apostles. He did not choose men from the religious Rabbinical Schools or the Levitical Priesthood. **Jesus made no distinction in calling and commissioning based on one's past professions or position in life.** Revelation regarding God's thoughts concerning fivefold ministers is going to revolutionize the present thinking and function of the old church order. **No scripture declares that a person must be the pastor of a church or have his own non-profit organization to be called as an apostle or prophet in the Body of Christ...God is raising up and giving recognition to His company of Joseph/Daniel-apostles/prophets.** The old order Church system or the government may never recognize them for who they are, but God is giving them His recognition and power to prosper."[5]

Jesus chose twelve men from the business world and ordained them as apostles.

Perhaps the following passage penned by Paul sums this up best: *"For he himself is our peace, who has made the two one and has **destroyed the barrier, the dividing wall of hostility,** by abolishing in his flesh the law with its commandments and regulations. His purpose was to create in himself one new man out of the two, thus **making peace,** and in the one body to **reconcile both of them to God** through the cross, by which **he put to death their hostility**...For through him we both have access to the Father by one spirit"* (Eph. 2:14-18, NIV, author's emphasis). Even though the Ephesian epistle is addressed to a predominately Gentile church, and the original context of this passage is referring to Jews and Gentiles, these verses are equally applicable to kings and priests, in my opinion. It's time for the barriers and walls to come down between clergy and laity, and the hostility to cease between five-fold officers in the Seven Mountains or spheres of culture.

Moreover, not only did Paul warn and admonish the 1st century churches to no longer make distinctions among believers after the flesh, to destroy the barriers and dividing walls that separate disciples from each other, to make peace, be reconciled, and put to death hostility; he also modeled that for us. After clarifying that the other apostles "added nothing to my message," and that he had received his revelation and apostolic calling and appointment directly from Jesus, Paul, along with his traveling companion and fellow apostle to the Gentiles, Barnabas, were given "the right hand of fellowship" by Peter, James and John—the pillars in the Jerusalem church, "when they recognized the grace given to me."

God's grace rests upon and saturates and permeates every true apostle, and gives witness to their apostolic calling, assignment, authority and commission. The end result of this historic meeting was that "They agreed that we should go to the Gentiles, and they to the Jews" (Gal. 2:6-10). The leaders of the early church agreed among themselves about their assignments and spheres of authority from the Lord, and agreed to work together and recognize and support each other and govern together in unity.

The Amplified translation says it this way: *"But on the contrary, when they [really] saw that I had been entrusted [to carry] the Gospel to the uncircumcised [Gentiles, just as definitely] as Peter had been entrusted [to proclaim] the Gospel to the circumcised [Jews, they were agreeable]; For He Who motivated and fitted Peter and worked effectively through him for the mission to the circumcised, motivated and fitted me and worked through me also for [the mission to] the Gentiles. **And when they knew***

(perceived, recognized, understood, and acknowledged)
the grace (God's unmerited favor and spiritual blessing)
that had been bestowed upon me, James and Cephas
(Peter) and John, who were reputed to be pillars of the
Jerusalem church, gave to me and Barnabas the right hand
of fellowship, with the understanding that we should go
to the Gentiles and they to the circumcised (Jews)" (Gal.
2:7-9, author's emphasis).

APOSTOLIC PARTNERSHIP
VS. PROPRIETORSHIP

In other words, the original apostles who were leaders of
the church in Jerusalem, and apparently who had some
degree of universal authority in the early church based
upon their sending delegations to Antioch, appointing
deacons and elders, convening councils to decide doctrinal
issues, and being given the keys to the kingdom of heaven
to steward, received Paul and Barnabas and their callings,
appointments, giftings, offices, assignments, and authority
as equal to their own, even though neither of these men
were among the 12 Apostles of the Lamb, and had very
different backgrounds. Today we might call this "ministerial
courtesy," or more accurately, "ambassadorial rank and
protocol" and "apostolic partnership."

The established apostolic leaders rendered a portion or
"tithe" of their mantle, mission and manifested power to
Paul and Barnabas, so they could "grasp" the full measure
of apostolic partnership in the distribution of kingdom
principles in the earth. This type of partnership is essential
today and builds the fellowship of apostles and apostolic
people into a cohesive union and function as the body
of Christ in the earth. Apostles help people to grasp or

"apprehend" what they have been called to function in. This example provides an excellent model for clergy-laity relationships today, particularly for apostles functioning in the workplace and those primarily in the Church or Religion mountain.

With the rise of a contemporary apostolate comes the prospect of regaining levels of significant influence which can affect the minds and hearts of masses of people. Whole communities, and ultimately entire people groups, will be swayed by the surge in righteousness, peace, and joy emanating from a kingdom-minded company of leaders. But, they must be leaders within the spheres which influence people's thinking. Of necessity, then, there will be and are apostles and apostolic leaders who function outside of the confines of Church organization and ecclesiastical perspective.

Accordingly, as I look at the dynamics of Christian leadership and consider the juxtaposition of apostles in both the Church and the workplace, I can only conclude that spiritually there is no such thing as a "workplace apostle" in contradistinction to an "ecclesiastical apostle." I am convinced, and scripture bears out my conviction, that there was no such distinction made in the early church. Furthermore, the use of such titles or categories is unnecessary, in my opinion, and creates or at least reinforces a disconnection between the Church and marketplace, and perpetuates the clergy-laity distinction. However, I do acknowledge the present truth revelation claim cited for these terms, and due to their widespread acceptance and use today by others, I will refer to these terms throughout my chapters.

THE CHURCH, THE MARKETPLACE, THE KINGDOM, THE SEVEN MOUNTAINS AND THE FIVE-FOLD

The development of a specific strategy for wielding influence in the Seven Mountains of cultural influence must not be separated from a purely kingdom of God dynamic. The Church, while an intrinsic part of the kingdom, is not the entirety of the kingdom. God's kingdom far outdistances the organizational, religious, and influential presence of the Church. It extends into every realm of culture, every corner of society, and every segment of ethnic identity. It is pervasive, manifesting its power and presence within the hearts and lives of those who have embraced Jesus Christ as Lord and King (Luke 17:21). Thus, every instrument of its order must be available to and functional in every place the kingdom of God is manifested.

> **The development of a specific strategy for wielding influence in the Seven Mountains of cultural influence must not be separated from a purely kingdom of God dynamic.**

One of the main "proof texts" cited for the existence and legitimacy of apostles and prophets in the church today is Eph. 2:19-21, with verses 20-21 quoted often about apostles and prophets being the foundation, and Christ Jesus being the chief cornerstone. I would like to suggest that verse 19 is also important in this whole discussion of the Seven Mountains or spheres of culture and five-fold functioning. Eph. 2:19 says (author's emphasis for all translations cited), *"Therefore you are no longer outsiders (exiles, migrants, and aliens, excluded from the rights of citizens), but you now share citizenship with the saints (God's own people, consecrated and set apart for Himself); and you belong to God's [own] household"* (AMP). The Message translates this verse as: *"That's plain enough, isn't it? You're no longer wandering exiles. This kingdom of faith is now your home country. You're no longer strangers or outsiders. You belong here, with as much right to the name Christian as anyone. God is building a home. He's using us all— irrespective of how we got here—in what he is building."*

Finally, the NIV says: *"Consequently, you are no longer foreigners and strangers, but fellow citizens with God's people and also members of his household."* The point I am making here and highlighting is that we as disciples and followers of Christ are not citizens of a church, but of a kingdom, as Dr. Myles Munroe has so adeptly and eloquently pointed out and written about in several best-selling books, and as The Message translation expresses best here. The Greek word for "citizens" is *"Polites,"* which means one from a particular governmental jurisdiction or entity, such as a city, town, colony or province. It also relates to the word *"Polemos,"* meaning warfare, battle or fight. As those whose "citizenship is in heaven" (Phil. 3:20, NIV), we war a good warfare for the expansion of the kingdom territory of God, while at the same time, we are members of God's own household, the Church. It is called a household because we are God's family as His sons and daughters.

From Ephesians 4:11, we are offered a taxonomy of authoritative leadership to direct and order the effective working of the kingdom as it is expressed in the world. These distinctive offices are known as the five-fold ministry and comprise the apostolic offices which are delegated to oversee and govern kingdom advancement. In some measure, they have recognition and utility within the Church, although not entirely. Some reject the offices of apostle and prophet, even within the Church, but the prevailing mindset is and has been that the "ministry" offices are isolated to ecclesiastical perspective (i.e., the Religion mountain or sphere).

This perception has changed dramatically as more and more apostles embrace and fulfill their responsibilities, and the obviously limited influence of the ecclesiastical community apart from effective marketplace ministry becomes apparent. In some ways, the "eyes of the blind" are being opened to see what has been missing from the picture, notably, that the presence and significance of a legitimate, justifiable, five-fold ministry presence and function in the marketplace is reasonable, logical, necessary, valid and undeniable. According to Glenn Shaffer, "Without a clear understanding of the five gifts in Ephesians 4:11 and the proper application of the foundational gifts of apostles and prophets, the hope of a strong, unified body of Christ will remain elusive."[6]

Rich Marshall outlined this perspective quite affirmatively when he wrote:

"A new breed of ministers is emerging in the world marketplace. These ministers are passionate about the Kingdom, and are people of integrity and high moral character. They think strategically and creatively about ways to impact the world for the Lord. They are called of God and know it, but not in the traditional sense of preaching, teaching, or even evangelism as we have known it. They serve the Lord, but not in church offices or mission headquarters. They serve Him in the marketplace. Why? Because they are business and professional people, and they know that their work is their ministry."[7]

Unfortunately, while the recognition of ministers in the marketplace has been elevated quite a bit in recent years, the spiritual significance and divine nature of their offices has not been advanced on an equal footing within the ecclesiastical mindset or interpretation and application of scripture. Many individuals who are called by God and know they are five-fold ministers in the workplace have not received recognition or acceptance on a level commensurate with ecclesiastical leaders, and sometimes, not on any level. This bias is understandable when one balances it against a centuries-old mindset and resultant historical practices and traditions. However, it is not defensible, given the marketplace origins of the Church and the necessity of reaching into the Seven Mountains of Culture with an undiluted five-fold ministry perspective.

In view of this, Ed Silvoso noted as follows:

> **"It is about time that people who are called to serve in the marketplace be validated as full-fledged ministers** because the last revival, the one predicted by Joel and quoted by Peter (see Acts 2:17-21), will happen all over the city, not just inside a building. It will be an outpouring of the Spirit of God upon all flesh."[8]

> **"When marketplace Christians are reduced to second-class status, the Church is automatically deprived of its most strategically-placed soldiers because they are the ones closest to Satan's command and control centers.** If properly equipped, they can do lethal damage to the systems by which the devil holds people captive in our cities (see 2 Cor. 4:4; Eph. 6:12). This is why he allocates so many of his resources to make marketplace Christians feel unqualified and inferior in spiritual matters."[9]

David Cannistraci agreed, stating, "The apostle may well represent the single greatest human threat in existence to the work of Satan."[10] Paula Price also pointed out that "the Lord's choice of the term *apostle* was calculated to inject a staggering force of laborers into God's kingdom."[11]

The ongoing assault on the importance of marketplace apostolic leaders can be primarily traced to their capacity to garner far-reaching influence within their operational spheres. Whereas apostles within the ecclesiastical arena are largely dependent on donor-based financial support systems, those in the marketplace are uniquely qualified to create significant wealth and use it to broaden their platform in the world. Yet, the prevailing perspective among marketplace leaders is that those in the Church look toward their ability to make significant amounts of money as their primary contribution to the kingdom.

In all honesty, that has been the case far too long and often as ecclesiastical leaders look to prosperous business leaders to fund their visions and underwrite their ministries. It is not unreasonable for apostolic leaders in the marketplace who have, and can gain substantial financial means, to participate in financing church operations, but that is not their principal function. They have so much more to contribute to God's kingdom advance than money, such as influence, wisdom, discernment, relationships, strategy, favor, reputation and authority, to name a few.

Again, I turn to Rich Marshall for a perspective we need to see in this regard:

"For years we have attempted to reach cities by means of nuclear church programs, outreaches, church planting, unity efforts, prayer movements, and every other conceivable local church concept. Yet, when Jesus speaks of authority in the city, He is referring to the impact that comes from businesspeople doing business. I am confident that when Marketplace Apostles are recognized for who they are, we will see new strategies and actions that will result in major, beneficial changes in the cities and nations of the world.

"...I need to emphasize that money is only one means of gaining authority for a Marketplace Apostle. Authority in a city or a nation also comes through political means, media, and wisdom. Sometimes God simply gives a level of authority that others respond to, yet it has an identifiable source. Being the Lord, God sometimes just does things that we cannot understand. In other words, it is possible for someone who does not have great financial resources to carry high levels of authority."[12]

APOSTLES ARE APOSTLES

One of the sincere and greatest concerns raised by ecclesiastical leaders with regard to workplace-oriented leaders is the lack of theological expertise they have. Of course, this is a self-fulfilling and self-perpetuating concern and circular argument, and even the theologians and ecclesiastical leaders cannot agree among themselves on many points of doctrine, such as eschatology and their debates about how many angels can fit on the head of a pin, so such concerns have limited validity and little if any bearing on the reality of the kingdom of God except to perpetuate an "us versus them" mentality and culture and separate class structure in the Church, and foster peer relationships and alliances among clergy, while pigeon-holing and labeling "workplace apostles" as second-class citizens, with superior doctrine and revelation being a primary focus or goal of their ministry.

It's no wonder that Peter Wagner calls workplace apostles "absolutely essential" and the "missing link" to Church growth, social transformation, and wealth transfer in the body of Christ. Wagner also noted, "I do not believe that we will see the social transformation we desire unless our workplace apostles are properly activated."[13] It is also important to note here that some workplace apostles have been "hidden" rather than "missing" for strategic, security and timing reasons, and that will continue until Christ returns due to the sensitive nature of their assignments.

In response, I want to say as clearly and humbly and respectfully and lovingly as I know how, that they are not actually "missing," but instead have been overlooked, ignored, neglected, misunderstood, underestimated, underutilized, undervalued, criticized, judged, insulted, dishonored and/or abused in some cases by ecclesiastical church leaders. I have experienced this personally on several occasions over the years in different churches.

I have also seen and experienced personally the flip side of this and heard some of the "war stories" from other senior pastors, bishops and apostles about the behavior, speech, busy schedules, pride, unavailability and lack of commitment of workplace leaders in their churches, their lack of respect and honor for church leadership and for tithing. I have scars from both and am standing in the gap for healing of this breach between kings and priests. Kent Humphreys has also addressed this dynamic at length in his writing and teaching, as have Nash and McLennan.[14]

So, while this tension and friction may always exist to some degree since we are human, especially in non-apostolic denominations, I call for this dysfunction to stop and cease now, whereever it exists in the body of Christ and Church leadership, and for relations to normalize and ideally harmonize between the five-fold officers of the Church as well as other ministers. And thankfully, that is happening in an ever-increasing number of cities, churches, ministries, businesses, agencies, and nations as the apostolic movement provides a new wineskin for the new wine of the Spirit to be poured into and flow through.

Certainly all true apostles are to know and steward not only the word of God, but the mysteries and revelation of God (Eph. 3:4-5). Paul told Timothy, *"Watch your life and doctrine closely. Persevere in them..."* (1 Tim. 4:16). This is certainly commendable for all apostles; however, the idea that a workplace professional such as a doctor/physician, lawyer/attorney, judge, engineer, nurse, teacher, social worker, computer programmer, accountant, pilot, plumber, salesman, electrician, actor, model, athlete, artist, musician, singer, soldier or CEO cannot learn or understand basic theology is ludicrous and laughable. Much of this notion stems from the increasing professionalization of the clergy, and the misconception of a class of "professional apostles."

Many Christian groups can and do agree on basic, simple doctrinal statements, such as the Apostle's Creed. That is not rocket science, and does not require advanced educational degrees, ordinations, or years of service in ministry to understand or explain. In this regard, Hirsch and Catchim noted that "...requiring a formal, classroom-based degree as a necessary basis for ordination, a concept itself completely alien to the New Testament, violates the calling and ministry that Jesus has clearly given to every disciple and lends itself to a professionalized elitism that Jesus himself detested."[15]

Furthermore, certain types or classes of doctrine are not foundational or primary, but rather secondary and less important. Still other doctrines are even further down the priority scale, so it is not necessary to "major in minors" to be an effective apostle. However, a basic understanding of systematic theology, hermeneutical principles, biblical exegesis, and foundational doctrines is useful for all apostles, just as a basic understanding of the principles of business and finance is useful for all apostles.

The fact that some individuals may not apply themselves in these areas with as much diligence or success as others is no excuse for discrimination, distinctions, and false judgment by either group of apostles toward the other. Each leader and apostle must be judged upon his or her own maturity, character and merit as well as sphere of influence and authority—whether workplace or ecclesiastical is the primary assignment—rather than being stereotyped as part of a group or class of five-fold officers.

Sound doctrine is a basic commandment and requirement of all apostles, but it is probably true that ecclesiastical apostles get more practice and spend more time on this area of study and teaching than workplace apostles as a whole, although there are no doubt exceptions in both groups. Further, it is true that workplace apostles tend to focus on the "bottom line," and the "big picture," and systems, processes, and results. This, however, does not make doctrine the sole province of ecclesiastical apostles any more than it makes finance the sole province of workplace apostles.

Such concerns are more about professionalization and empire-building than about ministry in my opinion. Each class of apostles should be willing to help the others with whatever special expertise or gifting they may have, so that we may all come to the maturity and fullness of Christ and be "jointly fitted." In fact, many modern, ecclesiastical apostles all came from and got their start in the workplace.

A small sampling of those today would include Dr. Chuck Pierce, Dr. Pat Francis, Dr. Peter Wagner, Dr. Paul (Buddy) Crum, Dr. John Benefiel, Dr. Rick Joyner, Ed Silvoso, Dr. Paul Costa, John Kelly, Naomi Dowdy, John Abercrombie, Dr. A.L. Gill, Dr. Paula Price, Dr. G. E. Bradshaw, Paul Keith Davis, Paul Manwaring, David Yarnes, Tim Taylor, Cal Pierce, Keith Miller, Danny Silk, Kris Vallotton, Georgian Banov, Patricia King, Faytene Kryskow Grassechi, Dr. Tim Hamon, Dr. Nasir Siddiki, Mickey Freed, Henry Falany, Mark Pfeifer, Dr. Joseph Umidi, Dr. Joseph Mattera, Dr. John Muratori, Doug Stringer, Joe Kelley, Dr. Philip Byler, Bob Hartley, Dr. Lance Wallnau, Kent Humphreys, Bart Pierce, Gene Strite, Sam Soleyn, Mike and Cindy Jacobs, Dr. James Boswell Sr., Larry Bizette, Linda Rios Brook, Ras Robinson, Larry Kreider, O. Michael Smith, Vance and Debbie Russell, Joe Morales, Bruce Gunkle, Dr. Kimberly Daniels, Ron DePriest, Willie Wooten, Barbara Yoder, Peter Nash, Dr. Larry Keefauver, Dr. Jonathan Hansen, Dr. Jack Sheffield, Dr. Sylvester Brinson III, Marcus Triplett, Joe Champion, Dr. Clay Nash, Randy Clark, Rick Wright, Dr. Kingsley Fletcher, Dr. Victor Choudhrie, Drs. Jerry and Isabella D'Souza, Bruce and Cheryl Lindley, David Hoskins, David Newsome, Norm Willis, John Fair, Indri Gautama, Luis Palau, Dr. Len Zoeteman, Ron McGatlin, Donald Alfred, Charles Flowers, Alan Vincent, H. Daniel Wilson, Dr. Bruno Caporrimo, Brian Simmons, Lorne Tebbutt, Jeff Beacham, Dr. Israel Kim and Johnny Enlow. Going back nearly two centuries, attorney-revivalist Charles Finney would be numbered among those also.

The nature of the workplace, particularly in the business and financial arena, not to mention government and politics, has been pock-marked with character flaws, sex scandals, greed, corruption, pride, control, and manipulative tactics, and Church leaders are all too ready to point this out, and routinely do so, disregarding and overlooking identical weaknesses within their own ranks which have tainted their image, provoked the same criticism and media attention, and become an outward show of hypocrisy. Joyner also points out that some Church leaders have fallen victim to financial investment Ponzi schemes and are seen as easy marks and prey by conmen and wolves in sheep's clothing.[16]

The majority of marketplace leaders are not called to function primarily as theologians; they are called to be leaders with godly influence whose lives and ethics help to shape the mindset and culture of their sphere(s) of authority and organizations. However, all apostles must have a solid grasp of scripture and biblical understanding in order to be effective and fruitful in their sphere(s) of assignment and authority. That alone is never enough, though, since knowledge puffs up but love never fails. Apostles must also know the heart of the Lord Jesus, and the person of the Holy Spirit. Their lives must be marked by intimacy. The underlying qualifications for ministry are not theological; they are practical, marked by stellar character, integrity, wisdom, courage, discernment, and maturity. This is a key issue in the development of apostles, one which Naomi Dowdy clearly stated as follows.

> "...there are specific types of Apostles who function with greater emphasis in certain areas. We cannot attempt to put them all in the same 'box,' saying, 'If you are an apostle, then you must do _____.' No, the functions of Apostles are as varied as the spheres of authority in God's Kingdom. **On the most basic level, an Apostle**

is an Apostle. When we know that a person occupies the office of Apostle by God's calling, with His grace, and with the character, mindset, and results of an Apostle, then we need to honor, respect, and relate to that person as an Apostle."[17]

Peter Wagner echoed that declaration:

"Sometimes in the New Testament we find the word ekklesia used for God's people gathered together. However, **an equal number of times it is used for God's people scattered wherever they might be.** To put it in modern terminology, when God's people are gathered together in their local churches on Sunday, they are the true church. And when they go out to the workplace Monday through Saturday, they are still the true church.

"... Once we realize that the extended church is a form of the real church, some interesting implications arise. One concerns church government. The foundation of the church, according to Ephesians 2:20, is apostles and prophets. **Up until now, we have associated apostles and prophets with the nuclear church, but there is no logical reason to think that church government stops there. Why not apostles and prophets in the extended church as well?**

"So let's take biblical church government to its logical conclusion. **Let's agree that there are workplace apostles."**[18]

In that regard, Dr. Paula Price has noted in agreement that **"there are non-ecclesiastical apostles assigned to handle the Lord's affairs outside the church, that is the business of the kingdom.** The narrow application of the word marketplace may well be a stricter way of saying 'world apostles' in which case the Great Commission's 'go ye into all the world...' does apply."[19] I clarify also that some apostles can function simultaneously in both the ecclesiastical and workplace dimensions, and that the two are not necessarily mutually exclusive, although some people perceive it that way.

Price also said that "apostles educate, organize, legislate, and strategize their jurisdictional spheres under Christ's leadership to steer current and future apostles' commissions toward God's ordained paths."[20] To whatever degree apostles and other five-fold ministers have authority within their own specific spheres of responsibility, they need to be identified and recognized as such. And while this chapter does not address the governmental implications inherent in the apostolic office, it is important to underscore in bold type that **apostles are apostles are apostles.** Wagner also stated:

> "Perhaps the greatest apostolic credential that Luke had was being inspired by the Holy Spirit to write over 25 percent of the New Testament. **Nothing in the New Testament would indicate that there is anything spiritually inferior on the part of workplace apostles.** In fact, it is noteworthy that Luke, the prototype of a workplace apostle, wrote the same percentage of the New Testament as Paul, the prototype of a nuclear-church apostle!
>
> **"Spiritually, then, workplace apostles and nuclear-church apostles are on the same plane. In matters of extraordinary character, the requirements for one are just as high as for the other. Most normal apostolic ministries would be observed in both."**[21]

I concur with Dr. Wagner on this point, and applaud his insight, courage and advocacy of workplace apostles, biblical church government, the Second Apostolic Age, and the New Apostolic Reformation. I differ with his viewpoint here only in one respect, and that is my belief that Paul was not exclusively or primarily a nuclear church or ecclesiastical apostle, per se. He was a tentmaker and provided both for himself and on many occasions for his traveling companions (see Acts 18:1-21, Rom. 16:3, 2 Thess. 3:6-10; see also 1 Cor. 9:10-15). In one instance, when in Corinth, he supported himself for a year and a half through this enterprise. He later took his partners, Priscilla and Aquila, with him to Syria and Ephesus where they continued their trade around their ministry schedule. From my understanding of scripture and early church history, all of the first century apostles were workplace apostles, and there were no ecclesiastical apostles as yet.

Only as the responsibility of oversight shifted toward city bishoprics several centuries later did the concept of a distinctly ecclesiastical leadership become a notable development in the changing infrastructure of the Church, and the terms "clergy" and "laity" were first introduced. Neither of these terms is found in scripture, and they are inventions of man to help institute, defend, maintain and enforce an artificial church hierarchy and class system that Jesus never intended, condoned or approved—despite certain denominational beliefs and teachings to the contrary.

Thus, if we identify or regard Paul as an ecclesiastical apostle, as Wagner suggests—and to be fair, he was sociologically and theologically trained in Judaism by a Rabbinical teacher named Gamaliel, who is mentioned as a Pharisee in Acts 5:33-40 and whose persuasive speech helped spare the lives of the apostles—this would mean Paul functioned as a *bi-lateral apostle* (a term to be discussed in a later chapter), holding authority in both the workplace and ecclesiastical spheres. In that respect, his background was a definite exception rather than the norm among the early apostles, and formal theological or sociological training was neither a requirement nor expectation of leadership, decision-making, doctrine, governance or calling in the early church. By necessity and practice, all of the early apostles were *bi-lateral apostles,* since they functioned both in the workplace and in church government and doctrinal matters. There was no dualism or bifurcation among the early apostles as we see practiced today in the Church.

Rich Marshall shares my viewpoint, stating:

> "The apostle Paul is a perfect example of a Marketplace Minister who heard from God. A builder, a tent maker, and a man who earned a living working with his hands, Paul wrote nearly half the New Testament. He is viewed as the greatest example of an apostle in the Church age."[22]

He then adds:

> **"As far as we know from Scripture, the apostle Paul never left his tent-making business."**[23]

I can find no separation of apostolic roles in the historical record until several hundred years into the Christian era. As the Church became institutionally oriented, bureaucratic, politicized and professionalized, a segregated clergy became prominent and the rules, culture and practice of church government changed drastically for the worse. None of the early church apostles attended a seminary or theological school. With the exception of Paul, none received religious training beyond the basic education required of Jewish male children within the synagogue system. To the degree that the system and culture was of itself theo-centric, they all had some level of theological perspective, but it was Jewish orthodoxy, not Christian evangelicalism.

The original apostles were perceived as ignorant and unlearned men (see Acts 4:13), but after receiving the indwelling power of the Holy Spirit, they showed no signs of ignorance or theological naiveté. Rather, they were given words to speak and ongoing access to divine wisdom and revelation whenever and wherever the occasion demanded. These and selected other first century apostles were the men who, inspired by the Holy Spirit, wrote the New Testament in the same manner as the prophets, judges, and kings of old scribed the Torah.

As Marshall has pointed out:

"**Not only were the first apostles all businessmen, it is highly possible that some (or all) remained in business while they fulfilled their call to follow Christ**... The first apostles were not only called from the marketplace; **they were also the first Marketplace Ministers.**"[24]

CONCLUSION

We will have a fuller discussion of the early church and first century apostles in Chapters 5 and 6, so I will conclude this opening chapter here and in summary, I have addressed several of the key scriptures and issues concerning ecclesiastical and workplace apostles, kings and priests, the church and the kingdom, and five-fold ministry in the Seven Mountains of Culture, which the Holy Spirit has highlighted to me in my study of this subject and instructed me to write about and release revelation on. The apostolic movement cannot fully mature and "go viral" again on a global scale, in my opinion, until these issues are recognized and corrected.

God moves in each generation through *"whosoever wills,"* and that is why every age has its apostolic reformers who start or lead movements. I suggest that there are two churches--not the workplace church and the ecclesiastical church, but the living church and the dead church, the Spirit-led church and the rules-led or sin-bound church. Make no mistake: the Spirit will find those in Christ who are yielded and obedient and work with them. May we be like Isaiah and say, *"Here am I; send me"* and like Mary, and say, *"Be it unto me according to thy word."* Then we will once again be an apostolic church. We turn now to Chapter 2.

ENDNOTES

1. Both Abraham and David offered sacrifices on occasion, but were never officially priests. Their friendship status with God seemed to grant them special favor and grace.

2. Aaron Evans, *The Emerging Daniel Company*, p. 91. Boxford, MA: The Emerging Daniel Company Intl., 2010. For a fuller description of the Order of Melchizedek, see Dr. Francis Myles, *The Order of Melchizedek: Rediscovering the Eternal Priesthood of Jesus Christ and How it Affects Us Today!* Leander, TX: Kingdom House Publishing, 2010.

3. Distinction and discernment are two very different things, and we will explore character and maturity in other chapters. We are to use discernment, but not distinction, in the church.

4. Ed Silvoso, *Anointed for Business*, p. 24, author's emphasis. Ventura, CA: Regal Books, 2002.

5. Dr. Bill Hamon, *Apostles Prophets and the Coming Moves of God*, p. 20. Shippensburg, PA: Destiny Image Publishers, 1997, author's emphasis.

6. Glenn Shaffer, *Apostolic Government in the 21st Century*, p. 10. Claremore, OK: Apostolic Teams Intl., 2005.

7. Rich Marshall, *God@Work*, pp. 1-2. Shippensburg, PA: Destiny Image Publishers, 2000.

8. Ed Silvoso, *Anointed for Business*, p. 12, author's emphasis.

9. Ibid, pp. 12-13, author's emphasis.

10. Dr. David Cannistraci, *The Gift of Apostle*, p. 79. Ventura, CA: Regal Books, 1996.

11. Dr. Paula A. Price, *Eternity's Generals*, p. 242. Tulsa, OK: Flaming Vision Publications, 2005.

12. Rich Marshall, *God@Work*, *Vol. II*, p. 70, author's emphasis. Shippensburg, PA: Destiny Image Publishers, 2005.

13. Dr. C. Peter Wagner, *On Earth as it is in Heaven: Answer God's Call to Transform the World*, pp. 138-139. Ventura, CA: Regal Books, 2012.

14. Kent Humphreys, *Shepherding Horses, Vols. I & II*. Oklahoma City, OK: Lifestyle Impact Ministries, 2006, 2009. Laura Nash and Scotty McLennan, *Church on Sunday, Work on Monday*. San Francisco, CA: Jossey-Bass, 2001.

15. Alan Hirsch and Tim Catchim, *The Permanent Revolution: Apostolic Imagingation and Practice for the 21ˢᵗ Century Church*, p. 240. San Francisco, CA: Jossey-Bass, 2012.

16. Dr. Rick Joyner, *The Apostolic Ministry*, pp. 28-29., author's emphasis Wilkesboro, NC: MorningStar Ministries Publications, 2004.

17. Naomi Dowdy, *Commissioning: The Process, Protocol, and Importance of Commissioning Modern-Day Apostles*, p. 12, author's emphasis. Dallas, TX: Naomi Dowdy Ministries, 2006.

18. Dr. C. Peter Wagner, *Apostles Today*. p. 110, author's emphasis. Ventura, CA: Regal Books, 2006.

19. Price, *Eternity's Generals*, p. 59.

20. Ibid, p. 12., author's emphasis.

21. Wagner, *Apostles Today*, p. 114, author's emphasis.

22. Rich Marshall, *God@Work, Vol. II*, page 103. Shippensburg, PA: Destiny Image Publishers, 2005.

23. Ibid, p. 45., author's emphasis.

24. Ibid, p. 45, author's emphasis.

Apostles must know the
heart of the Lord Jesus,
and the person of the
Holy Spirit. Their lives
must be marked
by intimacy.
The underlying
qualifications for
ministry are
not theological;
they are practical,
marked by stellar character,
integrity, wisdom, courage,
discernment, and maturity.

CHAPTER TWO

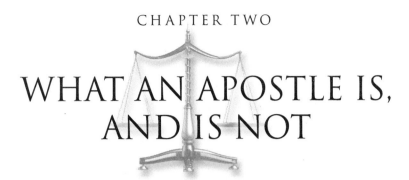

WHAT AN APOSTLE IS, AND IS NOT

It is my assertion that, with a Christian presence in the earth of more than two billion souls (closer to 2.5 billion), and some studies having estimated that 200,000 to 400,000 people per day are coming into the Kingdom worldwide,[1] **there are, in all likelihood, millions of apostles currently on the earth, and more on the way every day.** One ministry alone, Global Media Outreach, reports that one million people a month are finding and receiving Jesus through their efforts, or 12 million souls per year. Just multiplying 200,000 per day times 365 days yields around 73 million souls per year. Doubling that pushes the annual yield even higher, to 146 million. Some percentage of those will be called to five-fold ministry and leadership by the Lord and receive divine gifting and grace to function therein. Others will receive different spiritual gifts.

While some would dispute my opinion and estimate, and they are welcome to do so, it actually makes good sense to me, as well as others, since mathematically speaking, 97-98% of all Christians globally are either self-employed, employed by others or unemployed; the remaining 2-3% are vocational ministers who earn their economic livelihood and income as paid staff members of local churches, denominational organizations, or so-called "parachurch ministries."

According to Bob Fraser, for example, there is a great army of God comprised of "the 97% of believers who are not called to vocational ministry." He added, "97% of the pastoral, evangelistic, teaching, prophetic, and apostolic gifts are in Marketplace Christians and are to primarily operate in the marketplace. For Marketplace Christians, their field is their workplace, and their flock is the people they work with."[2]

Breaking this 97% down further, Drew Gentile noted:

"Robert Frasier {sic} has suggested that 3% of the body of Christ should be in vocational Christian service. He includes administrators, pastors, professors, secretaries, and teachers — anyone who is paid full-time. That leaves about 97% of the body of Christ in some other kind of vocation. ...There are probably something on the order of 6 million vocational Christian workers globally (of which 500,000 are foreign missionaries) and 2.2 billion Christians, broadly defined. That means that currently less than .5% of the Christians are in 'full-time Christian service' (1% in the US)." Gentile then summarized, "My point is that even if we had 10 times the number of pastors and missionaries, vocational Christian workers would still be a very small minority. The Christian work force for urban ministry is not going to be full-time workers, but people in the marketplace."[3]

Similarly, Dr. Bill Hamon makes this observation: "Church is in session wherever kingly and priestly Saints are operating, not just weekly in a building. We must activate and empower all Saints to bring the Kingdom of God to their realms of influence, including the 98 percent who function primarily outside the local church."[4] Hamon also stated, "Much research and evaluation have determined that only two percent of Christians earn their living and fulfill their ministry working inside the local church or non-profit ministries, while 98 percent of the Saints work and fulfill their ministry outside the local church. In other words, two percent are pastors and church staff...Ninety-eight percent of Saints earn their income, do their work, and fulfill their professions outside the walls of the local church."[5]

For our purposes, it makes little difference whether the actual number is 97% or 98%. The effect is essentially the same in either case, and when you factor in which job positions are actually listed or categorized under the heading of "vocational minister" or "vocational ministry," I suspect that Fraser and Hamon are saying the same thing. Marcus Hester also noted: "In God's first church, God had only a few apostles and prophets, but in God's end-time Church, He is restoring a 'company' of believers who will walk in the apostolic and prophetic anointing. I call this company the 'Joseph/Daniel Company.' **God is expanding His anointing from the original 12 apostles to thousands, even millions, of Christians in the years to come.**"[6]

This is a particularly reasonable assumption when one considers the presence of workplace apostles, who are not automatically recognized by church organizations or structures. I freely admit that many of those who function apostolically may not lay claim to a title or a position, especially an ecclesiastical one. In that regard, Peter Lyne noted, "...we need to recognize and release the apostles in business and give them our full support and encouragement."[7] Lyne added:

"I am convinced that there are many New World apostles across the earth, doing far greater work than we have ever achieved, and from whom we have much to learn.

I have…reports from China, but this is equally true of Africa, and South America, and countless other places. We may appear to be more sophisticated in our Western churches, but there is not one of us who would not covet the fresh anointing and dramatic results currently being experienced by these mostly un-named people … **Across the earth, God is raising up such an army, and they will be inspired and led by young, New World apostles who could easily be overlooked unless we have eyes to see and a heart to train and release them."**[8]

Therefore, understanding the nature of apostleship and the defining differences between what or who is and what or who is not to be considered an apostle is an important consideration, especially since Satan always tries to counterfeit every true plan, purpose and movement of God.

WHAT AN APOSTLE IS NOT

First of all, the apostleship is not primarily a title, although as Dowdy has noted, titles can be useful when used appropriately in five-fold ministry.[9] Neither is it a brand, a license, a franchise, a promotion, a benevolent dictatorship, or a club. The apostleship is a divine grace, a five-fold calling, a function, an assignment, a charge, a calling and an office. However, it is an appointed office rather than an elected or elective office. Apostles are chosen, called by God and validated through the affirmation and confirmation of other five-fold apostles and prophets who have proven character, track record, reputation and authority.

This unique structure of apostolic succession provides the kind of checks and balances which are necessary to preserve kingdom order. Without it, committees, boards, congregational elections, doctrines of generational or denominational succession, and personal advancement become the criteria for laying claim to the authority inherent within an apostolic or other five-fold ministry.

In this regard, Johnny Enlow observed,

> "...Apostleship can be a virtually wasted gift here on earth if no one discovers the gift of God that is in him. Many apostles themselves may not even know that they are apostles, as the Lord may or may not reveal to them that identity. The title of apostle isn't important; it's the function and anointing that must be restored. A legitimate prophetic ministry in its proper place is supposed to call out and validate true apostles. Even as John the Baptist announced Jesus, so too do we need the prophetic voice to call forth and confirm apostles."[10]

Receiving a call from the Lord is the beginning step in a journey to full-fledged, recognized and commissioned apostleship, but receiving a divine call is an imperative and prerequisite. Without that, an individual is left without personal assurance that his or her call is indeed genuine or legitimate. The remainder of the journey is designed to provide similar assurance to others, and is vitally necessary if an apostleship is to have effectiveness and acceptance from others in kingdom affairs.

DIFFERENCES BETWEEN BEING APOSTOLIC AND BEING AN APOSTLE

The beginning of the 21st century was accompanied by another beginning, what some are calling the Second Apostolic Age. This is a move of God which is provoking the most sweeping changes in the way the Church operates since the Protestant Reformation. This movement is currently the fastest growing and largest non-Catholic segment of Christianity throughout the world, growing even faster than the spread of Islam. Yet, there is a widespread lack of awareness and understanding of the apostolic ministry and function today beyond the recognition of the term *apostolic*, especially in the Western Church.

Staunch evangelicalism, fundamentalist groups, mainline Protestant denominations, Baptists, and even Pentecostals are only slightly aware, at best. A broader range of intentional training regarding both the relevance and the importance of the apostolic would diminish that lack and in the process, deepen the level of determination to expand the kingdom of God in a strategic and beneficial way. There is a spectrum or range of maturity within the apostolic, not unlike that which occurs in the development of the other five-fold gifts and offices. This will be discussed more fully in Chapters 3 and 4 in this section.

Perhaps first we should distinguish between the terms apostles and the apostolic, both of which are used extensively in this book, and included in the Glossary. According to Dr. David Cannistraci:

> "*Apostolic people* are Christians who support and participate in apostolic ministry, but are not actual apostles. Apostolic people work with apostles to reach the lost through dynamic outreach, church planting and nurturing. *Apostolic churches* are churches that recognize and relate to modern-day apostles and are active in varying forms of apostolic ministry. *The apostolic movement* is the Holy Spirit's worldwide activation of apostles and apostolic people to come together as a part of a great revival on earth."[11]

As we point out in several different chapters, Naomi Dowdy, John Eckhardt,[12] and many others, including Alan Hirsch and Tim Catchim, have noted that the entire Church should be apostolic, due to the Great Commission and the fact that Jesus and the Holy Spirit are sent ones, but that does not mean all are apostles, just as all prophetic people are not prophets, and all pastoral people are not pastors. Several writers have noted that the 70 Jesus sent out in Luke 10 were apostolic, whereas the 12 sent out in Matt. 10 were apostles. We see others in the New Testament who were full of the Spirit and did extraordinary miracles but were not apostles, such as Stephen, Philip and Apollos, to name a few. The same is true today. According to Dowdy:

"When we identify people as 'prophetic' or 'apostolic,' we are admitting that they have God-given gifts, but rejecting the idea that He has called them into an office in the body of Christ. According to the New Testament, He does indeed appoint and anoint certain people for certain offices so that the leadership structure of the Church can work together to empower, build up, serve, and strengthen His people (see Ephesians 4:7-12).

"Let me ask you: Do you believe every believer should be prophetic? In other words, do you believe all Christians should have the ability to hear the voice of God? Do you also believe all believers should be apostolic in the most basic sense of the word—being sent by God to make a difference in the world? If so, then all believers should be prophetic and apostolic. This tells me that the terms 'prophetic' and 'apostolic' are not sufficient for those individuals who are called and anointed of God to serve the Church out of their giftings."[13]

The bottom line and the commonality between the apostolic and apostles is that both have Jesus at the core and center. As Ed Delph has aptly noted, "All of apostolic ministry is meant to bring the church into alignment with the Chief Corner Stone ... **Apostolic ministry helps build Jesus in the person, a church, the church, the community, the city, the nations and ultimately, the world. Jesus is the wineskin which can hold the new wine of all of the emphases, offices, dimensions, character, and missions of Jesus."**[14]

Hirsch and Catchim have also done research and writing in this area, and concluded: "The apostolic role provides the key that unlocks the power of New Testament ecclesiology insofar as its ministry is concerned. In the power of the Holy Spirit, **apostles are given to the ecclesia to provide the catalytic, adaptive, movemental, translocal, pioneering, entrepreneurial, architectural and custodial ministry needed to spark, mobilize, and sustain apostolic movements.** Apostolic ministry is the appropriate form for missional movements. In fact, we doubt whether there can be significant movement in the church without it."[15]

Hirsch and Catchim also summarized the importance of the apostolic as follows:

"We have chosen to focus ... primarily on the nature and function of the apostolic ministry for good reason; we believe that in many ways, the apostolic plays the catalytic role in activating a fully fledged ministry appropriate for apostolic movement, maintaining the sending—purposive (missional) impulses that we organize around, and cultivating the ongoing adaptive aspects that the church needs to grow and achieve its purpose. In terms of the ministry and leadership of Jesus's people, the apostolic is the permanent revolutionary needed to sustain the permanent revolution that is the ecclesia.

"We believe that out of all the APEST ministries, the apostolic is the most generative and catalytic of them all, and because of this, it carries the most promise in helping to reverse the decline of the church. If this is correct, then the apostolic both initiates and maintains the permanent revolution at the root of the constant reformation of the church. This is also the reason that we believe that the apostolic is the key to unlocking Ephesians 4 and therefore all other New Testament forms of ministry. **It is not that prophets, evangelists, pastors, and teachers cannot function independently from the apostolic; rather, as far as we can discern, they are designed to function interdependently with it and each other. It is through their relationship with the apostolic calling that they will come into the fullness of their own role and purpose in Jesus's church.**

"...By initiating missional ventures, the apostolic provides the cohesive framework in which the other ministries can focus their seemingly disparate interests in collaborative ways. In essence, the apostle is the one who is most likely to facilitate the emergence of communitas, a particular kind of community that is shaped and formed around a challenge or compelling task."[16]

I also suggest there are different levels of gifting and maturity within each five-fold calling or other ministry gift in the body of Christ. Some have an apostolic gift, some have an apostolic spirit, some have an apostolic anointing, some have an apostolic mantle, and a few have all of these and are called to or functioning in the office of an apostle.

There are different levels of gifting and maturity within each five-fold calling or other ministry gift. Even then, there are different levels of maturity, as we will discuss shortly. It is difficult to understand the significance of the apostolic without first answering the question, what is an apostle? The simple answer to that question is a dictionary definition. However, a far more detailed understanding is necessary to be useful. So, we will begin with the simple and move to the complex.

WHAT IS AN APOSTLE?

The term apostle is a transliteration of the Greek word *apostolos*, which, according to Strong's means: a delegate; specially, an ambassador of the Gospel; officially a commissioner of Christ ["apostle"] (with miraculous powers): NT:652. It is a derivative of another word, *apostello*, a verb form which means one set apart, or one sent on a mission. It was not an uncommon word during New Testament times. It is comparable to the Hebrew word *sheliach* which has the same distinct meaning—a representative, an ambassador.

When Abraham appointed Eliezar to seek out a wife for Issac, he commissioned him to do so (see Gen. 24:2ff and 15:2). Eliezar was a noble and trusted servant of Abraham, selected specifically to go in Abraham's stead. Only after he took a solemn oath of loyalty and faithfulness, however, did Abraham send him to select and negotiate for Isaac's wife.

So, while Greek apostolos gives us the form of the New Testament apostle, it is the Hebrew Sheliach that provides the content. A Sheliach-Apostolos is the full representative of his sender. As the Rabbis said: "The Sheliach of a man is as the man himself" (Beraita 5:5). Gerhard Kittel says: "The Sheliach (of Jesus) is as good as his Sender in all he says and does in the execution of his mission" (K., TDNT, 1:415).[17]

AN AMBASSADOR

When Jesus used it to designate and delegate 12 of His disciples, He was making a bold statement regarding the kingdom of God. A Christian apostle is first and foremost, an ambassador, an emissary of God's kingdom, delegated with authority to communicate, orchestrate, and at times adjudicate the nature, order and administration of that kingdom. When Jesus chose the twelve (see Matt. 10:1-2), he gave them authority and called them apostles; then, he sent them out to proclaim the kingdom of God.

One of the earliest uses of this word *apostolos* can be found among the Greek historians, who employed it as terminology descriptive of an admiral over a fleet of ships. This fleet would be sent out with the express purpose of exploration, discovery, and conquest, so that the rule of the king who sent them could be established. Jesus did not carelessly choose this word, but applied it reflecting its emphasis as meaning "one sent from another," a fully authorized representative of the one who sent them— ambassadors (see 2 Cor. 5:20). It should also be noted here at the outset that Jesus is a sent one, as is the Holy Spirit. Thus, the entire nature and DNA of the kingdom of God is an apostolic kingdom. According to Hector Torres:

> **An apostle is a fully authorized representative of Jesus.**

"...*apostolos*, and its root is translated as someone who is sent from one place to another to accomplish a specific work. In ancient times it was used to describe a marine officer, generally an admiral or an individual responsible for a flotilla of ships. It was also used to refer to an emissary or an ambassador. When the ships set sail to establish a new colony, the admiral and his crew were called apostles."[18]

Jesus chose his apostles out of the company of his disciples. He did not go outside of the circle of dedicated followers who were students of his life and teachings. These individuals were specifically chosen because they had taken on the character and essence of Jesus. Through three-and-a-half years, he poured into them his very being—his life, his character, his wisdom, and his message, so that when he was ready to empower them, they were prepared to represent him faithfully.

We know there was a company of disciples far greater than the twelve. The thing that marked the difference in these men over all the others was their specific choosing and commissioning. To all the disciples he extended power (*dunamis*) so that they could accomplish supernatural ministry. To the apostles he gave a different power (*exousia*), which rightly translated means "the right to power." As apostles (*apostoloi*), they became the fully authorized, delegated representatives of the kingdom, the ambassadors of God's order.

GENERALS AND GOVERNORS

From the founding of the Church, beginning in Acts 2, we quickly realize that the original apostles were the founding overseers of the Church. Not only that, apostles maintained their responsibilities throughout the remainder of the New Testament period into the early centuries of Church history. As Christianity spread, the Church faced enormous conflict and persecution to the degree that it had to be recognized for what it was—war. Again and again in Paul's letters, we are reminded of the warring nature of the enemies arrayed against the kingdom. But we have been given weapons to war against the spiritual forces of darkness: *"The weapons of our warfare are not carnal but mighty...."* (2 Cor. 10:4).

Warfare in this verse is the Greek word *strateia*, indicating "military service." In other words, there is a military-like order to be effective in confronting the enemy. God has provided weapons, equipment (*hoopla*) which are powerful, capable of destroying every defense the enemy erects to deflect our advance. But battles and armies are led by generals, and equipment is ineffective without a commanding leader, an officer corps with rank, and an effective strategy.

In New Testament language, this is a *strategos*, a warrior-strategist-overseeing leader, a general or governor positioned to determine and direct advances against the enemy. Within ancient cultures, both Greek and Roman, the term *strategos* was often applied to a general who was responsible for devising a strategy and for carrying it to completion by his army. Another usage was the appointment by Imperial authority as an official, authorized representative to a territory, province, or region. As such, this individual was in charge, and was answerable to the Emperor for the legal operation of the Provincial government or the Temple government, whichever was his sphere of assignment.

In Neh. 2:5, Nehemiah asked the king to send him (*Shalach*) as his authorized representative-ambassador and "man in charge" to rebuild Jerusalem. He was asking to be an apostle-*Sheliach* on mission. In 2:6 the Word says, "So it pleased the King and he sent (Shalach) me." Letters were given to others already in the field and on assignment by the King so that they might recognize and assist Nehemiah in his mission. When he arrived, he took charge and became Governor (*Pechad*—overseer or Bishop) over Artaxerxes' work in all Jerusalem and Judea. The other rulers in the region dealt with him as with a head of state.

Here we have a strong example of what an apostle really is. Nehemiah was a *strategos*, an apostle-*Sheliach* to Artaxerxes to establish and maintain governmental order. Apostles today are God's representatives commissioned to represent His government in their assigned spheres. The apostle does not necessarily operate or administrate a church or micromanage its departments and activities. But he exercises the authority necessary to fulfill his assignment and stay true to its Kingdom purposes.[19]

Dr. Paula Price provided this historical insight:

"A single term was needed to classify those they sent out as ambassadors of the king's best interests and generals that conquered territories. The Romans drew on the Greek language for one. Research says they settled on **apostle** and used it in much the same way as the Greeks used it. To identify an order of high ranking ambassadors with military might, powers of persuasion and diplomacy; and the ability to disciple captives and converts to the culture and laws and the life of the Romans' kingdom. It seems these diplomatic generals were accorded enormous powers and comprised an elite commission to propagate the aims of the empire and unify its citizenry. In addition, they were to forcefully, if need be, enlarge and settle the king's territory, while at the same time, stabilize His holdings."[20]

APOSTOLIC JUSTICE

Ed Nelson has also noted the justice dimension of an apostle and the etymological origins and meanings of the Hebrew terms for apostle:

"Justice is at the heart of an apostle's purpose. In Hebrew, it is always helpful to see what other words are derived from the same root verb. By making this observation, we see that the root verb shaliach not only produces the word for apostle (shaliach), it also produces the noun shelach. By changing the first vowel sound "ah" to "eh" in the verb shaliach, we are introduced to shelach, another Hebrew word valuable to our understanding the intent of what an apostle does.

"The noun shelach gives us the biblical word used for "missile," "weapon" or "sword." A missile or weapon, like a sword, was used to execute justice in the hands of a soldier sent by a juridical authority. When the word is translated as a synonym for "war," the idea of a "just war" is implied. A just war is one in which a high court has ruled that war is necessary to execute justice upon a criminal people.

"In Nehemiah 4:17 we see such a use of the word to mean a "weapon" to execute justice: 'Those who were rebuilding the wall, and those who carried burdens, took their load with one hand doing the work and the other [hand] holding a weapon [shelach].' The weapon was typically a sword, in this instance, a sword of justice. The high court had ruled for all to defend themselves against their unjust enemies. In this case the instrument of justice is the sword which serves as an apostle in the hands of the defenders of Jerusalem.

"In 2 Chronicles 23:10 we find a similar meaning. The child-king Joash was set in place as the new king of Israel against treacherous foes. The Scripture tells us what action was taken to protect him from his enemies: 'And he [the high priest] stationed all the people, each man with his weapon [shelach] in his hand, from the right side of the house to the left side of the house, by the altar and by the house, around the king.'"[21]

PATRIARCHS AND MATRIARCHS

Spiritual fatherhood is a subject which has and continues to receive a great amount of attention within the apostolic community. Who is your spiritual father or mother? The patriarchal roles of Old Testament leaders have provided the apostolic community with a connectivity model that is both convenient and practical. Many of the Old Testament patriarchs are seen as prototypical apostles, though they could not truly be identified as such. Nehemiah, Ezra, Eliazer, and perhaps even Mordecai, Esther's cousin and mentor, would fill the capacity of a *sheliah*, but a patriarch was the leader of a tribe, that is a family of families. Still, the role of the apostle, particularly as we see it today, is such that many apostles oversee networks of leaders and of churches. These we call patriarchs and matriarchs.

"...**apostolic networks** (as contrasted to denominations) **are held together by personal relationships** instead of by legal, bureaucratic, organizational structures."[22]

The word patriarch (*patriarches*) is used four times in the New Testament (Acts 2:29; Acts, 7:7-8; Heb. 7:4), once referring to David, once referring to the sons of Jacob (Israel) and the other to Abraham. It is not used in any form in the Old Testament. Still, we see the pattern emerge in specific relationship within the New Testament. Paul was obviously a father figure to Timothy and others. Peter likely employed the services of John Mark in penning the Gospel bearing Mark's name. And while we do not have distinct connectedness revealed of other apostles to specific sons and daughters, we do have the evidence of an apostolic tribe in the work of Paul. He was the distinctive voice of authority to Corinth, Ephesus, Philippi, Thessalonica, Galatia, Colossae, and quite possibly to Athens and Rome as well. Through the book of Acts, and the letters he wrote, we are brought close to many in his tribe, namely Aquila and Priscilla, Philemon and Onesimus, Titus, Timothy, Apollos, and a host of others named throughout his writing.

It is because of the Old Testament type demonstrated within the 12 sons of Israel that the apostolic movement has so readily embraced the patriarchal-matriarchal model. It fits. It makes sense that the relationship between a senior or elder leader be somewhat like a parent to one of less maturity. So, they are called spiritual sons and daughters, and what that means is there is an intrinsic connection between leaders and followers akin to a spiritual DNA. The character, values, perspectives, and vision of the fathers is molded into the sons as the relationship is walked out in real-time circumstances.

Discipleship is the core element of kingdom expansion.

The framework for training and preparing emerging apostolic leaders seems best served by a relational connection. Discipleship is the core element of kingdom expansion, and the process of true discipleship is not such that it can be accomplished in a classroom setting. True understanding of ministry is caught as much or more than it is taught, and while formal training is an important and desirable part of one's preparation, nothing can be more significant than personal connectedness. As Naomi Dowdy notes:

> "In order for Apostles to function as God intends, and indeed for the entire five-fold to operate according to His plan, I believe we must have teaching and training in the areas of character, protocol, function (how offices work together and what they do), responsibility, relationships (how to relate to other ministry gifts), commissioning, and accountability."[23]

No responsibility should ever be delegated without two accompanying assurances. One is authority; the other is accountability. Responsibility without authority is vacuous, an empty command to accomplish a duty through some legalistic, ritualistic, or autonomous process. This ultimately leaves the delegated person in a type of personal bondage, obliged to accomplish tasks without personal initiative, creativity, intuition, or insight. No true apostle can long be bound to such servitude. He or she is compelled by the Spirit within to serve by leading.

No responsibility should ever be issued to a delegate without a structure for accountability.

The other factor in which the patriarchal-matriarchal model excels is the area of accountability. No responsibility should ever be issued to a delegate without a structure for accountability. It is the duty of the person delegating responsibility to insure that the delegate has the knowledge, equipment, motivation, and authority to accomplish the task. It is the obligation of the delegate to give account for what he or she does, is doing, and intends to do. However, there is much more to patriarchal-matriarchal leadership than this structure of accountability.

Accountability extends to the personal lives of sons and daughters, whereby the spiritual parent is both capable and determined to insure just and merciful responses in times of crisis, breakdown, weakness, or failure. The parental figure is also bound to provide encouragement, empowerment, development, and critical analysis of the progress of his or her spiritual offspring. If the patriarchal-matriarchal model is to have real effectiveness, it must be built on deeply-held, meaningful, and mutually-beneficial relationships. It should not be and cannot be superficial, else it becomes nothing more than a scheme to channel power and finances without a standard of love.

APOSTLES ARE MADE, NOT BORN

Knowing what an apostle is—particularly what the ultimate expression of an apostle is—provides a beneficial look at the whole concept of apostleship. The reality, however, is that apostles are not born, they are made. They are called by God, but they are developed within the crucible of ministry and relationship. They are crafted by wise and committed counsel in a process which begins in embryonic form and progresses through stages of development. No person is capable of functioning as an apostle from the moment they are called. It takes a time of seasoning, of maturing, or equipping, and of fashioning by the hand of the master.

The original apostles experienced three-and-a half years of intense, day to day training at the hand of Jesus. The apostle Paul was theologically trained in the school of Gamaliel, the greatest rabbi of his time. Then, after he was called out by Jesus, converted, blinded and healed, baptized and filled with the Spirit, he was apprenticed to Barnabas in the early years of his ministry before he was free to pursue his apostolic calling.

Dr. John Tetsola offers some revealing insights which bring a greater degree of real clarity to the maturing process in the development of apostles which I mentioned earlier in this chapter.

> "All apostles are not on equal plane or on the same level of maturity. There are five major levels of apostolic maturity and ranks. Each maturity level determines the depth of the anointing, the sphere of placement, the strength of gifting, the measure of blessing, and the measure of rule. It is important that the apostolic men that God is raising understand this concept and be willing to receive from one another. Jesus the Chief Apostle of all apostles went through these five levels of maturation in His ministry. Your level of authority as an apostle moves higher and becomes stronger as you move in maturity and rank...The journey and the process of maturation in everyone is different, but there are certain principles in everybody's process that are the same.

> "...You don't just become a mature apostle overnight. It does not come by hands being laid on you, or by any ordination. After the ordination and the laying on of

hands into the office of the apostle, you will have to go through the ranks of maturity."[24]

Understanding what an apostle is and how an individual grows into his or her apostleship is extremely important. Many who call themselves apostles have not embraced or endured the process. They have no legitimate apostolic oversight or accountability, have not been strategically placed by a *strategos*, and have had no validation of their calling or authority through a commissioning by those who are recognized and function as true apostles. According to Dr. David Cannistraci:

> "In measuring the dimensions of the apostolic office, we must be careful not to exaggerate the apostle's place of importance to the point of imbalance. Although apostles are primary in the Body of Christ, they are only human and as such they will be imperfect and fallible. Certainly neither apostolic people nor the apostolic movement will be perfect. Each apostolic person and each apostle represents only a fraction of the total equation. The Body is composed of many members, and it takes all of them working together to accomplish the will of God."[25]

An apostleship is not automatically an advancement in stature or significance, and is not necessarily the highest rung on the "ministry ladder," either. Unfortunately, it is easy to see the contemporary apostle as just that—the highest, most important, and most provided for minister in the kingdom. We must guard against deifying any of the five-fold offices or individual officers. The apostle Paul was quick to point out that he was no god (Acts 14:8-20), and offered a much different picture, one which should be considered as a warning to all true apostles. This is no game!

*"For I think that **God has displayed us, the apostles, last, as men condemned to death;** for we have been made a spectacle to the world, both to angels and to men. We are fools for Christ's sake, but you are wise in Christ! We are weak, but you are strong! You are distinguished, but we are dishonored! To the present hour we both hunger and thirst, and we are poorly clothed, and beaten, and homeless. And we labor, working with our own hands. Being reviled, we bless; being persecuted, we endure; being defamed, we entreat. We have been made as the filth of the world, the offscouring of all things until now"* (1 Cor. 4:9-13, NKJV, author's emphasis).

Certainly one requirement of apostleship is death, as this scripture indicates. This takes different forms for different apostles, and can include spiritual, emotional, physical, relational and financial death. Regardless of the individual mode of expression, this means a dying to self and a resurrection of Christ in us in a new dimension. Each of us must be willing to pay whatever price Christ requires. As we examine those who use the title apostle, we need to compare them to Jesus, and to see if there is a family resemblance. If not, we know they are either: 1) immature apostles, or 2) false apostles. Sometimes it can be hard to distinguish between the two.

False apostles typically have impure or unclean motives and a wrong spirit; they also tend to lack accountability or genuine concern and love for others; i.e, they are selfish, are usually-self-appointed, and have their own agendas. Deception and deceit are their tools, along with flattery, disguise, lies and lack of transparency. They are in ministry for the wrong reasons, and their fruit is dissension, strife and turmoil. According to Rev. 2:2 and 2 Cor. 11:13, there will generally be an evil pattern to their lives and a trail of broken hearts, homes, churches and relationships.

Immature apostles, on the other hand, may simply be ignorant, or lack experience, or need more wisdom or mentoring, or require correction, counsel, inner healing, deliverance, character development, study, preparation, and/ or maturation. True apostles will be quick to repent, quick to humble themselves, quick to serve, quick to promote and bless and honor others, quick to pray, and quick to protect and defend others who are weaker spiritually. Immature apostles will receive correction from true fathers and mothers of faith, will be aligned and covered spiritually, will be accountable to others and to God, will respect and honor legitimate authority, will pay whatever price is required, and will stay in the race and not quit and throw in the towel. They are willing to admit when they are wrong or make a mistake. I.e., they have a teachable spirit even though they may be lacking in one or more areas.

So, rather than focus on false apostles and study them, our model is Jesus and we are to imitate and follow Him and be rooted and grounded in Him, and have Christ fully formed within us. The U.S. Treasury Dept. teaches its agents assigned to investigate counterfeiting U.S. currency to study the U.S. currencies and learn the subtle nuances and distinguishing characteristics of such. When they know the true, the genuine and authentic, it becomes much easier to spot the bogus bills and impostors and to take appropriate action. That should be our approach in the apostolic movement. Paul said to mark those who walk disorderly among us, to warn them, and then if they don't respond to correction, to avoid them (Tit. 3:10-11). That should apply to every five-fold office and ministry, not just apostles and the apostolic. By a person's fruit, character, and motives, you will know them. We turn now to Chapter 3.

ENDNOTES

1. Dr. Rick Joyner. *The Apostolic Ministry*, p. 45. Wilkesboro, NC: MorningStar Publications Inc., 2004.

2. Bob Fraser, *Marketplace Christianity*, pp. 60-61. Overland Park, KS: New Grid Publishing, 2004, 2006.

3. Drew Gentile, Paradigms for Urban Ministry, Campus Crusade for Christ International, 2009. http://www.xpastor.org/ministry/theology/paradigms-for-urban-ministry/

4. Dr. Bill Hamon, *The Day of the Saints*, p. 243, author's emphasis. Shippensburg, PA: Destiny Image Publishers, 2002, 2003.

5. Ibid, p. 213.

6. Dr. Marcus Hester, *The God Factor*, p. 54, author's emphasis. Shippensburg, PA: Treasure House, 2003.

7. Peter Lyne, *First Apostles, Last Apostles*, p. 113. Kent, England: Sovereign World Ltd., 1999.

8. Ibid, pp. 126-128, author's emphasis.

9. Naomi Dowdy, *Commissioning: The Process, Protocol, and Importance of Commissioning Modern-Day Apostles*, pp. 3-5. Dallas, TX: Naomi Dowdy Ministries, 2006.

10. Johnny Enlow, *Seven Mountain Prophecy*, p. 66. Lake Mary, FL: Creation House, 2006.

11. Dr. David Cannistraci, *Apostles and the Emerging Apostolic Movement*, p. 29. Ventura, CA: Renew Books, 1996, 1998.

12. John Eckhardt, *Ordinary People, Extraordinary Power*, p. 35. Lake Mary, FL: Charisma House, 2010.

13. Naomi Dowdy, *Commissioning: The Process, Protocol, and Importance*, pp. 4-5.

14. Ed Delph, *Making Sense of Apostolic Ministry*, pp. 55-56, author's emphais. Christchurch, New Zealand: Net Work Ministries International Publications, 2002.

15. Alan Hirsch and Tim Catchim, *The Permanent Revolution: Apostolic Imagingation and Practice for the 21st Century Church*, p. xxxviii. San Francisco, CA: Jossey-Bass, 2012.

16. Ibid, pp. 92-93, author's emphasis.

17. Dr. Ronald E. Cottle and John P. Kelly, "Apostles are Ambassadors," ICA Website, 2011, www.coalitionofapostles.com

18. Hector Torres, *The Restoration of the Apostles and Prophets*, p. 113. Nashville, TN: Thomas Nelson Inc., 2001.

19. Dr. Ronald E. Cottle, "Apostles are Generals and Governors," ICA Website, 2011. www.coalitionofapostles.com

20. Dr. Paula Price, *Eternity's Generals*, p. 245. Tulsa, OK: Flaming Vision Publications, 2005.

21. Ed Nelson, "Apostles of God's Justice," http://www.ednelson.com/ modules.php?name=News&file=print&sid=32

22. Dr. C. Peter Wagner, *Apostles Today*, p. 92, author's emphasis. Ventura, CA: Regal Books, 2006.

23. Naomi Dowdy, *Commissioning: The Process, Protocol, and Importance of Commissioning Modern-Day Apostles*, p. 8.

24. Dr. John A. Tetsola, *The Apostolic Culture & Pattern: Understanding the Apostolic Ministries, Its Anointing and Its Applications*, pp. 35-36. Bronx, NY: Baruch Publishing, 2002.

25. Dr. David Cannistraci, *The Gift of Apostle,* p. 83. Ventura, CA: Regal Books, 1996.

True apostles are quick
to repent, quick to
humble themselves,
quick to serve, quick
to promote and bless
and honor others,
quick to pray, and
quick to protect and
defend others who are
weaker spiritually.

CHAPTER THREE

LEVELS OF MATURITY
AND TYPES OF APOSTLES

The original apostolic infrastructure of the Church was comprised of two specific categories of believers, namely, disciples and apostles. After the outpouring of the Holy Spirit in Acts 2 the growth rate of the Church exploded, and quickly outdistanced what the twelve could effectively accomplish themselves. It was time to delegate.

Acts 6 provides a narrative of the selection of seven unique men, filled with the Spirit and wisdom, approved of by the people, and appointed by the apostles to oversee the daily administration of Church logistics. They are often identified as deacons, but the recording of their functional ministry demonstrates something far beyond the ministry we currently see those appointed or elected to the office of deacon in the Church operating in. In some instances, especially among the more liturgical orders, they carry a significant ecclesiastical responsibility, but deacon (*diakonos*) was a widely-used term to indicate a heart and spirit of servanthood, more than that of a Church official.

By the time Paul wrote the books of Ephesians and 1 Corinthians, a much broader taxonomy of leadership was apparent. He provided a distinct naming of the five-fold offices in Eph. 4—apostles, prophets, evangelists, pastors and teachers, and an order of functional standing in 1 Cor. 12. There were other gifts listed in Rom. 12 as well. That we have no distinct chronology for the affirmation of prophets may well be ascribed to the fact that prophets preceded the Church. While there were approximately 400 years between the closing of the Old Testament and the beginning of the New Testament, there is no viable reason to believe there were no prophets during that period. None are recorded, unless one recognizes the Apocryphal books, which are included in the Catholic versions of the Bible, as scriptural.

The beginning days of Jesus' life were accompanied by prophets and prophecy. Both Simeon (see Luke 2:24-35) and Anna (Luke 2:36) were attested to as prophets and prophesied over the infant Jesus. Philip, identified as an evangelist, had four daughters who prophesied (Acts 21:8-9) and Agabus was identified as a prophet (Acts 21: 9). There are many more examples to note: prophets were sent from Jerusalem to Antioch, apostles and elders held council together concerning the redemption of the Gentiles, and Silas, who was joined to Paul following his separation from Barnabas, was a prophet.

The scripturally-identified offices during the New Testament era were apostle (*apostolos*), prophet (*prophetes*), evangelist (*euaggelistes*), pastor (*poimen*), teacher (*didasklalos*), bishop (*episkopos*), elder (*presbuteros*), and deacon (*diakonos*). These were all known within the structure of the Church, but it must be remembered that the Church was neither an institution nor an organizational hierarchy. It was a workplace-oriented, apostolically-led, dynamically-relational body of believers in Jesus Christ who lived, functioned, and communicated the message of the kingdom in their daily life as well as in their communal life.

With the coming of the Second Apostolic Reformation, the need for a taxonomy within the ranks of apostles became apparent, at least to a significant number of leaders within the movement. Thus, the contemporary terminology became vertical apostles and horizontal apostles, ecclesiastical or Church apostles and marketplace or workplace apostles, emerging apostles, convening apostles, territorial apostles, hyphenated apostles, congregational apostles, mobilizing apostles, foundational apostles, reformational apostles, ambassadorial, patriarchal, and governing apostles.[1] Rather than being an attempt to elevate one type of apostolic leader above another, this categorization was advanced as a way to identify apostolic roles and the functionality of individual leaders.

It has not always had that effect, especially as it earmarked the ecclesiastical community as being of a different caliber and significance from the workplace apostles. It is for that reason that I question the use of the term "marketplace or workplace apostle." We do not apply the descriptive or restrictive nomenclature of ecclesiastical, church, or nuclear church to apostles who function primarily within the ecclesiastical community. Neither should we do this with workplace apostles. To do so sends a message of second class status, whether intentional or not, since this phrase was coined and originated by ecclesiastical apostles.

I am not criticizing the terms "workplace apostle" or "marketplace apostle" per se, but simply suggesting that this was not the pattern recorded in scripture, or evidenced in the early church, but that is not to say that present-truth revelation (2 Pet. 1:12) by Marshall, Silvoso, Wagner, and others has not been helpful as a transitional strategy to awaken the church, bring attention to the need to commission righteous and anointed and authoritative and humble and wise workplace leaders, and to begin to acknowledge and recognize that leadership is distributed and disbursed throughout the body of Christ and throughout the Seven Mountains/spheres, and that likewise, anointing and authority and five-fold calling are similarly distributed and disbursed therein.

I am not advocating that we need to stop using these terms immediately, as it will take time for this to be accepted, circulated and implemented, but I am suggesting that a more scriptural and equitable and honoring approach is to simply use the biblical title of "apostle" and from there define, discern, discover and/or disclose spheres of authority and assignment for individual officers. Even military generals are all called generals despite the fact there are one-star generals, two-star generals, three-star generals, four-star generals, and five-star generals with different rank and authority and theater or sphere of assignment. The same approach applies to apostles.

With the integration of a Seven Mountain strategy, the importance of ministers wholly focused within the marketplace has taken on a much higher significance within the movement. Five-fold leaders there are being recognized more and more as commensurate in authority and responsibility with those in church-related ministries; they simply operate in different spheres. To that end, I would offer another page to the glossary of apostolic terminology, one which I believe the Lord has shown me. The nomenclature I am advancing is based on the sphere and span of authority in which an individual apostle operates. Many apostles are delegated with authority in only one or two spheres of influence, whether it be in the Religion mountain as a vocational ministry professional, or in one of six other societal spheres.

Scripturally, the sphere of the family is overseen by the head of household, with significant input and direction coming from a family leader's oversight. But, there are many church ministries and parachurch ministries that cater to, serve, and focus on the family. Some deal with marriage counseling, others deal with family counseling, some deal with abortion education and prevention and pro-life choices, then there are adoption agencies, orphanages, and many more.

An individual who exercises authority in only one sphere is a Unilateral Apostle, because his or her authority is one dimensional—within that particular arena. Someone who has a broader span of authority and influences two of those spheres is a Bilateral Apostle. Such individuals are fairly common, usually because an apostle has delegated authority in both the Religion mountain and in one of the others. Our kingly-priestly nature and design calls for that and is somewhat expected. Spanning three spheres of authority is much less common, but as the movement to restore apostles and prophets and thus legitimate church government grows larger and the strategy broadens, Trilateral Apostles and prophets are becoming much more prevalent. Only a very few apostles are given broad-based authority beyond those levels. If they should be recognized on that expansive of an area, they would be known as Multilateral Apostles.

The diagram on the following page offers a graphic view of how this terminology applies to the apostolic community and offers clarity to the concept I am advancing here. But, there is a much broader issue at stake than mere nomenclature. The realm of the apostolic extends to every corner of social and cultural experience for only one reason: authority. The apostolic dimension is primarily relational and missional rather than theological or doctrinal in nature and purpose, although each of these areas and foci is included within its jurisdiction and purview. As plenipotentiaries and ambassadors of the kingdom of heaven and government of God, apostles have been delegated authority by the King of the Universe. They exercise, release, impart and/or transfer power (*exousia*) from and on behalf of God, and function through the recognition and affirmation of individuals who either commend and commission their authority, and/or who respond, submit and are influenced by their authority. The same is true for each of the other five-fold offices— prophet, evangelist, pastor, and teacher.

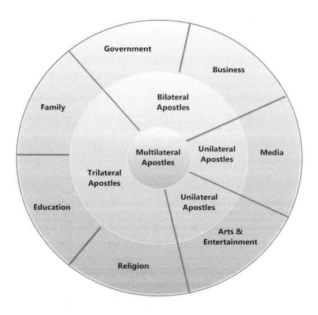

Figure 1. Span of Apostolic Authority in the Seven Mountains of Culture

The unique and specific assignments of those who are commissioned within a ministry office define where and in what manner their influence will be felt, and how much their authority will have impact. The Church, by virtue of its significance to the entirety of Christianity, is replete with five-fold ministers, but that does not minimize the importance, the quality, or the quantity of ministers in those mountains which are not governed by the Church realm. There is, as Walt Pilcher has described, a five-fold effect that is apparent beyond the confines of the ecclesiastical domain: "When we refer to 'apostolic practice' or 'apostolic leadership,' we are talking of course not just about apostles. We are describing organizations that understand and employ all of the gifts of the people involved."[2]

If this effect were not to be extended beyond the boundaries of Church structure, the kingdom of God would be limited to the Church. No one who has even the slightest understanding or appreciation of the apostolic believes that, even for a second. Both the kingdom of God and apostles preceded the establishment of the Church. The Jewish leaders of Jesus' day were convinced that the kingdom would be a reestablishment of the ancient Hebrew monarchy; thus, they came to Jesus seeking to know when the kingdom would be manifested and restored. His answer was simply that it already was. *The kingdom of God is within you*" (Luke 17:21). They didn't "get it" then, and many people do not get it now. It is a common misperception that the kingdom and the Church are synonymous terms, when they are anything but that.

The kingdom of God in the earth is not a physical expression of political power; it is a spiritual reality of incredible influence. Wherever, and in whomever, it is manifested, it is in place, resisting and repelling the dominions of this world system, establishing righteousness, peace, and joy in the Holy Spirit, transforming lives, communities, cities, and nations through the transformational process of changing lives. The kingdom of God to come—that is, the physical manifestation of the eternal kingdom—is prophetically assured in scripture, but that future does not characterize or minimize the presence of the kingdom in the earth today.

On trial before the Roman procurator of Judea, Jesus was asked if he was the king of the Jews. His cryptic answer was:

"My kingdom is not of this world. If My kingdom were of this world, My servants would fight, so that I should not be delivered to the Jews; but now My kingdom is not from here."

(John 18:36, NKJV)

The development of a Seven Mountain strategy to bring cultural transformation was, from its very beginning, an approach that, while using the Church as a vehicle of engagement, was meant to operate in the marketplace. Such an approach only functions within an apostolic framework; that is, it works through delegated authority (*exousia*) which is effective in and focused on the cultural structures that dominate society. (For a more detailed discussion of the difference between culture and society, and how they interrelate, see Robert Henderson, *A Voice of Reformation*).[3] To the degree the Church affects those structures, five-fold leaders are of significant importance. The Christian community has always looked to leaders within the Church to rightly instruct, train, and equip them for victorious living. The Church is an intrinsic part of the whole of Christianity. It was established by Jesus Christ and His promise was to build it.

The Christian community has always looked to leaders within the Church to rightly instruct, train, and equip them for victorious living.

However, it is an historical and theological reality that the Church made a wide-ranging and ill-advised departure from the apostolic moorings on which it was founded well over a millennium ago. Thereafter, in many ways, Christianity became another religion in a world filled with religions. Yet, the truth of God's redemption and the power of Christ's resurrection and the indwelling of the Holy Spirit have made the Christian message singularly different from every other religion, and the Church, despite its shortcomings and divergences, has been the vehicle God has used to sustain that message. With the present emphasis on a return to those apostolic roots, to do so without a commensurate return to cultural engagement at the marketplace level is unrealistic. Thus, it is vital and imperative that the marketplace—the entirety of the cultural landscape—be infused with dynamic, delegated, commissioned, and effective five-fold ministers. And increasingly, that is the case.

FOUR HISTORICAL GROUPINGS OF APOSTLES

In addition to functional types of apostles, we will also briefly examine four historical groupings of apostles now. These groupings were developed primarily from a review of the literature on apostles plus a review of scripture, but a portion of this grouping was developed in a discussion with Dr. Paula Price and so I would like to acknowledge her contribution to this process here.

1. **Apostles of the Lamb**[4] (the original 12 Apostles Jesus appointed and commissioned while on Earth, before His death, burial, resurrection or ascension). Their names are listed several places in scripture (Matt. 10-1-4, Mark 3:13-19, Luke 6:12-16, Matt. 19:28, Rev. 21:14). Matthias later replaced Judas in this group (see Acts 1:15-26 and also the 4th group below).

2. **Post-Commissioning Apostles** (Apostles that the 12 or Jesus appointed (if any) after their first

commissioning (Matt. 10:1-3, Mark 3:13-19, Luke 6:12-16, John 17:18-26). Scripture is silent in this regard.

3. **Post-Resurrection Apostles** (Apostles that the 11 (minus Judas) appointed after their second commissioning (Matt. 28:16-20, Mark 16:14-18, Luke 24:44-49, John 20:21-22, Acts 1:1-8) after the resurrection of Jesus, or that Jesus appointed between the 40-Day Period between His Resurrection and Ascension). The Scriptures are silent on who commissioned some of the apostles listed in the New Testament—e.g.., Andronicus and Junia, Luke, Jude, and numerous others. According to 1 Cor. 15:3-8, Paul provides an order of Jesus' appearing to various groups after his resurrection. Verse 5 mentions "the twelve," and Verse 7 says "all the apostles" as a separate category, with an appearance to more than 500 in Verse 6.

Since scripture does not define "all" or give a definite total of the number of apostles, we have no way of knowing how many apostles there were in the first century, except that there were apparently enough to get the job done. I have seen various estimates of New Testament apostles ranging from 19, 21, 24, 29, 32, and even higher, into the hundreds. There simply is no way to know for sure, and it is useless to speculate, in my opinion. Even Paul's account is not a complete listing of Jesus' appearances following his resurrection, because this list does not mention either the two men on the road to Emmaus (Luke 24:13-35), or his appearance to Mary Magdalene at the tomb (John 20:1-18).

4. **Post-Ascension Apostles** (Apostles that: a) Jesus called and appointed after His ascension, and after the

Holy Spirit was poured out on the Day of Pentecost, such as Paul [Acts 9:1-31—he was called by Jesus but not commissioned as an apostle until years later], and/or b) apostles who were summoned by the Holy Spirit and commissioned by church leaders, such as Paul and Barnabas by the Antioch church [Acts 13:1-3], and/or c) other apostles who were discipled and commissioned by these men or the 12 such as Titus, Timothy, Silas, Luke, John Mark, or Matthias [Acts 1:15-26], etc.). This group includes all apostles on the earth today, and all apostles since the ascension of Jesus and the outpouring of the Holy Spirit in Acts 2.

Although a few sources reference several examples of historical PostAscension Apostles in passing (most notably Barney Coombs, David Cartledge, Peter Wagner, Ulf Ekman, Elizabeth Hairston, and Lee Ann Marino)[5], there is no definitive or comprehensive list extant to my knowledge, and very little mention of workplace apostles historically, so we will leave that task to future historians (see Chapter 7 partial list).

We will take a moment before moving ahead to comment briefly on the primary Greek terms used in a few of these key commissioning passages which serve to inform us today. In Matt. 10:1-4 "appointed" is not used in the KJV but is instead the word "called"—"Proskaleomai" (Grk), meaning: to call toward oneself, to summon or invite. In Mark 3:13-19, again, the word "appointed" is not used in the KJV but rather the word "ordained"—"Poieo" (Grk), meaning: to make or do, **appoint,** agree with, purpose, **band together,** etc. In Luke 6:12-16, the word "called" is used again in the KJV, but this time a different root – "Prosphoneo" (Grk), meaning: to sound towards, to address, or **summon.** Also, in Mark 1:20, in the earlier part of Jesus' ministry, the word

there for "called" is "Kaleo" (Grk), meaning: to call properly
or aloud, bid, call (forth), or call by name.

Finally, in Matt. 19:28, the word "followed" is shown in
the KJV – "Akoloutheo" (Grk), meaning: to be in the same
way with, **to accompany, to become a disciple**.[3] Clearly, the
disciples were called by name and invited to accompany
Jesus, but the original 12 apostles were called and summoned
to the person, nature, revelation, teaching, doctrine, example,
mission, kingdom, sufferings, authority, power and glory of
Jesus, and appointed or ordained by Him to a governmental
office, position and rank in His kingdom.

LEVELS OF APOSTOLIC MATURITY

The most definitive summarization of levels of apostolic
maturity that I found in my review of the literature came
from Dr. John Tetsola. It would be an oversight and disservice
to overlook that in this discussion, so I have included some
rather extensive quotes from him here.

"All apostles are not on equal plane or on the same
level of maturity. There are five major levels of apostolic
maturity and ranks. Each maturity level determines
the depth of the anointing,
the sphere of placement,
the strength of gifting, the
measure of blessing, and
the measure of rule. It is
important that the apostolic
men that God is raising
understand this concept and be willing to receive from
one another. Jesus the Chief Apostle of all apostles went
through these five levels of maturation in His ministry.
Your level of authority as an apostle moves higher and

> **All apostles are not on equal plane or on the same level of maturity.**

becomes stronger as you move in maturity and rank. I am not talking about the authority of the believer or the ability to petition the Father and bind up devils. Anyone on any level can do that if they just believe God and move out by faith. There are certain levels of maturity in the development of the apostolic anointing that God puts a certain mantle, a certain cloak, a certain coat of God's presence, anointing, authority, influence, favor and opportunities that come on your life.

"...The journey and the process of maturation in everyone is different, but there are certain principles in everybody's process that are the same. We must not embrace the prophecy of our destiny, but we must be willing to accept the process of our destiny. If an apostolic man does not accept the process of his destiny, he will never enter into the prophecy of his destiny. In the earth we can make shortcuts, and wear titles and ranks that do not belong to us, but that does not mean we are that title or rank. Isaiah 28:9-10 shows us how God builds in our lives. He builds us bit by bit. We don't eat the cake all at once in a day. We eat it daily and gently. God serves His cake to us a slice at a time. You don't just become a mature apostle overnight. It does not come by hands being laid on you, or by any ordination. After the ordination and the laying on of hands into the office of the apostle, you will have to go through the ranks of maturity.

"Apostolic promotion does not come on the basis of the gifting in an individual's life, but it is on the basis of their maturity. As he begins the process of maturity, one of the things that evolves and grows in an apostle is his perspective. Your perspective begins to change. The apostle Paul at the beginning of his maturity said,

'I labor more than all of the other apostles.' Then in the middle of his apostolic development he said, 'I am the least of all of the apostles,' and at the end of his maturity he said, 'I am the chief of the sinners.' As he grew and matured in God, his thought of himself did not shoot through the roof, but instead he began to see himself in the light of God's holiness. This is a great place to be. That is why Paul was successful. The opposite of this is the obstacle to the development of most apostles today. That is why most of the apostles never get developed."[7]

This is how the pattern emerges as the process of development occurs in an individual's life, from a beginning to a place of mature and fulfilled function. It is slow, sometimes painful, and always deliberate. Those apostles who do achieve full maturity ultimately emerge as primary leaders, with deep insight, hard-won wisdom, and wide-ranging influence throughout large segments of culture, both within the Church and in the marketplace. Tetsola goes on to categorize these levels as follows:

1. **"The Nepios Apostle**. The word *Nepios* is a Greek word which actually means 'babe.' Sometimes in Scripture it is translated as child. Literally, what it means is 'no speech.' We have apostles that have the Nepios anointing. They are still a child, an infant, unskilled and untaught in the apostolic ministry and anointing. They are not babes in the sense of being newly born-again, but they are babes in that they are unskilled in the strength and maturity of their calling..."

2. **"The Paidion Apostle.** This is the stage of maturity where the apostolic anointing in the life of an

individual is in the formation stage. This is where the apostolic identity of an individual is formed. This is usually supposed to be a short stage of maturity before promotion is experienced, but sometimes some people never move out of this stage. The word *Paidion* in the Greek is translated as a younger child or a toddler..."

3. "**The Teknion Apostle.** The word *Teknion* in John 13:33 is translated in Scripture as an "older child." Sometimes it is translated son in Scripture, but the original Greek text of the word is an older child. In John 13, His disciples have been with Him for about three years now, and yet in verse 33 He addressed them as little children or little Teknions. He was not speaking about their age, but He was speaking about their maturity. Even though they were growing, they had not fully grown or matured to carry or walk in a certain measure of the anointing..."

4. "**The Huios Apostle.** The word *Huios* speaks of a fully matured son that is now able to walk and function in his own capacity, his own measure of rule and sphere. He is able to understand some of the principles that govern his walk, without stumbling every single day. It is only when you get to this level of development that you get your placing and your appointing of God. You get led, and always remain tutored, in all of the previous levels, but it is only when you get to this level do you really step over concerning your personal life. In a sense, it is stepping over Jordan into the promised land of your life. This is where you get commissioned, placed and appointed in what He has called you to do..."

5. **"The Pater Apostle.** *Pater* is a Greek word that is translated 'father.' The degree of your authority will be determined and be indicative of the degree of your maturity. The Pater apostle is a very mature apostle. They are regarded as true fathers. These are apostolic men that have gone through the stages of development and recognize them in their lives, and then are able to recognize it in the lives of the emerging apostles. The training processes of the Pater apostles are very rigorous and painful. It is in these processes that God develops the fatherhood anointing in them."[8]

Without regard for sphere or cultural perspective or assignment, it is necessary for apostles to go through this maturation process. Some seemingly mature faster than others, but they all must go through the process. For those who are just beginning, this leveling often proves to be a source of frustration because they have already been involved in ministry and have enjoyed a measure of recognition, acceptance, and effectiveness. They are ready... at least, they believe they are ready, the moment they embrace an apostolic call or respond to the first suggestion or prophecy that they are apostles. However, the breadth of responsibility that falls on the shoulders of a mature apostle is crushing if that individual has not matured to the point he or she can bear the burden.

It is an unfortunate reality that many who claim the title apostle are ill-prepared to bear the weight of apostleship. They proclaim themselves to be what they are not capable of accomplishing, and it is the body of Christ which suffers for their impatience, immaturity, ambition, ego, pride or lack of knowledge. These would-be apostles are most prevalent within the Religion mountain for the simple reason that in the marketplace, their lack of effectiveness and immaturity are measured by their productivity, not their proclamations.

In the same way in which we began, it must be made clear that apostleship is based on function and character and calling, and not on titles, positions, personal press releases, websites, business cards, blogs, self-promotion or peer patronage. As we said earlier, "By their fruit you will know them." There is no substitute for the real thing. Imitations are a dime a dozen and easy to spot for those who by use of exercise have trained their senses to discern between good and evil (Heb. 5:14).

A final test of apostolic maturity is honor. Numerous Scriptures command us to esteem, prefer, and honor one another, and to give honor to whom honor is due. Robert Henderson has captured the importance of this core value:

> "Alignment is first and foremost about honor. It is honor that brings real alignment. In fact I would say that you cannot be in alignment without honor. Alignment is not organizational, it is spiritual. It is a spiritual connecting that allows forces and powers of God to flow through the bonds and ligaments of the body and the kingdom. Honor is what makes these connections.

> "...Honor is the thing that makes the connection that allows what is in the Head to flow down to the body. We know that Jesus is the Head.

> "...When we honor that which is apostolic, we are honoring the Headship of the Lord."[9]

To that I would add a hearty amen! True apostles understand, embrace, demonstrate and apply honor in their relationships, just as they do love. We turn now to Chapter 4.

ENDNOTES

1. Dr. C. Peter Wagner, *Spheres of Authority: Apostles in Today's Church,* pp. 75-100. Colorado Springs, CO: Wagner Publications, 2002. See also Dr. C. Peter Wagner, *Apostles Today,* pp. 88-100, 133-136. Ventura, CA: Regal Books, 2006.

2. Walt Pilcher, *The Five-Fold Effect: Unlocking Power Leadership and Results for Your Organization,* in press. Bloomington, IN: WestBow Press, 2013.

3. Robert Henderson, *A Voice of Reformation: An Apostolic and Prophetic View of Each of the Seven Mountains in a Reformed State,* pp. 9-11. Colorado Springs, CO: Robert Henderson Ministries, 2010.

4. The Apostles of the Lamb received at least as much (if not more) of the so-called "ascension gifting and calling" as those apostles who came after them, plus the estimated 15,000 hours of personal instruction by the Lord on earth during his 3.5 year ministry and after his resurrection.

5. See Barney Coombs, *Apostles Today,* pp. 203-204; David Cartledge, *The Apostolic Revolution,* p. 250; Dr. Peter Wagner, *Apostles Today,* pp. 7, 89; Ulf Ekman, *The Apostolic Ministry: Can The Church Live Without It?,* p. 23; Dr. Elizabeth Hairston, *Apostolic Intervention;* and Dr. Lee Ann Marino, who includes numerous historical female apostles in a powerpoint teaching she has developed titled "Female Apostles in History" which is available on her website at http://www.slideshare.net/powerfortoday/female-apostles-in-history.

6. *Strong's Concordance with Hebrew and Greek Lexicon.*

7. Dr. John A. Tetsola, *The Apostolic Culture & Pattern: Understanding the Apostolic Ministries, Its Anointing and Its Applications,* pp. 35-36. Bronx, NY: Baruch Publishing, 2002.

8. Ibid. pp 42-51.

9. Robert Henderson, *Consecrated Business: Apostolically Aligning the Marketplace,* pp. 143-147. Colorado Springs, CO: Robert Henderson Ministries, 2008.

CHAPTER FOUR

APOSTOLIC AUTHORITY: A TWO-EDGED SWORD

UNDERSTANDING APOSTOLIC AUTHORITY

Of all the perceptions which people have toward the apostolic and apostles, nothing generates greater questions or concerns than the issue of apostolic authority. The exercise of authority—whether in the political, business, religious, judicial, educational, military, family or any other arena—is generally a mixture of styles, perceptions, expectations, goals, objectives, rules, laws, values, applications, outcomes and responses. People do not have a universal understanding of apostolic authority, whether that is in the exercise of it or the submission to it. As a result, people are often confused about how to respond to it, both as people in positions of authority or as those who are under authority in given situations (that includes all of us at one time or another). So, we will now address this important topic in some depth and detail to try and change those perceptions.

First, an apostleship is a functional responsibility, limited to a specific measure (*metron*), beyond which the *de facto* authority diminishes proportionally to those who willingly respond to that authority. And although an apostle has great authority in the spiritual realm, and can make decrees and declarations into that realm as needed, he or she cannot exercise that authority directly over or on behalf of others without the willing and conscientious participation of those under his or her authority. This holds true in every sphere of culture, though in some spheres it is enforced by words, in others by economics, and sometimes by both.

According to Glenn Shaffer, "...the subject of God's authority is paramount in the proper functioning of the Church. **Experience reveals that most church conflicts arise from an authority issue in one form or another.** Authority issues often emanate from those who attempt to take on authority not rightfully theirs or by some who abuse a position of authority."[1]

All authority is derived from God; on that we should all be in agreement (Rom. 13:1). Jesus was unequivocal on this point. He said, *"All authority has been given to me, both in heaven and in earth"* (Matt. 28:18, NKJV), and in light of that statement, he commissioned the apostles for their upcoming assignments to establish the kingdom through the process of discipleship. They were not given authority to overthrow kings, to raise armies, to develop a currency, or to create nations; instead, they were given authority to make disciples, to influence individuals with the message of transformation, to destroy the works of the devil, to proclaim the gospel of the kingdom, to set the captives free, loose the prisoners, open the eyes of the blind, etc.

Only then did they assemble them into congregations which gathered together, and that more for equipping or preparing them than for establishing enclaves of focused interest. The establishment of an expanded leadership was accomplished out of necessity more than anything else, although it was a natural by-product of organic growth, and the Holy Spirit was working with them—using them to achieve the purpose for which they had been commissioned.

APPLYING THE 12 DIMENSIONS OF SPIRITUAL AUTHORITY TO APOSTLES

All spiritual authority is defined by, exercised within, and distributed along or across 12 distinct dimensions as follows: 1) Appointed, 2) Delegated, 3) Positional, 4) Spherical, 5) Maturational, 6) Relational, 7) Accountable, 8) Approachable, 9) Benevolent, 10) Revelational, 11) Demonstrable, and 12) Generational, authority.

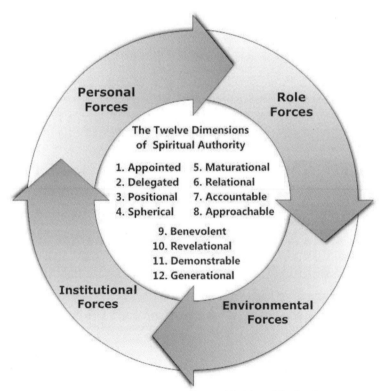

Figure 2. The 12 Dimensions of Spiritual Authority

Around these 12 dimensions of spiritual authority are four boundary constraints—1) Personal Forces, 2) Role Forces, 3)

Environmental Forces, and 4) Institutional Forces.[3] I will discuss the 12 dimensions first and then the four boundary constraints.

First, the initial apostles were all **Appointed** by Jesus to function in those roles. Apostleship is not an elected or elective office, cannot be self-appointed, and cannot be chosen or assumed by an individual; rather, the call to this office is a divine one, with other five-fold leaders confirming this independently and established, senior apostles commissioning the new apostle. The first century apostles carried out their responsibilities to the extent that they compassed the whole known world. Obviously, they soon found themselves overwhelmed by the sheer enormity of their task, with the rapid spread of the gospel and growth of the Church, and quickly found it necessary to appoint others in various capacities to share the burden and authority of leadership responsibility.

Second, all authority is **Delegated** by or from God (Rom. 13:1-2). The authority Jesus had while on earth was delegated to him by God even though it was universal in scope, and included "all authority in heaven and earth." in order for those individuals selected by the early apostles for appointment to function with effectiveness, they delegated to them the same authority which had been appointed unto them by Jesus; thus, they commissioned them to serve. In at least many if not most cases, as recorded in scripture, this included the laying on of hands and impartation of gifting. In thus identifying them, they recognized their capacity and endorsed it to those who followed their lead. Ultimately, all apostolic authority comes through the process of delegation, whereby the authority held by one or some is properly passed along to others.

Third, spiritual authority is **Positional**—that is, it is affected by the five-fold office, gift or calling of an individual disciple. There is a whole body of social science called Role Theory which deals with this. The heads of households have spiritual, legal and financial authority for their families based on their position. Similarly, apostles and other five-fold officers have authority within and for their assignments, calling, and destiny.

Fourth, spiritual authority is **Spherical**—that is, it is linked not just to a position or assignment, but to a particular sphere or multiple spheres of society and culture. Apostles are recognized within their sphere or metron as they begin to function effectively. Paul the Apostle said,

> *"Of course we shouldn't dare include ourselves in the same class as those who write their own testimonials, or even to compare ourselves with them! All they are doing, of course, is to measure themselves by their own standards or by comparisons within their own circle, and that doesn't make for accurate estimation, you may be sure. No, we shall not make any wild claims, but simply judge ourselves by that line of duty which God has marked out for us, and that line includes our work on your behalf. We do not exceed our duty when we embrace your interests, for it was our preaching of the Gospel which brought us into contact with you. **Our pride is not in matters beyond our proper sphere nor in the labours of other men. No, our hope is that your growing faith will mean the expansion of our sphere of action,** so that before long we shall be preaching the Gospel in districts beyond you, instead of being proud of work that has already been done in someone else's province"* (2 Cor. 10:12-16, Phillips, author's emphasis).

Apostolic authority is limited both in scope and capacity, which has been difficult for some to accept. Having been identified as apostles, some have reached beyond their measure, have become domineering and implacable in the application of their responsibilities, and have not been held to account by their overseers.

Fifth, spiritual authority is **Maturational**. There is an old saying in leadership that you can have as much authority as you are willing to be under. In general, people who are power hungry and are seeking authority are not good candidates for or stewards of it. These are self-promoters. God does not call such people to spiritual leadership because they cannot be trusted and are still selfish and egocentric and spiritually immature. Instead, he calls those who have put to death or are in the process of putting to death or soon will put to death such things as well as the carnal nature and fleshly desires so that Christ might dwell and reign in their mortal bodies by faith. Apostles must be meat eaters and not just milk drinkers (Heb. 5:11-6:3). They should be able to say like Paul: "Follow me as I follow Christ." Personal maturity is a boundary constraint on spiritual authority.

> You can have as much authority as you are willing to be under.

Sixth, spiritual authority is **Relational**. In that regard, David Cannistraci quotes Dick Iverson as follows: "Relationship, not hierarchy, is the basis of spiritual authority. Holding a position, filling an office, or being elected to a place of importance is not how spiritual elders are made—they earn it! One qualifies to be a leader by developing relationships."[2] If we cannot lead in our own homes and our own churches and businesses or government agencies or NGOs, how can we lead a network or council? Leadership starts at home, and locally. As we are faithful in the little, He adds the much and the rulership of it. Relationships are the currency of the Kingdom, and promotion comes from the Lord. If we cannot love others as ourselves and as unto the Lord, we cannot be trusted with spiritual authority. Relationships are not a side show or coming attraction, but the main event. As we can be known and tested and trusted, we will gain authority.

Seventh, spiritual authority is **Accountable**. By this, I mean teachable and correctable and submitted. True apostles voluntarily and willingly submit to other genuine, authentic, fatherly, apostolic authority. The real challenge is that such fatherly leaders and authority figures are rare and hard to find, and in great demand. Count yourself blessed when you find one that you can connect with at a deep level. I am fortunate and favored to have several such apostles in my life, and inner circle, who I draw strength and counsel from on a regular basis, and vice versa. These are reciprocal, mutually beneficial, and mutually accountable relationships.

In addition to such trusted and covenantal peer-level relationships, apostles also can benefit from association and alignment with one or more apostolic networks, and national or international councils of apostles. Despite all the recent talk about alignment versus covering as the new model of apostolic relationship, I suggest that apostles still need both dimensions—horizontal and vertical.

Of course, God is the ultimate covering for all apostles and converts and disciples of Jesus, but that is too often used as an excuse by immature leaders to isolate and separate and detach or run from accountability and transparency with other leaders. On the other hand, having someone's name on a piece of paper as a spiritual covering offers no guarantees either. You might spend 15 minutes a year with such a person if they are really busy or preoccupied or have the "favored father" or "mentor mother" title at the moment. What really counts is finding other leaders with whom you can have authentic, intimate, and healthy communication and exchange in a safe, trusted and confidential relationship, and where there is a shared spiritual DNA and core values, as well as personal connection, affinity or chemistry. Mutual honor and respect are also things to look for in accountable relationships and a willingness to pray for one another.

Every apostle needs a spectrum and continuum of such relationships where he or she can respectively be a father, son and brother, or a mother, daughter and sister to other apostles, and in some cases, to other five-fold officers. As scripture says, "in the multitude of counselors there is wisdom, and in numbers there is strength, and a three-fold cord is not easily broken," much less a seven- or ten-fold cord. Having accountable relationships is a safety net and an early warning system and a reality check. It is finding a few leaders who understand your calling and your heart, and that can love you as you are and see your potential, but are willing to walk with you, help you to grow, and speak life into you. Accountability is not being under someone's thumb or being their slave or indentured servant or apprentice or guinea pig or whipping post or ego booster or door opener or doormat or personal ATM or another notch on someone's spiritual gun. Avoid such leaders whenever possible. That is abuse rather than

Accountable relationships are never meant to be abusive.

accountability, and mature apostles will know and discern the difference between the two, and proceed accordingly.

Eighth, spiritual authority is **Approachable**. By that, I mean humble, other-oriented, and servant-minded. Those who influence or lead others must be servants of all, and there is no room for pride or ego in God's service. That is a luxury, and a sin, which neither He, nor we, can afford. Busy leaders cannot meet every person, nor should they, as we all must give account to the Lord for our stewardship of time, talent, treasure, and testimony, but there is a difference between being Approachable and Accessible. Many leaders have layers of staff and layers of insulation or protection around them to allow them to focus, stay on track, and be obedient to and effective with their assignments. However, in our busyness, we must never forget our roots, and where we came from, and who we represent, nor lose sight of our humanity.

Leaders need margin in their lives and schedules to allow for the unexpected, the unplanned, and divine interruptions. Those who are driven and controlled by their schedules to the exclusion or detriment of relationships, must find a proper balance between responsibility and relationships. Jesus was touched by the pain and suffering of those around him, and we must each find the balance and the boundaries in our lives between wisdom, diligence, effectiveness and obedience, and not hardening our hearts to and isolating ourselves or "cocooning" from those around us.

Ninth, healthy spiritual authority is **Benevolent**. A few definitions of this term include: "characterized by or expressing goodwill or kindly feelings; desiring to help others; charitable." Scripture says that God is long-suffering, not willing that any should perish but that all should come to the saving knowledge of His Son, Jesus. Believing that God is a benevolent God who loves us unconditionally and has our best interests at heart in every situation and circumstance is often a personal prerequisite to trusting Him fully and/or having an intimate relationship with Him. This is more difficult for some than for others who may have had faulty or failed father figures in their lives or experienced abuse from authority figures or had absentee fathers or mothers. Spiritual fathers and mothers, and apostolic leaders, must be other-oriented with a genuine desire to help others and represent Jesus to them to the best of their ability. These are true shepherds and not hirelings, and are healthy, "safe" people to be around emotionally, physically, spiritually and financially.

Just like a parent will go to great lengths to protect and nurture and train and discipline a child, so God is toward us, and apostles must have this same heart of love and compassion for those they serve, while at the same time having healthy boundaries and priorities so they don't burn out or neglect their own families or health. We can endure the occasional discipline and correction when we know that we are loved. Eph. 4:15 exhorts us to "speak the truth in love" with one another, and that is more art than science.

Tenth, effective spiritual authority is **Revelational,** meaning that the spiritual leader has a continual or ongoing source of revelation from God to bring to bear in and on different circumstances and situations. Included within this dimension would be Strategy, Direction, Counsel and Discernment, among others. One of the main jobs of an apostle is to counsel and advise others and to receive counsel and revelation from God and from trusted fellow leaders. This would include such things as divine timing, spiritual confirmation, understanding of the mysteries and secrets of God, revelatory understanding of scripture and doctrine as well as current events and political landscape, investment decisions, and even military, business and financial strategy, etc.

King David received strategy and revelation from God on a regular basis, including specific plans for battles and military campaigns, and specific plans for the design of the first temple. Moses, Joshua, Abraham and other great leaders also received revelation from God on a regular basis and had an ongoing dialogue and intimacy with Him. The leaders of the short-lived, misguided and so-called "shepherding movement" of the 1970s abused this dimension of spiritual authority and were highly criticized for it, evoking a wave of backlash, criticism and negative repercussions against the apostolic movement that finally is fading and diminishing after many years. Revelational authority is not optional for today's apostle, and is directly linked with intimacy with God in the secret place. Prov. 29:18 says, *"Where there is no revelation, the people cast off restraint."*

Eleventh, real spiritual authority is **Demonstrable,** i.e., there is fruit and there is power. It is not mere talk but love in action. This term means clearly evident, obvious, capable of being proved or demonstrated. As James says, *"Do not merely listen to the word, and so deceive yourselves. Do what it says…But the man who looks intently into the perfect law that gives freedom, and continues to do this, not forgetting what he has heard, but doing it—he will be blessed in what he does"* (James 1: 22, 25, NIV). Paul also says, *"The things that mark an apostle—signs, wonders and miracles—were done among you with great perseverance"* (2 Cor. 12:12).

Jesus demonstrated his authority to His apostles and disciples by teaching, wisdom, example, miracles, healing the sick, raising the dead, overturning the tables of the moneychangers in the temple, rebuking the religious leaders, calming the storm, turning water into wine, casting out demons, telling them where to catch fish, interpreting Old Testament prophecy and scripture, His own resurrection and ascension, and many other proofs. We today are to be doing the works of Jesus, and even greater works (John 14:12-14).

And twelfth, appropriate spiritual authority is **Generational**. Many cultures revere and honor the elderly for their years of experience and wisdom and life mastery. The Bible says that a good man will leave an inheritance for his children's children (Prov. 13:22). This includes not only a financial inheritance but a spiritual inheritance. Prov. 16:31 says, *"Gray hair is a crown of splendor; it is attained by a righteous life."* Prov. 20:29 says, *"The glory of young men is their strength, gray hair the splendor of the old."* And Prov. 21:21 says, *"He who pursues righteousness and love finds life, prosperity and honor."* God told Abraham that his seed and offspring would be as numerous as the stars in the sky and the sand on the seashore. He also told David that there would not fail a man from his lineage to sit on the throne and rule over Israel. That prophecy was fulfilled through Jesus. That is real generational authority.

So, it is in the context of these 12 dimensions of spiritual authority that we must consider, understand, apply and administer apostolic authority. It is not just policy-making authority, but more often polity-serving authority. Apart from such a context of safeguards and protocol, spiritual authority can and will be abused by some, whether intentionally or unintentionally, knowingly or unknowingly.

Scripture says to "know those who labor among you" and we must each discern whether our spiritual fathers and mothers and apostolic leaders measure up to these criteria and standards of effective and healthy spiritual leadership in terms of proper use of authority, keeping in mind that all leaders are human, are being perfected, and need our mercy, patience and grace at times just as we need theirs.

Referring back to Figure 2, around these 12 dimensions are four boundary constraints that mitigate and influence the use of spiritual authority by leaders. Personal Forces include habits, preferences, expectations, self-talk, leadership style, personality traits, experiences, needs, attitudes, values, beliefs, and interpersonal skills, among other things. Role Forces include both internal (role holder) and external (role sender) expectations, duties and responsibilities of specific positions, roles, or offices.

Institutional Forces include traditions, history, culture, norms, sanctions, taboos, rituals, rewards, and other aspects of organizational life, since an institution such as a church or corporation is a complex and dynamic social organism and not a static and lifeless machine. Institutional Forces can also include wealth, constituencies, capabilities, strengths and weaknesses, market position, size, maturity, prestige, and quality.

Finally, Environmental Forces include the Seven Mountains or spheres of culture, proclivity of the surrounding area to natural disasters, unemployment rate, inflation rate, state of the economy, federal tax policy, government policy toward freedom of religion, public opinion toward Christianity and morality, economic incentives for entrepreneurs and job creation, etc.

Leadership has its stresses, pressures and challenges, and extra measures of divine grace, favor and wisdom are needed to cope and be effective in such positions of influence. Likewise, apostolic authority, like all authority, must operate within defined boundaries if it is to be effective. John Tetsola offers a significant insight here which provides those kinds of boundaries.

"God is raising up apostles in various nations and they must begin to come together to form apostolic councils.

"There are three forms of apostolic councils that must be established and embraced for the Church to really see the growth of the apostolic ministry and anointing in the body. The Church is still scratching the surface of the apostolic movement. The first council is the local church apostolic council, sometimes called the apostolic team or the eldership team of a house which provides apostolic rulership to that house. This local church apostolic council is comprised of men that have been spiritually selected in accordance to biblical principles and put together to govern and rule the local centers. The numbers of the members of this council vary and it is normally in direct proportion to the need, gifting, anointing, and the size of the congregational membership of the center. The second form of council is the regional apostolic council. This council is comprised of selected apostolic men with valid apostolic anointings from various valid apostolic centers within a region to form a council to represent that region. These men are prayerfully selected by their peers according to their spiritual ranks, maturity and influence. Some of the job of this council is to bring accountability, correction, order, structure, and sometimes make policies. They also establish doctrinal foundations in the churches.

"Then, finally, we have the national apostolic councils. These are made up of men that are usually selected from valid recognizable regional apostolic councils to form a national council of apostles. These men tend to be matured and often are highly regarded with a national influence. They work and make contacts with other national apostolic councils that represent other nations. As a result of their level of influence, maturity and placement, they are able to formulate policies and strategies for nations. They pioneer and verify new moves of God. They also establish and restore doctrinal foundations, structure and order for the body."[4]

Such councils, once effectively placed, would be able to address at least some of the abuses and oversights which have fostered suspicion or apprehension held by some in the body of Christ about apostles and the current apostolic restoration movement. They would be able to deal lovingly but firmly with those who call themselves apostles and are not, provide guidance to those who have not matured in their offices, and direct the collective efforts of many while encouraging the initiatives and resourcefulness of those within the scope of their council.

There may be those who object to such councils as unnecessary or overreaching, but without a more uniform structure of authoritative oversight of the apostolic movement, some cases of abuse and misuse of apostolic authority will likely continue and may increase. Standards of conduct and ministry, assessment testing, best practices, mentorship, and apostolic education and training are possible foci and outcomes of such groups. In that regard, Dr. Paula Price has developed some excellent assessment testing and curriculum for apostles and other five-fold officers. Others working in this area of apostolic education and training include John Kelly and Jonas Clark as well as Drs. Stan DeKoven, Che Ahn, Kluane Spake, Mark Virkler, Ron Cottle, Philip Byler, James Boswell, Sr. and Lee Ann Marino, among many others. Most apostolic networks, councils and associations also offer or provide this as a service to their members.

An alternative or perhaps parallel mechanism to Tetsola's proposal is apostolic networks. Individual networks with capable, mature leadership are able to address issues or problems that may surface or arise among individual members as long as there is a covenantal bond in place, and mutual honor and respect, and a willingness to remain in relationship and be teachable and correctable. The proliferation of apostolic networks in recent years seems to suggest that many apostles prefer this more decentralized approach over national councils, although clearly there is a place and a need for both in the body of Christ.

EVIDENCES OF APOSTOLIC FUNCTION

As the apostolic movement continues to expand globally, there will be a commensurate expansion in the number of apostles. Recognizing who they are places a demand on those who eventually will commission them to function apostolically. This will not happen automatically, but rather will force greater collaboration between apostles who function in very different ways and in very different spheres of ministry. In this regard, Naomi Dowdy has stated:

"In order for Apostles to function as God intends, and indeed for the entire five-fold to operate according to His plan, I believe we must have teaching and training in the areas of character, protocol, function (how offices work together and what they do), responsibility, relationships (how to relate to other ministry gifts), commissioning, and accountability."[5]

In some segments of the apostolic movement, training for apostles has been woefully overlooked. In others, unskilled and underdeveloped apostles have merely duplicated their own weaknesses and lack of perspective. This may seem like a harsh criticism, but the viability of an effective apostolate depends on those who hold authority to wield it with the grace, wisdom, and depth of insight that will sustain the transformation process. Reproducing those perceptions and functional weaknesses which failed in the past will guarantee failure in the future. So what are the core evidences of an apostolic ministry? Wagner has summarized them as follows:

"There are 12 ministries that we can expect of all apostles. They won't perform them the same way or to the same degree, but they will be characterized by these activities: They receive revelation. They cast vision. They birth. They impart. They build. They govern. They teach. They send. They finish. They war. They align generations. They equip."[6]

It stands to reason that it is not necessary for every apostle to perform every aspect of these differing ministry applications, or at least to the same degree, but the list provides a working platform for evaluating those who function apostolically and for those who are being called into the apostleship. Dr. Jonathan David also listed 12 functions of apostles and John Eckhardt's list of apostolic functions is more than double that, literally spanning from "A" to "Z." Dr. Paula Price has succinctly summarized apostolic function as to Guard, Guide and Govern.

Several others mention the Fathering dimension and still others list the functions of Ambassador and *Architekton* (master builder). Hirsch and Catchim added Foundation Layer and Planter to these three to round out Paul's apostolic roles. They also listed Interpreter of Gospel, Agent of Doctrinal Integrity, Designer, Innovator, Change Agent, Networker, and Founder as apostolic roles. Ernest Gentile's list of apostolic functions included Planters, Growers, Encouragers, Expanders, Supervisors, Overseers and Invaders. Mike Breen suggested Pioneer, Planter, Bridger and Builder. Dr. David Cannistraci named seven functions: Planting Churches, Developing Leaders, Ordaining Ministries, Overseeing and Strengthening Churches, Managing Crisis, Networking with Other Ministries, Supervising and Coordinating Ministries.[7]

It is a lengthy job description and the Holy Spirit will give different graces and assignments to different apostles, as He did with Peter, James, John, Barnabas and Paul. Even there, the assignment and grace shifted over time in each of them. And just for good measure, Paul wrote Titus that he should *"set in order the things that are wanting..."* (Titus 1:5, KJV) such as appointing elders, etc. That is a broad mandate indeed.

Apostles are at the forefront of biblical leadership, as is indicated in 1 Cor. 12:28. Their positioning as first (*proton*— first in time, place, order or importance) in scripture and in the ministry of Jesus carries with it the clear indication that they also carry the most authority within their respective spheres. They are positioned in the most accountable role before God in what they teach and preach, and in what they allow to be taught and preached within their *metron*. The responsibility structure of Kingdom assignments is delegated in levels, based upon the increasing measure each individual leader holds. Within each of these structures one finds other five-fold ministers occupying positions of authority as well, but the apostolic leader is foremost in both the extent and the liability of that authority.

Therein lies a great paradox. Apostles are the only five-fold ministers who predated the church and were entrusted with its birth and growth and administration; they are also the only officers with an eternal ministry, having their names written on the foundations of the walls or gates in heaven and being appointed to judge the 12 tribes of Israel; they are also the only members of the five-fold charged and delegated with overseeing and interpreting doctrine; and they are the only members of the five-fold called to be ambassadors, governors and generals; also, they must spend time in the presence of the Lord on an ongoing basis to know His heart and receive His revelation and carry not only His presence but represent His person.

With this great authority must of necessity come great humility, great intimacy, great love, great faith, great character, great wisdom, and great service and selflessness; otherwise, a Frankenstein or Jekyl and Hyde might result. As Scripture notes, "To whom much has been given, much shall be required." Paul de-fended his apostleship based on his calling, his authority, his revelation, his having seen and heard Jesus, his fruitfulness and harvest, his self-sacrifice and hard work, his personal lifestyle and example, his acceptance by other high-ranking apostles, the things he had suffered, the marks borne in his own body, and the churches he had planted.

> **With great authority must come great humility, great intimacy, great love, great faith ...**

Wagner had this to say: "An apostle is distinguished from others in the Body of Christ by extraordinary authority."[8] He also stated, "Apostles are distinguished from other leaders, **more than anything else**, by their God-given authority."[9] Similarly, Dr. Paula Price added:

"Apostles exude authority. Active or dormant, their authority is difficult to disregard. It is the first obvious distinguishing feature. Whatever the situation the apostle inevitably stands out. He unavoidably finds himself in charge or it is thrust upon him. He competently makes decisions and often casts the deciding vote. Apostles lead when they do not try to; are looked to and relied upon when others seek a strong hand. **They command attention and provoke obedience because of God's blatant authority upon them.** Extended involvement with an apostle puts you face to face with authority."[10]

Johnny Enlow has also addressed the issue of apostolic authority as follows:

"An apostle is called and anointed to take the tops of the mountains. That anointing is not based on their charisma, their moneymaking ability, their networking, their personality type, their speaking skills, or any other naturally-understood ability. It is authority with heaven based on a specific call — and then an obedient response to that call. It is moored in **profound intimacy with the Godhead.**

"...Apostles are some of the greater gifts God gives us — often hidden, but anointed with power. And the greater of them will be **some of the most unlikely individuals imaginable**. In heaven they are very well known, mostly because of their **cloak of humility**. An apostle will have untold thousands of **angels working with him** because of the call upon his life, and many will be major territorial angels with a displacement anointing."[11]

In addition to being generals, guardians and ambassadors, apostles in the first century, and prophets even earlier in history, were on a few occasions executioners, as in the case of Ananias and Sapphira when they came before Peter with their gift and lied about it. This also happened with Elijah on more than one occasion, and with Moses as well. God dealt harshly but justly with lying, rebellion, idolatry, and other sins like witchcraft, sorcery and paganism. Technically, the Holy Spirit was the executioner in the case involving Peter and on several occasions with Moses, but Elijah used a sword to help the Israelites kill all 850 of the prophets of Baal (450) and Asherah (400) following his victory over them on Mount Carmel, and on at least one occasion, Moses sent the priests through the camp with swords drawn at God's command.

Only prophets and apostles were given this kind of life and death authority by God historically (other than judges and kings), and that is one of many reasons why they are the foundation of both the kingdom of God and the Church, being positioned and aligned next to the Chief Corner Stone, Jesus (Eph. 2:20-21). Both roles are also revelatory in nature.

Today, however, apostles are rarely if ever used in this manner by God, and it is much more common that an apostle would be used to resurrect someone from the dead, as in a case made famous through a video recording involving Reinhard Bonnke, or in the ministry of David Hogan and his team in Mexico which has reported some 1000 resurrections in recent years, or Heidi and Rolland Baker in Mozambique. Make no mistake about it: Spiritual rank is a reality. There is rank within the five-fold, and there is rank within the kingdom of God and the kingdom

All authority and power is based upon rank.

of Darkness, even though some choose to ignore it or do not believe it. Passages of scripture such as Eph. 6 and Col. 2 list some of the ranks of darkness. Paul even referred to rank within the apostolic when he spoke of the "super apostles" in 2 Cor. 11:5 and called Peter, James and John "pillars of the Jerusalem church" in Gal. 2:9. John Eckhardt has summarized this well:

> "*Rank* is defined as a degree or position of dignity, eminence, or excellence, a grade of official standing (Webster). Even though we are all equal in Christ as to salvation, there are different ranks in the spirit. Different ranks carry different degrees of authority and power. One of the definitions of 'first' is *chiefly*. This means according to the highest rank or office, of greatest importance, significance, or influence.

> "Just as there is rank in the military, there is also rank in the 'army of God.' There is rank in the spirit realm. There is a rank in the Godhead. There is rank among angels. There is even rank among evil spirits. All authority and power is based upon rank. We must be able to receive, walk in, and discern different rankings in the spirit.

> "Evil spirits recognize spiritual rank. Every believer has rank to cast out devils. Apostles walk and minister in the highest rank. Evil spirits and angels much recognize and respect their rank. They have enough rank in the spirit to command, decree and rebuke with authority.

> "Their rank is within their *sphere of authority*. In other words, they have rank in the areas they have been assigned to by God."[12]

The individual configurations of apostolic authority structures, known variously as apostolic teams or apostolic networks, depending on their size and scope, can be as different as the individuals who lead them. Within them one generally finds an apostolic council, comprised of apostles and prophets and possibly other five-fold ministers. Furthermore, several apostolic networks may collaborate to form a regional or even a national council, which will also be comprised of apostles and prophets. According to Wagner:

> "Whereas denominations were once upon a time the new wineskins into which God was pouring new wine, apostolic networks now appear to be the new wineskins of the Second Apostolic Age."[13]

KINGS AND PRIESTS

As the marketplace movement began to gain traction within the apostolic movement, it also was gaining momentum outside of the movement. Both denominational and non-denominational churches became increasingly interested in conducting business-oriented events. The Men's Movement had a significant impact on men across denominational lines. This interest seems to have been instrumental in elevating business and marketplace issues into places of importance within Church perspectives. The apostolic movement, however, though lagging behind the para-church world in focusing on the marketplace, was quick to recognize the necessity of fully-functional ministers within those spheres.

The apostolic movement experienced its initial thrust within the Church world, largely due to an elevated recognition of the necessity of a functional five-fold ministry within its ranks. The Prophetic had drawn significant impetus from the earlier Latter Rain revivals, which occurred largely in the 1940s and early 1950s. That movement rightly embraced the theology of a contemporary apostolate but failed to fully understand or establish a working structure for the emergence of apostles within the Church. It would take almost another half-century before the apostolic would gain sufficient momentum to become a true spiritual movement.

One of the unique distinctions which was made in those early days was between those who were called priests and those who were called kings. Scripture informed us that God had intended Israel to be a kingdom of priests unto God (Ex. 19:6). And the apostle John, in his prelude to the Revelation, wrote these words in praise to Jesus: *"To Him who loved us and washed us from our sins in His own blood, and has made us kings and priests to His God and Father, to Him be glory and dominion forever and ever. Amen"* (Rev 1:5-6, NKJV, author's emphasis). Thus, a defining language was established, assigning to those who were ecclesiastical, professional, Church-oriented ministers as priests, and those who were marketplace, business-oriented ministers as kings.

Rich Marshall, a marketplace leader, former pastor, and an apostle, explained this language in 2000 when he wrote:

> "In the coming revival we need to identify the apostolic leaders in the marketplace arena. God is going to begin to reveal the five-fold ministry gifts to them as they operate in the marketplace. I believe we will soon see prophets and apostles in business, government, and all facets of society. As these **apostolic kings** begin to operate, we will have the opportunity to see the revival I have been describing.
>
> **"Who are they? They are kings. They are called. They walk in a power and authority that can break the grip**

of bondage and oppression holding many. **They are a new breed of ministers that God is raising up for this day.**[14]

"Kings also come in all shapes and sizes. However, they are all selected in the same way. **God chooses them!** He selects—anoints—appoints. They may have different attitudes about their roles...

"The common ingredient is this: **They know that God has called them, and that God will enable them. They know the power is from the Lord**, and they know they can **walk humbly** before the Lord **with a boldness that defies human reasoning.**"[15]

In 2000, this was ground-breaking insight. The marketplace community was, and continues to be to some degree, identified more for its capacity to finance Church operations than to be deeply engaged in directed, hands on ministry, both within the Church and in the workplace. Marshall directed attention to that as well.

"Apart from finances, **businesspeople are calling out to the Church to be fully recognized for their value and giftings for the Kingdom of God**. The business community is a very important resource for this work. Some businesspeople hold powerful positions in society, and can use their influence on behalf of the Kingdom. **If the Church began to reach out to, equip and release businesspeople, God's earthly Kingdom would look much different.**

"...**Businesspeople have indeed been overlooked** for the multitude of talents, skills, and gifts that could be utilized on behalf of God. **It is a huge oversight. The**

spiritual and physical magnitude of what they have to offer is endless."[16]

The distinction between kings and priests is not as pronounced as these perspectives indicate, but the separation they describe has been such for some time. But this perspective certainly has carried a great deal of weight and, agreeing with that perspective, Peter Wagner characterized his observations in that vein, indicating that in his opinion, the propensity of apostolic leadership lies within the nuclear church: "Based on my observations, **I would estimate that ecclesiastical apostles constitute the largest number of all the categories of apostolic activities."**[17]

Despite my great respect for Dr. Wagner, based on my own observations and understanding, I am convinced there are many more apostles in the workplace than there ever will be or can be in the ecclesiastical sphere. I therefore cannot agree with Dr. Wagner's estimate and find it mathematically and factually suspect, based on the rationale and assumptions I shared earlier in Chapter 1. I make this point simply to underscore what is a prevailing perspective within the ecclesiastical community. Almost everyone there would agree with Dr. Wagner's statement. In a recent personal correspondence with Dr. Wagner, he stated that he has since changed his mind about this point and now agrees with me.[18] I am happy to report this as I believe we all owe Dr. Wagner a debt of gratitude for his leadership of and contributions to the apostolic movement.

There are several reasons to think differently, but if there were no other reason, the clear-cut mathematical reality indicates otherwise. On a global scale, it is estimated that 97-98% of all Christians are not on a vocational ministry payroll, either as professional ministers, staff personnel, or in any other capacity. The vast majority of people in this world, and in the Church, are employed in the workplace, own their own businesses, or are simply unemployed. That in itself is an overpowering reason for a preponderance of five-fold ministers operating within the marketplace arena.

The question lingers, however, concerning kings and priests. Are kings marketplace and priests ecclesiastical? Or, are we, as saints made to be both kings and priests, after being born again and made to be joint heirs with Jesus Christ? While this may be a theological conundrum for some, it seems obvious to me that the latter question expresses a more biblical viewpoint for New Covenant believers, as I shared more fully in an earlier chapter. Regardless of your perspective, however, there is no case or justification for minimizing apostolic authority or failing to recognize and affirm those five-fold ministers whose sphere is in the workplace.

WIELDING AUTHORITY AND ENGAGING IN SPIRITUAL WARFARE

Two distinct characteristics accompany the apostolic regardless of the arena in which one functions. One is oversight or the right and proper exercise of authority, and the other is spiritual warfare. When exercising oversight it is difficult to maintain the appropriate balance between command and influence. Of course, command is one form of influence, but its connotation here is to rule by giving orders and demanding obedience. When an apostle functions from the position as a general, command and obedience are both necessary and practical. Obedience and submission are closely aligned responses, but it is all too easy for obedience to become austere subjection rather than willing submission. Too many who call themselves apostles have resorted to "my way or the highway" tactics, when relational ties would provide a much greater and more effective path to achieving success and biblical outcomes.

True spiritual fathers tend to lead by relational connectedness and influence rather than by force or compulsion.

True spiritual fathers tend to lead by relational connectedness and influence rather than by force or compulsion or ultimatums, relying on the intuitive nature of those under their authority or within their sphere to be responsive based on practiced knowledge of their vision, mission, character, selflessness, reputation and purpose. Philip Byler has summarized some of the current dynamics in the apostolic community as follows:

"Most ecclesiastical leaders believe and assert that they carry the greatest weight in most, if not all, situations. Realistically though, this is not so cut and dried as it may seem. Remember, the defining quality of apostolic leadership is relationship. Apostles lead by influence. They lead by command only in the most extreme of circumstances. True apostolic generals should recognize which among them has the greater effectiveness in a given set of circumstances and yield to that one. An individual's sphere is not threatened when he yields. Rather it is strengthened. Usually, when numerous apostles are on scene, an individual leader will, without political positioning, be recognized as the lead voice. Their experience, influence and relational connectedness to the group will establish them in that position. In turn, they will usually have the intelligence and the wisdom to know when to speak and when to hold their peace. In the process, a lot can be accomplished.

"Pulpit leaders need to know their boundaries and limitations, their levels of expertise and experience, and the lack thereof. They must be willing to yield in the face of greater insight, wisdom and skill.

"Workplace leaders should also recognize their boundaries. They must know how and when to yield to pulpit leaders and be led in those areas where they are not fulfilling their particular assignments. Every individual Christian needs an overseer. We might call that person pastor, but that person could just as well be an apostle or a prophet. Regardless of title, they will be in a position of spiritual authority and need to be accepted in that role. Furthermore, a person may be under one authority structure in one area of life and ministry and under a completely different one in another area.

"Regardless of which mountain or sphere an individual is assigned to, they must be under authority, connected with authority, and committed to authority. Those who are not under authority need to be shunned and their voices quieted by common consent."[19]

APOSTOLIC WEAPONS

Paul writes in 2 Corinthians 10 regarding the weapons of our warfare as being mighty through God. The weaponry of an apostle, apart from the strength of his or her authority, is significantly different from that of other saints. Likewise, the understanding, deployment, and effectiveness with which apostles use that weaponry is also different. Having been delegated as an authority, and holding the accountability and responsibility for a contingent of other Christians, apostles carry a "bigger stick," so to speak. They need one!

One of the weapons an apostle may receive is often called an "apostle's rod." It is not a tangible, physical tool like the one Moses carried, but rather, it is a metaphorical indicator of the immense authority that an apostle carries, and exists in intangible, invisible form. Other typical examples of apostolic spiritual weapons include signet rings, crowns, mantles, scepters, robes, swords, gavels, keys, etc. Such items are typically bestowed upon or presented to an apostle by angels or the Lord himself in a vision, trance, personal visitation, spiritual experience, or third heaven encounter, and each of them is directly related to authority and rank.

Very little is written on this topic because most leaders are too humble to even speak of such things, and also consider such experiences and authority as something holy and not to be grasped, or "spoken of lightly or publically," but to wield sparingly and privately. They may also be concerned about being considered prideful, crazy or extreme by others who are less prophetic or spiritually discerning, or have not yet experienced or understood such matters.

Rick Joyner has touched on some of this in *The Final Quest*, as has Tudor Bismark in a videotape teaching series on Spiritual Warfare where he described battling and defeating a dragon over the city of London in the spirit dimension with an apostle's rod. Ian Clayton, a Kingdom businessman and workplace apostle from New Zealand, ministers around the world and has shared a number of personal experiences in this area in his teaching and ministry. Kathie Walters also teaches on these areas, just to reference a few sources.

Recently I ministered at the U.N.K.A.P. conference[20] in Grande Prairie, Alberta, Canada from 12-12-12 to 12-16-12 with 12 apostles and prophets. On the last night of the conference Dennis Wiedrick shared a vision he had seen while there of a heavenly treasure room with the following 10 items: Peter's Fishing Net, Moses' Rod, Elijah's Mantle, David's Harp, Solomon's Crown, Gideon's Sword, Mary Magdalene's Alabaster Box, Joan of Arc's Armor, Martin Luther's Pen, and Jesus' Cup of Suffering (Chalice). Dennis said to the conference leaders and speakers that Jesus had spoken to him that He was making those precious, priceless items available as gifts to use by the speakers for ministry purposes and that Jesus was inviting us at that moment to choose one or more of these treasures as we prayed and sought the Lord. Wow! Talk about a holy hush that fell in the room. It was an historic moment and everyone present could sense it. Whatever God's purpose, I am sure much fruit will result from it. I only mention this as an example of the type of divine encounters apostles can have today.

Rather than belabor this point, however, which may be considered exotic or esoteric by some, I would rather encourage our readers to apply and master the basic fundamentals of warfare, which many yet lack. These would include having an effective intercession team, discerning and commanding angels, and receiving revelation and strategy by the spirit on an ongoing basis. Such things are considered basic for apostles, but some are not even operating in these yet. They are available. Just ask God.

Whether generals or patriarchs, *nepios, teknion, paidios,* or *pater,* apostles are ambassadors of the Kingdom, duly appointed and commissioned to carry out the duties of their office. They need the strength of their weaponry, and they need to be able to use it effectively in times of warfare and in times of peace, with righteousness, peace, and joy in the Holy Spirit being the operable status of Kingdom relationships.

Spiritual warfare engages the enemy, whether on the field of battle in the heavenly realms or against the strongholds that gain dominance of people's lives, individually or collectively. To be able to hear and distinguish the voice of the Lord and to plan and execute a strategic plan under the guidance of the Holy Spirit is a vital apostolic quality. Thus, apostles are given to strategy, they are profound in leadership, and they are sensitive to the realm of the spirit.

This is much more pronounced in the marketplace than people are prone to believe, not that the marketplace has less spiritual chaos, but that warfare must be accomplished at the ecclesiastical level. The battle is there, in the avenues of daily living, and there is where the enemy must be engaged. Jesus did it, both in confronting demons and in tearing down the theological and ideological strongholds that were built up in people's minds. The early apostles practiced open warfare in the marketplace as well, confronting both demonic spirits, sorcerers, magicians and cultural power brokers. It is no different today.

SIGNS, WONDERS, AND ATTENDING ANGELS

Positions of power are complicated. They pose complex demands on those who hold them, especially those who are commissioned as apostles of the Kingdom. The balance they must maintain, the integrity of their relationships with God and with those who are under their authority, and the depth of wisdom and knowledge they must constantly apply, make the apostolic a challenge to the most venerable of saints. They need help, and lots of it.

Buried deep within the arsenal of a truly effective apostle lie four vital weapons often overlooked by less effective leaders: intercessors, angels, revelatory strategy and the supernatural. The power of effective intercession, to my knowledge, is never challenged in apostolic and prophetic circles. In fact, quite the opposite is true. The number of apostles who have inadequate prayer shields is staggering. It is extremely important to develop the kind of relationships with prayer warriors that will enlist them in the overall vision and strategy of an apostolic ministry. An entire library of books has been written regarding the importance of and intervention brought about by prayer, especially apostolic-prophetic intercessory prayer. Underlining that necessity should be totally beyond the scope of this material, but unfortunately, it remains one of the overlooked weaknesses of many apostles and other five-fold ministers.

Another one of those overlooked benefits is the presence of angels. Hebrews 1:14 poses the telling question, *"Are they not all ministering spirits sent forth to minister for those who will inherit salvation?"* They are, and those who have been given the privilege of seeing angels will readily tell you of their presence, their power, and their number. Even a popular, award-winning television series called *Touched By An Angel* was created to document and focus on this phenomenon.

Because they are unseen to the vast majority of believers, angels go unnoticed and unheralded again and again. Assigned to protect, promote, and influence the atmosphere of transformation, they await directions from heaven and from heaven's delegates, the five-fold officers. What would be the effect if apostles took the presence of angels more seriously, and engaged them in the unseen warfare they have been commissioned to fight?[21]

Tetsola notes in that regard:

"The apostle is governed by an entirely unequal set of circumstances. He is mandated for purposes the typical bishop has little knowledge of. The apostle is a founder, a builder, and a restorer of the lost or stolen dominions of God. He must initiate and instigate, and be the originator or restorer of his own movement. He has a mandate to overthrow, inflame, and inspire. The apostle's goal is to return to God His flock and His kingdoms. The Lord's reign is regnant to the apostle's purpose, a definition that fundamentally crafts his move and mission. As such, the apostle has an enormous spiritual backing from God and His heavenly host. His ministry is backed with supernatural powers."[22]

The third overlooked weapon in the apostle's arsenal is revelatory insight and strategy. Bob Fraser provides a great example of that as follows:

"I was trained as a computer engineer and considered myself a craftsman of code. I loved writing code to the glory of God. I wrote code that people said was impossible to do. I would sit for hours quietly before my computer and craft the very finest code. I fellowshipped with God, and at times we wrote together. Several times when I was stumped, I asked God to help me, and I had a dream that showed me where the problem was! I worked hard to improve my craft and become the best engineer possible, and as a result, wherever I went, I quickly became one of the top engineers in the company."[23]

Apostolic Revelation also extends to other areas, including scripture, doctrine and teaching. As Jonathan David has noted: "The Apostolic mantle provides the apostle with the ability to teach and preach present truths by the revelation of the Holy Spirit. These revelations will take people higher into their abilities and giftings and deeper into the truths and experiences God has for them."[24] I depend heavily on this weapon every time Holy Spirit asks me to write a book.

The final poorly-used weapon is the supernatural, engaging with the gifts of the spirit, healing the sick, casting out demons, discerning spirits, and exercising words of knowledge. Every possible scenario has with it an accompanying solution which becomes far less formidable when engaged at the supernatural level. At least 10 different passages of scripture attest to the presence of signs and wonders accompanying the message of the kingdom and the early apostles, apart from the record of miracles and healings that were performed at their hand.

Today, many apostolic "signs and wonders" occur within a church-related setting, a special service of healing or miracles, or an "altar call" following a particularly inspirational sermon. Those which occur in the marketplace are unheralded and often unnoticed for the most part, despite a large and growing number of exceptions, and even new terms like "treasure hunts" are being used to describe this. It is there, however, that signs and wonders follow ministry in the marketplace. Generally, the wise leadership or the informative counsel or the personal influence or breaker anointing of an apostle opens the doors of success.

The gentle touch of friendship or the honest confrontation of iniquity in the marketplace produces results that are not measured in church growth statistics.

Dr. Alan Pateman offered this observation in that regard:

"Many end time apostles are walking in the earth again, so dead to self, so yielded to obeying Jesus and so perfected in the love walk that the authority they have is unparalleled. Nations are listening to them because God has granted them a genuine 'VOICE' that can be heard." [25]

Jesus taught that the kingdom of God is to be compared with an almost imperceptible growth cycle: *"What is the kingdom of God like? And to what shall I compare it? It is like a mustard seed, which a man took and put in his garden; and it grew and became a large tree, and the birds of the air nested in its branches"* (Luke 13:19, NKJV).

This is the nature of the apostolic in the marketplace, almost unnoticed, barely perceptible to the culture that surrounds it. It grows and expands until it becomes a mighty force, filled with integrity, utterly reliable even to those who oppose it, unassailable in the face of challenge, and empowered with divine strategy. That apostolic force becomes the catalyst for transformation of culture, of individuals and companies, of communities and cities, of ethnic prejudices and national mindsets. It is the challenge which faces the Church, to be sure, but far more, it is a challenge which is met with the kingdom dynamic called the Second Apostolic Reformation. We turn now to Chapter 5.

ENDNOTES

1. Glenn Shaffer, *Apostolic Government in the 21st Century*, p. 9, author's emphasis. Claremore, OK: Apostolic Teams Intl., 2005.

2. Dr. David Cannistraci, *Apostles and the Emerging Apostolic Movement*, p. 153. Ventura, CA: Regal Books, 1996, 1998.

3. Adapted from Cook, Bruce and Lasher, William, The Four Forces Model of Presidential Fund Raising in Higher Education, in "Toward a Theory of Fund Raising in Higher Education," published by the *Review of Higher Education*, 20(1), 33-51. Copyright 1996: Association for the Study of Higher Education (ASHE).

4. Dr. John A. Tetsola, *The Apostolic Culture & Pattern: Understanding the Apostolic Ministries, Its Anointing and Its Applications*, pp. 171-172. Bronx, NY: Baruch Publishing, 2002.

5. Naomi Dowdy, *Commissioning: The Process, Protocol, and Importance of Commissioning Modern-Day Apostles*, 2006, p. 8. Dallas, TX: Naomi Dowdy Ministries, 2006.

6. Dr. C. Peter Wagner, *Apostles Today*, pp. 28-29. Ventura, CA: Regal Books, 2006.

7. See John Eckhardt, *Moving in the Apostolic*, pp. 96-99 and 50 *Truths Concerning Apostolic Ministry*; Dr. Paula Price, *Eternity's Generals*; Bill Scheidler, *Apostles: The Fathering Servant*; Dr. David Cannistraci, *The Gift of Apostle*, pp. 100-103; Mike Breen, *The Apostle's Notebook*; Dr. Jonathan David, *Apostolic Strategies Affecting Nations*; Ernest Gentile, *Why Apostles Now?*, p. 246; Alan Hirsch and Tim Catchim, *The Permanent Revolution: Apostolic Imagination and Practice for the 21st Century Church*, pp. 103, 106.

8. Dr. C. Peter Wagner, *The Church in the Workplace*, p. 117. Ventura, CA: Regal Books, 2006.

9. Ibid, p. 32, author's emphasis.

10. Dr. Paula A. Price, *God's Apostle Revived*, p. 95, author's emphasis. Tulsa, OK: Flaming Vision Publications, 1992, 1993, 1994, 2003.

11. Johnny Enlow, *Seven Mountain Prophecy*, p. 65. author's emphasis, Lake Mary, FL: Creation House, 2008.

12. John Eckhardt, *50 Truths Concerning Apostolic Ministry*, p. 4. Chicago, IL: Crusaders Ministries, 1994.

13. Wagner, *Apostles Today*, p. 91.

14. Rich Marshall, *God@Work*, pp. 124-125, author's emphasis. Shippensburg, PA: Destiny Image Publishers, 2000.

15. Ibid., p. 135, author's emphasis.

16. Ibid., p. 108, author's emphasis.

17. Wagner, *Apostles Today*, pp. 90-91, author's emphasis.

18. Personal correspondence with Dr. C. Peter Wagner of 12/10/12.

19. Dr. Philip Byler, *The Changing Church in the Unchanging Kingdom*, pp. 155-156, author's emphasis. Keller, TX: Palm Tree Productions, 2008.

20. U.N.K.A.P. is an acronym for Unlocking Nations through the Kingdom Apostolic and Prophetic. Charlie and Lisa Fisher and Dr. Doug and Shawnee Atha hosted this event in cooperation with K.E.Y.S., held in Grande Prairie, AB Canada from 12-12-12 to 12-16-12. Each of the five-fold ministry gifts and offices was "uncapped" by a different speaker, and other   ministries such as healing, worship, intercession and youth were also uncapped in the Spirit realm.

21. Related books include *Angels on Assignment,* by Perry Stone; *Angels on Assignment,* by Roland Buck; *Angels that Gather,* by Paul Keith Davis; *Angelic Encounters: Engaging Help From Heaven,* by James and Michal Ann Goll; *Entertaining Angels: Engaging the Unseen Realm,* by Randy Clark; *Surrounded by Angels,* and *Under His Wings,* by Theodore Mistra, and *Keys to Heaven's Economy: An Angelic Visitation from the Minister of Finance,* by Shawn Bolz.

22. Tetsola, *The Apostolic Culture and Pattern, Understanding the Apostolic Ministries, Its Anointing and Its Applications,* pp. 81-82.

23. Bob Fraser, *Marketplace Christianity,* p. 43. Overland Park, KS: New Grid Publishing, 2004, 2006.

24. Dr. Jonathan David, *Apostolic Strategies Affecting Nations,* p. 411. Johor, Malaysia: Destiny Heights, 1997, 1999, 2007.

25. Dr. Alan Pateman, *Apostles: Can The Church Survive Without Them?,* Amazon Kindle, Introduction, 2% -- 43 of 2029. Florence, Italy: APMI Publications, 2012.

CHAPTER FIVE

ORIGINS OF THE PATRIARCHS AND JUDAISM ARE FOUND IN THE MARKETPLACE

INTRODUCTION

Judaism, like all religions, developed more as a work in progress than it did as a distinct moment, or even a period in history. What we do know of it is derived from a wide variety of historical records, expositions, and assumptions, some profoundly defending Judaism as having been derived from Adam, through Noah, and the renewed rise of humanity after the flood. Others who are less sympathetic to a biblical point of view connect it with the Ancient Semitic religions. What we do know is that Judaism traces its own foundational perspectives to Abram, who began life as a Chaldean from Ur.

We are also confident that this man had a viable, communicational relationship with God, one of such a nature, depth and importance that their conversations were recorded by Moses. Following the death of his father, Terah, God reassigned and relocated Abram, sending him from Haran to Canaan, a land far removed from his motherland. There, he became the progenitor of the Hebrew people. Thus, the God of Judaism is known as the God of Abraham, his son Isaac, and his grandson Jacob, the latter being renamed Israel (Gen. 32:28), and to Jacob were born 12 sons who became the tribal chieftains of the nation named for their father.

The book of Genesis provides historically important glimpses into the worship of God before the establishment of the Hebrew religion. It spans a time frame of approximately 2,100 years, from the creation until the death of Joseph, one of Jacob's 12 sons. It is followed by Exodus, which tells of Israel's slavery in Egypt until they were delivered to freedom by Moses, after some 400 years of captivity. From there they traveled as a nation into the wilderness and spent 40 years wandering in the desert. Moses was their principal leader, perhaps the most notable prototype of a governing or ruling apostle, who for the entire wilderness journey maintained a position of divine delegation as the signal leader of the nation.

During this time, the Hebrew religion was formalized as God gave Moses specific instructions regarding a house of worship (the tabernacle), a priesthood (Aaronic), an ecclesiastical order (Levitical order), a pattern for worship (the sacrificial system), a moral code (the ten commandments), a structure for memorialization and celebration (the seven feasts) and a specific day of worship and rest (the Sabbath).

Prior to this definitive religious structure, the acts of worship recorded in the Bible are somewhat subjective, and are probably based on the personal communications between God and individual people. Adam and Eve had distinct, personal conversations with God. Cain and Able did as well, and the record shows that they came to bring sacrifice to God. In the Old Testament, sacrifice and worship are synonymous concepts, a point which must not be overlooked. Cain offered the labor of his hands, an offering of fruit from the ground. Able sacrificed the first-born of his flock, a blood offering which was pleasing to the Lord.

Nothing in scripture outlines God's instructions to these two men, yet the author obviously interprets God's response to those offerings in accordance with later sacrificial law. Some might say it was interpreted in the light of the later establishment of a sacrificial system. It is more likely that worship prior to the Exodus was aligned with God's will and communication to man, requiring an animal sacrifice as a mediator for sin.

Thousands of years later, the apostle Paul, writing under the inspiration of the Holy Spirit would pen, *"without the shedding of blood, there is no remission"* (Heb. 9:22). It is impossible to separate the God of redemption from sacrifice, even in a pre-Jewish era, resulting from the fall of man and the initial animal sacrifice God made to provide covering for man's nakedness (Gen. 3:21). God, in the form in which He appeared to Adam and Eve, made the first blood sacrifice of a living creature in response to mankind's sin.

There are numerous instances of sacrifice recorded prior to the time of Moses. Following the flood, Noah built an altar and sacrificed animals and birds, but only those which we considered to be clean animals (Gen. 8:20-21). Who told him to do that, and who told Noah they were clean? Prior to loading the ark, Noah had been instructed to take animals into the ark, but of clean animals he was to take seven. The biblical revelation of clean and unclean animals is not offered until Leviticus 11 and Deuteronomy 14, yet Noah had a specific understanding of the differences between those that were clean and those that were not.

The book of Job, which is often considered to be the oldest biblical book, records that Job was a man of stellar character, a man without evil, who also sacrificed on a continual basis. And Abram, even before his name was changed to Abraham, erected altars and called on the name of the Lord numerous times. All of this underscores one significant perception. The historical origin of man's relationship with the true and living God was not formulated in a dedicated structure, a religious institution, or under the ministration and mediation of a priesthood. It was an ongoing occurrence of personal relationship between God and mankind, fleshed out in daily living as those individuals carried out their daily re-sponsibilities and embraced the rising opportunities. In other words, worship of God by man was begun in the marketplace, the arena of everyday life.

> **The historical origin of man's relationship with God was an ongoing occurrence of personal relation between God and mankind.**

When God established a religious structure for the nation of Israel, he did so in the setting of their daily living. At the Exodus, the Hebrew people were accustomed to Egyptian forms of worship. How they worshiped God during the 400 years of slavery is not revealed in scripture; however, it is clear that at least some of them were faithful to God. When ordered to kill all male babies as they were being born, the two midwives of Israel refused because they feared God (Ex. 1:15-20). More than 80 years later, as Moses was confronting Pharaoh, again and again he requested that the people be allowed to go into the desert and sacrifice (worship) apart from the abominations of the Egyptians. After 400 years of slavery, there remained in Israel an awareness of and a faith in the Lord God Almighty; yet, it was never separated from their day to day living.

To the extent that it is possible to connect the concept of marketplace with that of daily living, Judaism is firmly rooted in the marketplace, not in the temple or the tabernacle. Tabernacle worship was instituted after the Exodus, 2500 to 3000 years after Creation and temple worship did not begin until the 4th year of Solomon's reign, approximately 1000 years before the birth of Christ. The generationally-significant Levitical priesthood was instituted after the Exodus (Ex. 28:1-3). Prior to that, individuals operated as priests over their own households (Noah, Abraham, Jacob, Job). The Bible speaks of pagan priests, of Egypt, priests of Baal, and of other gods. It speaks specifically of Poti-Pherah, the Egyptian priest of On, (Gen. 41:45) and of Jethro, Priest of Midian and Moses' father in law (Ex. 3:1) and Melchizedek (Gen. 14:18), who many scholars believe to be an Old Testament appearance of Jesus—called a *theophanes*.

The conclusion is obvious; the Jewish priesthood was an extension of the institution of the Hebrew religious order, and the separation between priest and people was made necessary by the refusal of the people to actually be the priesthood God had called them to be (Ex. 19:6).

RABBINIC JUDAISM AND ELDERSHIP

The origins of the Rabbinic form of Judaism, like that of synagogue worship and practice, are primarily traced to the sixth century B.C., during the Babylonian captivity. There was no temple, and thus there was no place for sacrifice, for since the institution of the Hebrew religion in Moses' day, all mediatorial sacrifice had been performed by priests, on the altar of sacrifice, either in the tabernacle or in the temple in Jerusalem. With the destruction of the temple and the deportation of Jews to Babylonia, there was no means to maintain the religious nature of Jewish culture. Hence, the rabbis (teachers of the law) became the predominant religious figures, and their influence within the Jewish community was immense.

From the time of the patriarchs, tribal elders had been the governing leaders of Jewish life, and although a monarchy was established, the influence of elders was not diminished. Historically, most cultures maintained a high degree of submission to elders, regardless of religious orientation. Age, prior to the "Enlightenment," was venerated, and people intrinsically knew that wisdom came from age. Thus, elders formed the primary structure of local governments, and in many parts of the world, still do.

As the early Church found its moorings, the apostles provided both the governmental and the didactic elements which determined its direction; however, as local congregations were established, the need for wisdom and insight, and the oversight of those assemblies needed to be recognized. The appointment of elders was only natural. Dr. Philip Byler noted this as follows:

> "We are confident that the form of ecclesiastical government that was best understood among early Christian leaders was that of the Jewish community. When the apostles needed to expand the governmental order, they quite naturally followed this familiar pattern. This was not a violation of the Spirit's leading. It was in keeping with how God had established the culture long before the time of Jesus. So, elders (Gk. presbuteros) were appointed.

"Jewish cities and communities had elders. They were not necessarily religious leaders, but were the wise leaders of the community who provided insight and counsel in matters pertaining to almost everything. There was a long-standing tradition of elders among the people of Israel that was not dogmatically religious. However, ancient Israel was a theocratic society in which the Temple, the Priesthood, and the Levitical order played a huge role. No member of Jewish society would have been totally disengaged from religious life.

"The appointment of elders (or overseers in the church) beginning with the appointment of the seven in Acts 6, was an obvious progression. The church needed leadership, and that leadership took on the roles of oversight. We can be confident that early church polity closely resembled that of its Jewish counterpart. However, the original apostles filled the leadership roles, rather than the priests or the rabbinical councils."[1]

The earliest body of Christians was Jewish, gathered from the wide-flung regions of the Roman Empire to be sure, but Jews, nonetheless. At some juncture, perhaps as early as Paul's inclusion into the faith, they began to be excommunicated from Jewish synagogues. As they formed Christian gatherings and local congregations, the obvious forms of worship they knew were those of the synagogue. It would have been a great stretch for them to adopt differing forms of congregational worship or government. The simple fact is they didn't.

The apostles appointed elders, they preached the kingdom, and they equipped the saints to do the work of ministry wherever they went and whenever they could. Like the earliest evidence of Judaism, the earliest evidence of the Christian community was deeply immersed in the day-today cultural experience of their time. They were what we call today, "Marketplace or Workplace Christians."

OLD TESTAMENT PROPHETS WERE OF THE MARKETPLACE

The prophets of the Old Testament were not primarily of the tribe of Levi, not even Samuel, who was an Ephraimite. Their ministry was not ecclesiastical in nature; that is, they were not their ministry, per se. Prophecies are recorded from as many as 45 different individuals in the Old Testament, from the time of Adam until the close of the canon. It is doubtful that all of them would be considered to be prophets, but even if they were, only the smallest percentage could be traced to the Levitical order.

By and large, the known prophets of the Old Testament were inspired preachers, proclaimers of the oracles of God to the people of a wayward nation. Sometimes they had access to the court of the king, like Nathan and Micaiah and Elijah, but most of them delivered their messages directly to the people or through a written prophetic word. Many of them were farmers and herdsmen, such as Elijah the Tishbite and his successor, Elisha. They prophesied of coming captivity and also during times when Israel was enslaved. They prophesied of a coming Messiah and of the kingdom He would establish. They were feared and sometimes behaved in ways which were socially unacceptable, but their ministry was to the marketplace, to the people of the workplace and within the halls of government.

SYNAGOGUE WORSHIP AND THE MARKETPLACE

Synagogue is a transliteration of a Greek term which means a house of prayer. The origin of synagogue worship is not clear from historical records, but seems to have emerged in full force during the time of the Babylonian captivity, a 70-year period in the sixth century B.C., after the destruction of the first temple which had been built by Solomon. There, prayers to God, the reading of the Torah, and discussions of the law were a prominent means of maintaining the solidarity of the Jewish faith. In later years, synagogues became the seats of education, providing training for Jewish boys in reading, prayers, and the maintenance of their theocratic way of life.

While ancient synagogues were separate from the workplace per se, it is important to remember that everything in Jewish life revolved around their religious structure. Every day, every business transaction, every family process, and every verdict of their courts was governed by their perception of who God is and how He wanted them to live. The "so-called" marketplace and the "so-called" mountain of religion were so powerfully intertwined that to try to separate them would do violence to the historical reality of the Hebrew nation.

Everything in Jewish life revolved around their religious structure.

Even during the time of Jesus, when Judea was under the dominating rule of Rome, the Jews maintained a high degree of self-determination and allegiance to their religious faith. This was not permitted in other provinces of the Roman Empire, but so intertwined was Jewish faith with Jewish life that the Romans could not extricate the Hebrews from their beliefs. The courts of the temple were given the freedom to administer Jewish justice, Jewish merchants established a reliable mercantile system which was relied on throughout the Empire, and children were educated with Jewish literature, Jewish ethics, Jewish morality, and Jewish faith.

The broad separation of religious Judaism and secular Jewish culture was a gradual development as late as the 19th or 20th century, as the people began to define their faith apart from their daily living. Still, the Jews have largely been a persecuted people throughout their history, and have maintained an ethnic identity which has never been far removed from their faith. Orthodox, or Hassidic Judaism, as a religious force, remains as intertwined with daily life today as it did in the sixth century before Christ.

THE ORIGIN OF THE PATRIARCHS WAS THE MARKETPLACE

Few believers have difficulty identifying the notable patriarchs of scripture. Apart from the 12 sons of Israel whose progeny became the 12 tribes, others are recognized as patriarchs as well. Abraham, Isaac, Jacob, Moses, and Noah, as well as the antediluvian patriarchs, are notably not connected with any formal religious order or structure. Whatever their relationship with God happened to be, it was clearly mingled with their daily living. A primary example is Abraham. According to Fernando Guillen:

> "Abraham, as the faith forefather, is an apostolic type and figure, since one of the true apostle's characteristics is to establish generations or a lineage, because the seed potential which is upon his shoulders. So, we see in the processes which Abraham went through, an apostolic plan or model of entrepreneurship...

> "The apostolic always draws the alignment with eternal purpose. In Abraham's seed is the blessing for

the earth's families, and consequently the provision and the financial plans and strategies. It was a royal or governmental generational seed; so, it had an apostolic manifestation. That purpose established in Abraham's seed was going to transcend generationally so that all God's governmental plan was fulfilled."[2]

Banished from the Garden of Eden, humanity was largely agrarian, either as tillers of the ground or hunters. In time, men became workers in metallurgy, merchants, masons, and tradesmen of every sort. Historical records and oral tradition mingle with myth, memory, and supposition to help us discover how religions were formed. Temples were erected, priesthoods were developed, and pagan worship rituals were instituted; even among animistic religions there was ritual and ceremonial "worship" conducted by shamans, spiritual holy men, and priests. Yet, from a historical point of view, people did not separate their religious or spiritual life from their daily or work life until a much more recent past.

People did not separate their religious or spiritual life from their daily life until a much more recent past.

Humanism or secularism was largely a product of the "Age of Enlightenment" which emerged in the late 17th and 18th centuries A.D., occurred primarily in Europe and the American colonies. In Africa, Asia, and South America, the integration of the secular and the sacred was a mindset which remained deeply embedded until much later, and in some regions remains strong today. Even the Roman Catholic Church, with its ornate houses of worship and its set apart priesthood, was, and in many parts of the world, still is deeply embedded in the daily lives of its people. Parish priests are trained to consider themselves to be pastors to entire geographical regions, regardless of the religious preference of those who live in their assigned locales. Where Roman Catholic influence is broad, that perspective is projected even within the United States.

The monastic segments of Christianity are also very ancient in origin, as men tried to separate themselves from the world and live out their days in quietness, contemplation, and reverence, whether in caves, cloistered monasteries, desert and mountain strongholds, or even on top of poles and ledges (the so-called stele ascetics). But even in their sequestered lifestyles, they could never separate their work life from their religious life. As they became self-sustaining as a way to provide for their own nourishment and freedom, they became entrepreneurial and industrious, creating special breads, wines, and beers, growing gardens, and raising livestock. Note the lack of separation experienced by one famous monk:

> "...No conceited scholar was Brother Lawrence; theological and doctrinal debates bored him, if he noticed them at all. His one desire was for communion with God. We find him worshiping more in his kitchen that in his cathedral; he could pray, with another,
>
> > *'Lord of all pots and pans and things...*
> > *Make me a saint by getting meals*
> > *And washing up the plates!'*
>
> "And he could say, 'The time of business does not with me differ from the time of prayer, and in the noise and clatter of my kitchen, while several persons are at the same time calling for different things, I possess God in as great tranquility as if I were upon my knees at the blessed sacrament.'"[3]

MARKETPLACE ORIGINS
OF THE APOSTLES

The disciples who followed Jesus during his earthly ministry were noticeably removed from the religious community. The major opponents to Jesus, and later to the emerging Church, were the more religious elements of Judaism, the priests, the Pharisees, and the Sadducees. His disciples came from the streets, the hillsides, and the lakesides of Judea. They were men of business, merchants, fishermen, and professionals who held responsible government posts. There were a few among the religious community who sought out the Master, such as Nicodemus, but their fear of social reprisal was sufficient to keep their activities more clandestine than straightforward.

None of the original apostles were part of the religious orders of Judaism. With the exception of Paul, who trained under Gamaliel as a Pharisee (see Phil. 3:4-6), none of the later apostles were either; in fact, some of them were ethnic Gentiles, birthed into the kingdom, equipped with Paul's teachings, and commissioned by Paul, Barnabas and other apostles to be overseers of congregations.

The new Church had to define its culture, much of which was modeled after elements of Judaism, and teach new converts and disciples the law of the Spirit and the New Covenant, versus the Law of Moses. It was then, and still is, an ongoing process. The mind and the religious spirit demand New Moon celebrations, religious festivals, Sabbaths, circumcision, ceremonies, rituals, tabernacles, temples, priests, sacrifices, etc. to try and materialize and make manifest the invisible God and His invisible kingdom (Luke 17:21). Invariably, such efforts are futile, lead to disappointment, and end in frustration and/or disillusionment. Repeatedly, the early apostles and New Testament writers described such practices as "a shadow of the things that were to come," "a copy and shadow of what is in heaven," "the copies of the heavenly things," and "a shadow of the good things that are coming—not the realities themselves;" instead, "the reality, however, is found in Christ" (Col. 2:16-23, Heb. 8:1-10:18).

After the death of Stephen, a "great persecution" had broken out against the church in Jerusalem, led by Saul, who "began to destroy the church. Going from house to house, he dragged off men and women and began to put them in prison" (Acts 8:1-3). Even that did not satisfy this religious zealot, and he was "still breathing out murderous threats" against the church, even as far as Damascus (Acts 9:1). Once he met the Lord on the way there and was converted, "then the church throughout Judea, Galilee and Samaria enjoyed a time of peace" (Acts 9:31).

Persecution eventually escalated against the Church throughout the Roman Empire, but not before the church at Antioch had been established, Paul and Barnabas were dispatched by the Holy Spirit, and Christianity had "gone viral," and the good news spread to major centers of cultural influence by the early church leaders, primarily apostles and their apostolic teams, which included prophets and teachers, as well as historians such as Luke the physician. Philip the Evangelist was also active and through his ministry and conversion of the Ethiopian eunuch, a royal court official responsible for the Queen's treasury, an entire nation was impacted with the Gospel. According to Joyner:

"These persecutions against the Church did not just last a few months or even years, but for almost three centuries! The most intense persecution of all came during the last ten years of this period. On February 24, 303, an imperial decree was issued requiring the destruction of all Christian property, all copies of the Bible, and a reduction of all Christians to the status of slaves. With these civil rights revoked, the entire populace of the empire was free to attack and afflict Christians in any way they desired. Their property was seized, their persons violated in every conceivable way, and multitudes were slaughtered. Yet, the faith continued to grow and prevail, and the faithful grew even bolder in their witness."[4]

Had the Emperor Constantine I not had his fateful vision of the cross before a crucial battle nearly a decade later, history would certainly have been very different for the Church. For that reason, we will now touch on the circumstances surrounding this important event.

As background, he was the eldest son of Constantinus Chlorus and Helena, and first distinguished himself as a soldier in Diocletian's Egyptian expedition (296), and then under Galerius in the Persian war. In 305 the two emperors Diocletian and Maximian abdicated, and were succeeded by Constantine Chlorus and Galerius. Constantine joined his father, who ruled in the west, at Boulogne on the expedition against the Picts, and before Constantinus died (306) he proclaimed his son his successor.

Galerius did not wish to quarrel with Constantine, yet he granted him the title of Caesar only, refusing that of Augustus. Political complications increased, until in 308 there were actually no fewer than six emperors at once— Galerius, Licinius and Maximin in the east, and Maximian, Maxentius his son, and Constantine in the west. Maxentius drove his father from Rome and Maximian committed suicide (309). Maximin died in 311 and Galerius in 313, leaving Licinius in sole control of the East.

Maxentius threatened Gaul with a large army and in AD 312 Constantine and his army crossed the Alps and invaded Italy. Maxentius is believed to have had up to four times as many troops, though they were inexperienced and undisciplined. Brushing aside the opposition in battles at Augusta Taurinorum (Turin) and Verona, Constantine marched on Rome. Constantine later claimed to have had a vision on the way to Rome, during the night before battle. In this dream he supposedly saw the 'Chi-Ro,' the symbol of Christ, shining above the sun, with the words "in this conquer."

Seeing this as a divine sign, it is said that Constantine had his soldiers paint the symbol on their shields. The next morning, Constantine went on to defeat the numerically stronger army of Maxentius at the Battle at the Milvian Bridge (Oct. 312). Constantine's opponent Maxentius, together with thousands of his soldiers, drowned as the bridge of boats collapsed over which his force was retreating.

Constantine saw this victory as directly related to the vision he had had the night before, and henceforth saw himself as an 'emperor of the Christian people'. Whether this made him a Christian is the subject of much debate. But Constantine, who only had himself baptized on his deathbed in 337 A.D. by Eusebius, bishop of Nicomedia, is generally regarded as the first Christian emperor of the Roman world.

Constantine ended the persecution of Christians in 313 A.D. when Constantine and co-Emperor Licinius issued the Edict of Milan, which proclaimed tolerance of all religions throughout the Empire and granted or reinstated civil rights to Christians. Over a decade later, after defeating and killing Licinius and consolidating his power in the Eastern Empire, Constantine legitimized Christianity across the Roman Empire in 324 by decreeing it as an official state religion (one of several, with pagan worship still tolerated). That same year he renamed Byzantium as Constantinople and made it the Eastern seat of his vast Empire.

The following year, in 325, Constantine convened the Council of Nicaea to help resolve certain doctrinal questions among the churches and their leaders, and create a unified statement of faith for Christianity which was signed by 318 church leaders present (mostly bishops) and known as the Nicaean Creed. Thus, a segregated priesthood began to emerge, which was legitimized by the state. That priesthood was given privilege commensurate with those which, prior to that time, had been held by pagan priests. But a separation was instituted which has affected the Church ever since.[5]

In that regard, Peter Lyne noted:

"The Church still manages to promote a dualism of the sacred and secular that is completely misleading, leaving so many talented people with a second-rate feeling and nowhere to go...Priesthood is an Old Testament concept, along with the special clothes, special days, sacred buildings and fancy ceremonies. In Hebrews we are told that all these things were only a shadow of the reality that was to come, which is Christ (Hebrews 10). Equally important is the New Testament concept of the priesthood of all believers, as encouraged by the Apostle Peter (I Peter 2:4). As long as we perpetuate priesthood, and create an artificial division between the sacred and secular, we will always leave so many talented people outside of the church, shackling them with a powerful 'them and us' feeling. Those pursuing a business or career calling are left feeling like second-class citizens where the Church is concerned."[6]

This dualism introduced professional or at least politically-appointed clergy, and notably absent were apostles and prophets in the new Church government, which was administered by priests, bishops, archbishops, chancellors, and cardinals, who eventually established their own schools and instituted the study of "canon (church) law," and later began the practice of issuing indulgences and "papal bulls." The center of this bureaucratic Church shifted from Jerusalem to Rome, as politics and law dominated the scene.

The Western Empire fell first, in 476 A.D. and it would be nearly 1000 years later before the Eastern Empire, centered in Constantinople, would meet a similar fate in 1453 A.D. The Catholic Church became so powerful at one point that the popes and kings of various nations raised opposing armies and vied for political power and financial and military control with each other—both officially and unofficially—when they were not otherwise preoccupied with a series of Crusades during the Middle Ages.

For example, Pope Innocent III refused to accept King John's choice of a new archbishop of Canterbury in 1207. No English king since the Conquest had failed to get an archbishop he wanted. Innocent would not give way, asserting his right not only to rule the Church but to influence the Empire as well. In 1208, he put England under an "Interdict," which meant all churches were locked and no services held except baptism of infants and confession for the dying. King John reopened some monasteries and sent the clergy packing. The pope then excommunicated John and put England under a Church law that stated that no christening or marriage would be legal until the time the pope said that they would be. Church law said that only christened people could get to Heaven while children born out of marriage were doomed to Hell. This placed people in England under a terrible strain and they blamed one person for this—John. In 1213, King John had to give in and surrender the spiritual well-being of the whole country to the pope. Not long after this, he died a broken man.

This period is also known as the Middle Ages, and despite a few bright spots such as St. Patrick evangelizing Ireland, and Charlemagne reuniting Western Europe, and the rise of medieval hospitals and universities in Europe, and the signing of the Magna Carta in 1215, and the invention of movable type and the printing press in 1439 by Johannes von Gutenberg, it was generally a period of war and conquest, empire building, and cultural disruption.

A low point was Ferdinand and Isabella's rise to power in Spain, and their decree of forced expulsion or conversion of Jews and Muslims to the Catholic Church in 1492, upon penalty of death. This occurred around the same time as Christopher Columbus and his crew set sail on their historic voyage to discover the New World. The Spanish Inquisition had been founded in 1478 by Ferdinand and Isabella to maintain Catholic orthodoxy in their kingdoms and was under the direct control of the Spanish monarchy; it continued for 350 years until 1834.

In contrast, The Renaissance was a cultural movement that spanned the period roughly from the 14th to the 17th centuries, beginning in Florence, Italy in the Late Middle Ages and later spreading to the rest of Europe. Còsimo di Giovanni degli Mèdici (1389 – 1464) was the first of the powerful Medici political dynasty, de facto rulers of Florence during much of the Italian Renaissance. Cosimo inherited both his wealth and his expertise in business from his father, Giovanni di Bicci de' Medici. In 1415 he accompanied the Antipope John XXIII at the council of Constance, and in the same year he was named "Priore of the Republic." Later he acted frequently as ambassador, showing a prudence for which he became renowned. He was also a patron of the arts as well as an astute businessman. Upon his death, he was given the title *"Pater Patriae"* (Latin: 'father of the nation'), and his son succeeded him.

Though availability of paper and the invention of metal movable type sped the dissemination of ideas from the later 15th century, the changes of the Renaissance were not uniformly experienced across Europe. As a cultural movement, it encompassed innovative flowering of Latin and vernacular literatures, beginning with the 14th-century resurgence of learning based on classical sources, which contemporaries credited to Petrarch; the development of linear perspective and other techniques of rendering a more natural reality in painting; and gradual but widespread educational reform.

In politics the Renaissance contributed the development of the conventions of diplomacy, and in science an increased reliance on observation. During this period Copernicus, Galileo, Isaac Newton, John Calvin and Martin Luther made notable contributions in their respective fields, among others. Historians often argue this intellectual transformation was a bridge between the Middle Ages and the Modern era. Although the Renaissance saw revolutions in many intellectual pursuits, as well as social and political upheaval, it is perhaps best known for its artistic developments and the contributions of such polymaths as Leonardo da Vinci and Michelangelo, who inspired the term "Renaissance man."[7]

The rise of a secular, humanistic, philosophical mindset during the 17th and 18th centuries greatly adjusted the cultural climate, both of Europe and of the American colonies. The sacred and the secular were no longer integrated, and the separation of Church and State became a founding principle. Ironically, this principle was put forth to protect the Church from the State, and not the State from the Church, as is commonly misunderstood, misapplied and judicially interpreted today.

The byproduct of such thinking has been the rise to power *(exousia)* of influential leaders from outside the Church who have shaped and are shaping social attitudes for major segments of the population. The mountains of cultural influence have become dominated by influences far removed from the biblically-based, Judeo-Christian perspective, values, morals, and ethics which once held sway over societies and cultures.

As a result, this Second Apostolic Reformation which is now taking place, must be wholly integrated into every structure of social and cultural influence. We must recognize, affirm and encourage existing apostles and help develop and raise up new ones in every arena, not just in the ecclesiastical realm. Educators, government workers, artists, manufacturing workers, business leaders, professionals, accountants, architects, engineers, doctors, lawyers, nurses, financiers, jurists, journalists, writers... whatever position, whichever vocation, there must be a dedication to the outworking of the kingdom of God.

The Second Apostolic Reformation must be wholly integrated into every structure of social and cultural influence.

There must be apostles and other five-fold leaders who embrace their callings and gain their commissions to lead, to strategize, to equip and to mobilize the people of God. The good news is they are there, in place and strategically positioned, much like Joseph, Daniel and Esther of old. The problem is the Church does not recognize them, and is looking in the wrong places, through the wrong lenses and filters. Now the Church must stop waiting for them, acknowledge their existence, and embrace them as equals, not just as sons and daughters, but as "joint heirs." The hour demands it, the kingdom requires it, and the world in which we live is desperate for it. We turn now to Chapter 6.

ENDNOTES

1. Dr. Philip Byler, *The Changing Church in the Unchanging Kingdom*, pp. 50-52. Keller, TX: Palm Tree Productions, 2008.

2. Fernando Guillen, "Apostolic Entrepreneurism," in *Aligning with the Apostolic, Vol. IV.* Leander, TX: Kingdom House Publishing, 2013.

3. Brother Lawrence, *The Practice of the Presence of God*, pp 10-11. Grand Rapids, MI: Spire Books, 1958, 1967.

4. Rick Joyner, *The Apostolic Ministry*, pp. 147-148. Wilkesboro, NC: MorningStar Ministries Publications, 2004.

5. History of Emperor Constantine, the Roman Empire, the Medicis and the Middle Ages excerpted from several different entries in Wikipedia online and from my doctoral dissertation, *Courting Philanthropy.*

6. Peter Lyne, *First Apostles, Last Apostles*, p. 110. Kent, England: Sovereign World Ltd., 1999.

7. History of Emperor Constantine, the Roman Empire, the Medicis and the Middle Ages excerpted from several different entries in Wikipedia online and from my doctoral dissertation, *Courting Philanthropy.*

CHAPTER SIX

ORIGINS OF THE CHURCH AND CHRISTIANITY ARE FOUND IN THE MARKETPLACE

JESUS WAS A MARKETPLACE MINISTER

Jesus the Christ, the promised Messiah, the Son of God, the Redeemer of mankind, was not born to privilege or priesthood. He was born in a shelter for cattle, to working-class parents who lived, worked, and served God in a marketplace setting. Jesus' earthly father was a carpenter by trade, and Jesus was reared according to the culture and social structure of his time. He learned the craft of his father, was apprenticed to the trade, and as the eldest son, inherited ownership of the family business.

He joined the other boys of his native home, studied the law and the Hebrew language at the local synagogue, observed the religious rituals that were merged into daily life, and faithfully pursued life as a Jewish youth was want to do. As he came to the time of manhood, his parents presented Him at the temple in Jerusalem, as was the custom and the most desired manner for a boy to enter manhood. His wisdom and insight, even at that age, astounded the ecclesiastical leaders (Luke 2:41-50), most likely because of his distinctly marketplace culture, rather than that of a boy raised to be a religious scholar.

When Jesus began his public ministry, he did so in the marketplace. He was approximately 30 years of age. Prior to that time, we have only the temple incident as an indicator of anything remotely different from everyone else in Nazareth. He was baptized in the Jordan River, was led by the Holy Spirit into the wilderness, and there he fasted for 40 days and nights. There he faced his most recorded temptations and withstood them by his knowledge of and his confidence in the Word of God he had learned while growing up.

Very soon after his baptism, Jesus drew together a band of disciples who became his closest companions during his years of public ministry. Some of their stories are reported in scripture, though many others are not. We know of these 12 because these he would specifically name to be his apostles, and these he would train to carry his message to the whole world. Every one of these 12 men were products of the marketplace, raised in Jewish culture much as Jesus had been reared; several were apprenticed to their father's trade as commercial fishermen; one was a government employee who collected taxes for the Roman government; and one was a politically-active opponent of Rome—Simon the Zealot.

At Cana in Galilee, Jesus and his family attended a wedding where he performed his first recorded miracle; he turned water into wine. It seems only fitting that he would do so. The One who came to earth to establish a new covenant with men, would eventually compare that covenant to a new wineskin, illustrating that the old wineskin, which represented the old covenant, could not contain the new wine. Thus, the new and more excellent wine which he created at the wedding feast was but a foreshadowing of the more excellent way which He would establish through his death, burial, and resurrection, and the outpouring of the Holy Spirit upon all who would receive Him.

Later in Jesus' life, perhaps in the third year of his ministry, he faced rejection among those with whom he had grown up. Returning to Nazareth, as was his habit, he taught in the Synagogue (Mark 6:1-6), a custom which was highly approved among the Jews, but many were offended by his teaching. *"Where did this Man get these things? And what wisdom is this which is given to Him, that such mighty works are performed by His hands! Is this not the carpenter, the Son of Mary, and brother of James, Joses, Judas, and Simon? And are not His sisters here with us?"* (Mark 6:2-3, NKJV).

How could he be what people claimed him to be? After all, he was from the marketplace, everyone knew his family, and they were certainly not among the religiously important; in other words, He was "wrong"— wrong for their expectations of who a Messiah should be, wrong for their social acceptance, from the wrong tribe, from the wrong city… How could someone from the marketplace be the one who would redeem Israel? He was just wrong!

As one reads through the Gospel accounts, it becomes readily apparent that Jesus' ministry activities were marketplace-oriented, though he faithfully attended the synagogues where he traveled and went to the temple daily to teach when he was in Jerusalem (Luke 19:7). The biblical record of his preaching, teaching, healing the sick and working of other miracles is almost all located in open spaces and market places, not in synagogues.

On the day of Pentecost, in Acts chapter 2, the church was birthed through the apostles in the marketplace.[1] The original 12 apostles were all from the workplace, men of business and labor and government. None were Priests, Levites, or Rabbis. None were drawn from the ranks of the spiritually-elite Sanhedrin or the theologically-privileged party of the Pharisees. Jesus himself was a carpenter, raised in the home of a workman and craftsman, apprenticed to a trade. His band of disciples included professional fishermen, tax collectors, doctors, socialites, and wealthy women who funded his ministry (Luke 8:1-3). Moreover, from a distinctly scriptural point of view, Jesus was most critical of the ecclesiastical community, calling them a "brood of vipers," "whited sepulchers," and "blind guides," while showing compassion to the people of the marketplace as "sheep without a shepherd."

It is easy for the contemporary mind to overlook the importance of the temple to the Jewish people of Jesus' day. In the temple, the essence of the Jewish religion found its focus. There, and there alone, sacrifices were offered—the sin offerings, the grain offerings, the peace offerings, the trespass offerings, the burnt offerings, and the offerings of consecration. Annually, on the Day of Atonement, the High Priest offered a sin offering, entered the Holy of holies, and mediated forgiveness for all the people. The temple was the focal epicenter of Judaism, and Jerusalem was the heart of the nation.

As an orthodox Jew, it would have been unthinkable for Jesus not to go to the temple. As a descendant of Judah, however, he was not permitted to go beyond the Court of the Jews. He could not enter the place of sacrifice, the Holy Place behind the door of the temple, or the Holy of Holies beyond the veil. Thus, his ministry in the temple was entirely conducted outside of the strict confines of the priestly ministrations. Scripture mentions Solomon's Porch (John 10:23) and history records that this was an area where Levites resided and the doctors of the law met to hear and answer questions. Here was a gathering place where Jewish people from every walk of life could listen and be taught, but it was also a place surrounded by merchandisers of every sort.

Offerings could only be made with specially-approved temple coins. Roman coins were struck with images of the Caesar, and foreign coins bore images repugnant to Jewish law. Money changers sat at tables, selling temple coinage for significant profits, while animal venders marketed sacrificial animals to travelers who could not bring their own sacrifices. Something about this process, the lack of integrity, the violation of personal engagement with worship, the loss of sanctity and reverence toward the reason for the temple's existence ... something about the process unleashed a response from Jesus unlike any other moment in his life.

As His earthly ministry was drawing toward a point of completion, the last time Jesus entered Jerusalem, He came as a king, riding on a foal of a mule (donkey), after the tradition of Israel's kings, and was declared by the people as "He who comes in the name of the Lord" (Matt. 21:1-11; Mark 11:1-11; John 12:12-19). "Hosanna," they cried—which translated means, "Save, we pray!" But soon, the shouts of joy would turn to the ranting of an angry mob as the eternal Lamb of God was prepared as the ultimate sacrifice for sin.

Once back in Jerusalem, Jesus went again to the temple and there, moved with passion and offense at the abusive and dishonest merchandising he had so often witnessed, he went into the temple area and violently drove the moneychangers and merchandisers out of the house, His house that was dedicated to prayer and the expiation of sins (Mark 11:15-19; Luke 19:45-48; John 2:13-22). It cannot escape our attention that Jesus truly honored the temple and the Jewish faith, but at the point where the Jewish faith reached its most significant expressions, Jesus only functioned in the marketplace areas of the temple.

THE CHURCH WAS BIRTHED AND ESTABLISHED IN THE MARKETPLACE

Even on the Day of Pentecost, when the Church was born, it was birthed by apostles and the Holy Spirit, in the marketplace, in a large home where the 120 disciples were staying and praying. It was not birthed in a synagogue or the temple, or a religious setting, but in the Upper Room of a large house, a private residence (Acts 1:12-13, 2:1-2). As the church grew in Jerusalem, they continued to meet from house to house and in the temple courts (Acts 2-5).

The original 12 apostles were all men of the marketplace without formal theological training.

The point has already been made in earlier chapters that the original 12 apostles were all men of the marketplace and that none of them had formal theological training. That there were no women in that original band of intimate, core leaders has produced a great deal of concern in our modern, politically-correct culture. However, it is not a significant problem when one considers the cultural climate of Judea. It was such that having women be part of Jesus' public ministry team would have been untenable and an open door for speculation by critics. When he healed and delivered known harlots, he was called a whoremonger, and because he drank wine, he was called a winebibber (a drunken sot). Having a band of women as camp followers would have further undermined his reputation.

Even contemporary ministers have to exercise the greatest levels of propriety because of the popular hunger for sexual scandal and the insatiable appetites of tabloids, talk shows, and religious critics. It was not much different in the times of the New Testament. Scripture does reveal, however, that several highly-placed and wealthy women maintained a distinct connection to his ministry and supported it with their substance. No doubt they were able to afford private quarters when they traveled with Jesus on some of his trips.

"He continued according to plan, traveled to town after town, village after village, preaching God's kingdom, spreading the Message. The Twelve were with him. There were also some women in their company who had been healed of various evil afflictions and illnesses: Mary, the one called Magdalene, from whom seven demons had gone out; Joanna, wife of Chuza, Herod's manager; and Susanna—along with many others who used their considerable means to provide for the company" (Luke 8:1-3, MSG). And the fact that Jesus needed a treasurer for his ministry and that there was a moneybag speaks to adequate provision.

THE PRIESTHOOD AND THE MARKETPLACE

From the time of Moses, the Jewish priesthood was a well-established order. Genealogies had been meticulously maintained, and the Levitical order preserved. The priests were specifically ordained to function within the boundaries of the temple, offering sacrifices, maintaining the laver, the lampstand, the showbread, and the altar of incense, but the priestly function in the temple was limited. Divided into 24 divisions, they served for only one week at a time. Added to that were the feasts of Israel, when all the priesthood was required for temple service. Two weeks out of the year, and the time of the feasts, left a significant amount of time available for priests to do other things. Little is revealed in scripture concerning the off-duty lives of priests. However, in Numbers 35 we are told they were allotted land on which to live and raise their livestock (agrarian), and that they were to have control of 48 "cities of refuge" where someone who had killed another person could find refuge—likely to obtain a fair hearing in a judicial setting, rather than be caught and punished in an act of revenge or vigilante justice.

Zechariah, father of John the Baptist, had an angelic visitation during the order of his division or course (Luke 1:8). To what degree the priests could receive compensation from non-priestly functions I was unable to discover; however, any level of work they would have performed had to fit within the ritual, ceremonial, and cleanliness laws surrounding the priesthood. Theirs was a unique situation within the Jewish culture; yet, it is obvious that they maintained some level of marketplace perspective beyond their duties as priests.

THE EARLY CHURCH OPERATED IN THE MARKETPLACE

Until the development of the basilica, during the time of Constantine, the only facilities used by Christians were either gatherings in the outer courts of the temple, in Jewish synagogues which were populated by believers, or in obscure gathering places out of the public eye—homes, caves, catacombs, etc. In the days following the outpouring of the Holy Spirit at Pentecost, the Christian community expanded very rapidly. Some 3000 were converted on the day of Pentecost, and they were adding numbers to the contingent of believers on a daily basis (Acts 2:42), and by Acts 21:20 the population of Christians reached many thousands of people, all within the context of daily living— marketplace. Ed Silvoso adds this insightful observation:

> "Acts records 40 major supernatural actions, many of which are dramatic power encounters. It is interesting that only one of them took place in a religious setting: the healing of the lame man at the Temple gate called Beautiful (see Acts 3:1-10). This highlights the fact that the Early Church was not confined to a building or to a prearranged schedule of meetings. In Acts, the Church was a movement that shook or took cities. The 39 supernatural actions...took place in the marketplace."[2]

How many Christians there actually were in this early period is not recorded, except in heaven, but by a reasonable, conservative estimate of a 40% cumulative growth rate, by the time the Church became a legal institution within the Empire of Constantine, there could have been between six and seven million Christians in the known world, possibly more. Estimates from various sources indicate that the population of the world at that time was close to 300 million. If this is an accurate estimate, the Christian population at the time of Constantine would have been two percent or less.

The history of how Constantine the Great transformed Christianity into an empirical religion was discussed in detail in Chapter 5 so we will not repeat it here, except to share a few additional details. Suffice it to say that his contributions to a radically-altered Church were far-reaching and long-standing, and are still being felt today. According to Dr. Philip Byler:

"The priesthood became a hierarchy with ecclesiastical titles that were quite removed from the responsibility assignments once understood by the Christian community. Ritual and tradition rivaled (and eventually outpaced) Scripture as the standard of authority. The division between clergy and laity became as distinct in Christianity as it was in every other religion. The hierarchy of the church exercised vast power—both religiously and politically. Sadly, the western world slid gradually into a time of superstition, fear, and subservience to papal prerogatives that lasted for more than a thousand years."[3]

Many of the ideas Constantine brought to the Christian community were never a part of the Church's original design. The introduction of the basilica as an architectural prototype remains largely in place, even in Protestant, Evangelical, and Pentecostal churches. The separation of the clergy area from the congregational area with an altar in between is distinctly Catholic in origin, but lingers in the form of a communion table between pulpit and pew.

The veneration of the original 12 apostles was also a design element implemented by Constantine. In his great basilica, statues of the twelve were erected with another one of himself included, though his was of greater magnitude—a direct contradiction to the Jewish abhorrence of statuary and images. No matter to Constantine; he disliked the Jews more than most people hated Christians. He changed the day of Christian worship from Saturday to Sunday, amplifying the distinct separation between the Christians and the Jews. He also instituted the professional status of the clergy, allocating to Christian priests the privilege which had been reserved for pagan priests, notably an exemption from taxation and the ability to possess land, a prohibition which had been upheld against Christians for centuries.

This pronouncement changed the status of the priesthood and the distinction between clergy and laity was profoundly felt. Summarizing this period of Church history, Dr. Philip Byler noted:

> "...The first three centuries of church history are a bloody record of prejudice against and persecution of the church. The period was marked by the rise of numerous heresies and heretical teachings. Such teaching espoused everything from overt sensuality to the denial of Jesus' deity or humanity.

> "The passing of time also brought a distinct decline in the use of the term apostle with a commensurate rise in the use of the term bishop."[4]

Elaborating on this last point in greater detail, Roger Sapp commented:

> "Historically, the decline of the apostolic ministry occurred as the unscriptural role of bishops was embraced by the Church. Which came first, the decline of apostles or the rise of bishops is a matter of debate. However, it is not a matter of debate that the Church suffered greatly as a clear decline in its supernatural functioning occurred during that period. By the end of the fourth century, the unscriptural bishops were fully in control, and the Church was beginning to embrace the world. It entered a serious moral decline, and the thousand years of the Dark Ages began. For that

thousand years the function of bishops did little to bring the Church out of the Dark Ages. There is no doubt that there were godly men who served as bishops; however, many were simply politicians who used religion to further their own ambitions and greed. In fact, it was a break from their unscriptural authority that began the Protestant Reformation and began to use to bring the church back into the light of God's Word. Now, a new Reformation is needed among Evangelicals. We need to embrace all that God's Word reveals and to hold back nothing. A 'new wineskin' of apostolic strength will be needed to hold the gracious amounts of new wine that the Lord wishes to pour out upon the Church in our day. Nothing less will sustain the revival God is bringing forth.

"As we have already established, the actual role of the overseer is the role of the elder, which is generally correctly understood within the modern-day Church. An elder is a subordinate leader within a local church who functions with other overseers to take care of a local church. He is an elder because he exercises authority collectively with other overseers in spiritual government over a local body of believers. The overseers function together possibly with the leadership of a single local apostle and possibly a senior elder. Other apostles, not local to this fellowship may also properly influence as they did in Corinth. Together they seek to hear the Lord's word and will for a particular local church. The ministry of the overseer is clearly not a translocal ministry with oversight over many churches; that is the role of the apostle and not the bishop.

"Perhaps it would be better to altogether dispense with the term bishop. It has been so strongly tied to traditional and historical misuse that its use will continue to perpetuate confusion and make the apostle's role more difficult. Perhaps we simply need to use elder or overseer to describe this local church ministry to avoid confusion...

"There are those who presently allow others to call them bishops because of their reluctance to embrace their actual correct ministry name of apostle. Perhaps the Church needs to reassure them of our acceptance of what the Word of God reveals about this ministry. If they have the characteristics and call of the apostle, then they should be identified as apostles of the Church without hesitation or fear. There will surely be those who will misunderstand because of traditional teaching, yet to submit to their unscriptural understandings and perpetuate confusion is certainly a worse choice for any man of God who is a bishop, but is not an apostle, there is no alternative but to repent and refuse to usurp the ministry of another. Only the truth will set the Church free to become His Bride."[5]

Another Church historian who wrote on this unfortunate state of affairs is Peter Wagner:

"In some circles, people prefer the title 'bishop' to 'apostle.' This is more due to religious tradition than biblical precedent. The Catholic Church has used the title freely for centuries, and some Protestants continue to use it. The word 'bishop,' however, only appears four times in the New Testament as a synonym of 'pastor' or 'elder,' but never for a senior church leader. And no one in the Bible is specifically identified as a 'bishop.'[6]

Jonas Clark added the following observations and historical narrative:

"Sometime around Constantine's placement as Emperor in 306 A.D. and the Council of Nicaea (modern Iznak in Turkey) in 325 A.D., the priesthood of all believers (1 Peter 2:9) was usurped by the institution of a series of bishops. These bishops were thought to be direct descendants of the 12 Apostles, particularly Saint Peter, through a ceremony conducted by the laying on of hands. This ordination ritual for choosing bishops was called apostolic succession. By the Council of Nicaea in 325 A.D., there were more than 1800 bishops.

"This institution of bishops had nothing to do with a direct calling from God but rather participation in a religious ceremony.

"These bishops were wrongly said to be the 'sole successors of the apostles as ordainers of other ministers and governors both of pastors and people. They were uniquely different from others and possessed a special, almost mystical, authority. The unbroken lineage of bishops were said to be the only ones that possessed the keys to the Kingdom.

"This institution of bishops took the ministry and priesthood away from the believer and threw the Church into the Dark Ages. No longer could Christ sovereignly call His own apostles. Gradually this institution became known as the Roman Catholic Church.

"Just as the Protestant Reformers of old, we strongly oppose the religious system of apostolic succession.

"The call of God on any ascension (doma) gift belongs solely to God's sovereign will.

"Therefore, apostleship is a direct call of God by His sovereign will alone and has nothing whatsoever to do with apostolic succession through the laying on of hands."[7]

ORIGINS—CHURCH AND CHRISTIANITY | 155

John Eckhardt has also made similar comments regarding the history and role of bishops, and adds this perspective:

"During the second century, the church came under threat from false teachings, primarily the teachings of Gnosticism. These heresies posed such a threat to the church that Irenaeus proposed the concept that the true churches must be able to trace their leaders back to the apostles. He taught that an unbroken succession of bishops founded by the apostles guaranteed the truth that a church possesses. In this way, one could differentiate true churches from the false ones led by heretics. Churches were therefore considered apostolic if they could trace their leadership back to the apostles. This is found in Irenaeus's writing *Against Heresies* (ca. 185).

"The African orator Tertullian, in his treatise *On the 'Prescription' of Heretics* (ca. 200), proposed that a church need only have the teaching of the apostles in order to be apostolic. In other words, there was no need to have apostolic succession in order to be a legitimate church. Clement of Alexandria (ca. 150-215) similarly proposed that a succession of doctrine rather than a succession of bishops is the most important characteristic of a true apostolic church.

"Cyprian, the bishop of Carthage (ca. 205-258), was perhaps one of the strongest proponents of apostolic succession. He maintained that the apostolate (the apostles) and the episcopate (the bishops) are one. In his view the bishops were the successors to the apostles, and the apostles were the bishops of old. By the mid-third century, the difference between the apostles and bishops disappeared with Cyprian."[8]

Clearly the rise of unscriptural bishops, particularly in denominational churches, and the hijacking of the Church into a bureaucratized, hierarchical, religious structure, coupled with the corresponding scarcity and lack of recognition of apostles and prophets in the Church for 1700-1800 years, with a few notable exceptions, has had a significant detrimental effect on the body of Christ, and on the kingdom of God. According to Hirsch and Catchim: "As far as we can discern, it is simply not possible to be the church that Jesus intended if three (APE) of the five constitutional ministries are removed. According to the explicit teaching of Ephesians 4:1-16, it cannot be done. But in fact it has been done, and the tragic consequences are dramatically demonstrated in and through the history of the Christian church through the past seventeen centuries."[9]

Wagner provided the following summary of and perspective on this phenomenon:

> **"Here's what happens with a state church. Instead of the church transforming the government, the government transforms the church.** Under Constantine and his successors, the church became spiritually impotent and ended up in what we know as the Dark Ages. **The church is called to influence the government, but not to rule over society. This is one reason why the threat of Muslim sharia law is so terrifying...**

> "Neither Luther nor Calvin took steps to disband the structures of the state church, which Constantine instituted. Both before and after the Reformation, it was assumed that the government should be in charge of the church. Churches like the Roman Catholic Church, the Lutheran Church, the Reformed Church, the Anglican Church, and the Church of Scotland (Presbyterian)

were the only churches in their nations recognized and supported by the government. It seems strange to us today that pastors, for example, would be government employees, but such a thing commonly happens with state churches...

"The U.S. Constitution, ratified in 1783, and the Modern Missionary Movement, pioneered by William Carey when he went from England to India in 1792, fostered some of the first significant alternatives to state churches. The Constitution prohibited a state church in the United States. Also, when missionaries from state churches went to Hindu, Buddhist, Muslim or animistic nations, state churches were no longer possible. The result was the emergence of what we now know as denominations."[10]

Regarding denominations, David Cartledge has provided the following explanation of why many of them dismiss, ignore or feel threatened by apostles and prophets:

"It has generally been considered in most denominations that apostles and prophets no longer exist, and only the pastoral, teaching and evangelistic gifts are still available. This attitude has been developed for two main reasons:

"A reluctance to recognize the ministries of apostles and prophets in case there is undue elevation of these persons. Bureaucratic church officials cannot cope with the attraction that is generated by these two ministries, because they have desire to conform all ministries to a set type. Denominations prefer clones rather than charismatic leaders.

"Apostolic and Prophetic ministries carry a greater level of authority than the others and this is hard to accommodate in a 'democratic' system of Church government. Many church organisations have developed a bureaucratic administration rather than dynamic leadership raised up by God. The natural tendency is to suppress such gifted ministries, or to force them out of the fellowship because they cannot conform to the "norm." The end result of this policy is to inhibit the emergence of apostles and prophets by reducing every minister to the level of the lowest common denominator."[11]

Cartledge also astutely noted:

"Both the apostle and prophet are inconvenient ministries within a democratic organization... They just emerge under the sovereign appointment of the Lord through His blessing on their ministry. As such, they often have more influence and leadership than the organization can cope with as their very existence tends to create another centre of gravity in the movement."[12]

In other words, many deacon-led churches and man-pleasing organizations want to "dumb down" the leadership structure of the Church and the kingdom so that ceremony, ritual, bureaucracy and rules prevail and control the institutional culture, identity, atmosphere and direction.

This concludes our brief historical review for this chapter. To extricate the marketplace from the Church would take a millennium and a half, but by the beginning of the 19th century, the major influences of Western culture had become largely secularized. The Church was spiritual; the rest of culture was secular.

With the development of the Seven Mountain strategy in recent years, a significant challenge has been directed at this separation. Many local churches and pastors have taken a position of including the business community and the marketplace perspective as a part of their mission and mandate. Unfortunately, they have tried to organize and operate their initiatives from the Religion mountain at the expense of those who are called to be leaders within the other spheres of influence.

If the Christian community and the apostolic leadership of the 21st century are to have broad reaching cultural influence, two distinct things will have to take place. First, there will of necessity be a much broader embracing of a marketplace Christianity, unbounded by the constraints of Church-controlled authority structures, schedules, and boundaries. Second, there must also be a determined and broad recognition of apostles, prophets, evangelists, pastors, and teachers whose spheres of influence and responsibility are uniquely or primarily marketplace in orientation. That does not negate the importance of, or the vital connection to, the Church.

The Church is the pivotal point of convergence between the various mountains of culture. It is the epicenter of Christian activity, the outposts of kingdom dynamic. In all the territory occupied by the world system, the Church, rather than functioning as an addendum to society, must function as an embassy of the kingdom of God. When local churches see themselves in this way and become willing to equip people to minister in every arena, using recognized, commissioned, five-fold ministers whose expertise and training is utterly marketplace to do the training, the level of godly influence and increase in each of these mountains will begin to rise as in the days following the outpouring of the Holy Spirit. We turn now to Chapter 7.

ENDNOTES

1. I am aware of other viewpoints which have interpreted Jesus' declaration to Peter in the Gospels that upon this rock (confession) Jesus would build the church as a type of birthing, or at least spiritual insemination in preparation for birthing. However, the New Testament or covenant could not become official or legal or go into effect until after Jesus' death, according to Heb. 9:1-28. Also, the Holy Spirit had not yet been given or sent to men (John 14:15-26; 16:5-15) and was a direct promise and necessity for divine power and counsel (Acts 1:4-8).

2. Ed Silvoso, *Anointed for Business*, p. 115. Ventura, CA: Regal Books, 2002.

3. Dr. Philip Byler, *The Changing Church in the Unchanging Kingdom*, p. 55. Keller, TX: Palm Tree Productions, 2008.

4. Ibid, pp. 50-52.

5. Roger Sapp, *The Last Apostles on Earth*, pp. 158-159. Southlake, TX: All Nations Ministries and Publications, 1995.

6. Dr. C. Peter Wagner, *Apostles Today*, p. 63. Ventura, CA: Regal Books, 2006.

7. Jonas Clark, *Advanced Apostolic Studies: Transitioning Every Believer into Apostolic Ministry.* p. 42. Hallandale, FL: Jonas Clark Ministries, 2008.

8. John Eckhardt, *Ordinary People, Extraordinary Power*, p. 8. Lake Mary, FL: Charisma House, 2010.

9. Alan Hirsch and Tim Catchim, *The Permanent Revolution*, p. 16: *Apostolic Imagination and Practice for the 21st Century Church*, San Francisco, CA: Jossey-Bass, 2012.

10. Dr. C. Peter Wagner, *On Earth as it is in Heaven: Answer God's Call to Transform the World*, pp. 46-50 author's emphasis. Ventura, CA: Regal Books, 2012.

11. David Cartledge, *The Apostolic Reformation*, p. 232-233. Chester Hill, NSW, Australia: Paraclete Institute, 2000.

12. Ibid, p. 231.

CHAPTER SEVEN

APOSTOLIC REFORMERS IN THE MARKETPLACE

A CALL TO A VAST ARMY—ACTIVATE, AWAKEN, ARISE, ACCLIMATE, ASSEMBLE, ARM, ALIGN, ASSIGN, ACCELERATE

A MODERN-DAY APOSTOLIC CALLING IN THE WORKPLACE

What does an apostolic calling look like? It's good to be reminded, and to keep our callings fresh and alive in our minds and hearts even as the years roll by. Moses and the burning bush comes first to mind, then Gideon and the angel of the Lord in the winepress. Or what about Noah and his call to build an ark over a 120-year period when it had never rained before? Then how about Abraham, or Joseph, or Samuel, or Jeremiah, or Ezekiel, or Daniel, or Isaiah, or Saul, or Mary, mother of Jesus? Some callings are more dramatic than others, accompanied by unusual signs with bells and whistles and fireworks, while others simply hear the still, quiet voice of the Good Shepherd speaking to them and calling their name (John 10).

I chose to start this chapter with a modern-day example of an apostolic calling, even though the person involved does not even admit to being an apostle or see himself that way. That is irrelevant for our purposes, since I know the person and the call upon his life, and his fruit. Next, I will share part of my own calling for the marketplace and how God has worked with me, and then we will present an overview of the modern marketplace movement, and how it coincides, intersects and correlates with the apostolic movement to conclude this chapter. I want this encounter to inspire you, to encourage you, and to remind you…what it was like when Jesus called your name. It still happens today…and every day…for someone…somewhere. Now here is Chuck's remarkable and dramatic testimony:

"I walked over to the front of the stage where a group of worship singers and musicians were gathered. Soon, more than a hundred people filled the room.

"Suddenly I heard God speaking to me: *I want you to prostrate yourself before Me.*

"Right there, I lay down on the floor and closed my eyes. A vision like a movie began playing in my head. I was lying down in darkness. Before me were seven rising steps. I lifted my head to see where the steps led, and there, sitting on a golden throne, was Jesus. Brilliant light shone all around Him. He looked down at me, and with two fingers beckoned me forward.

"I rose and stepped toward Him. Now light was all around me. I tried to keep my knees from shaking.

"A crown leaned against Jesus' throne. He picked it up and stood. Then He motioned with a flat hand for me to put my head down, and He placed the crown on me.

"*Chuck*, He said, *this crown represents the authority I have given you to go into your sphere of influence in the marketplace. I want you to take this authority, go into the places I have called you to go, and use it to tear down the strongholds that the enemy places before you.*

"I glanced around me. On the floor surrounding the throne were hundreds, maybe thousands, of golden crowns. 'Lord, thank you for what You just did for me,' I said. 'But I'm confused. What are all these other crowns doing here?'

"*Turn around,* Jesus said. He put His left hand on my shoulder and pointed into the darkness with His right. In the shadows, I could see the outlines of figures moving away.

"*My children have walked away from the throne and the authority I want to give them,* He said. *Others have received their crowns, brought them back, and left them here. They said, 'It's too hard' or 'I can't do this.' I want you to call them back to the throne to receive their crowns.*

"*Wow,* I thought. *Here is my commission from God.*

"*There is only one time when you will lay your crown down,* Jesus said. *That is when you come to worship Me. Don't forget to take it with you when you leave.*"[1]

This is a workplace leader, a former salesman and banker, and now commodities trader, having an encounter with Jesus. A husband, a father, and an elder in his church. A very ordinary, no nonsense kind of guy. Hanging out with Jesus. Receiving a calling and commission and crown. And doing something godly with it. That's what it's all about.

Since receiving this calling, he has prayed for over 100 people in the bank he formerly worked at who were healed and helped the bank to grow and prosper financially. Oh, yes, he was also featured in a cover story of the *New York Times Magazine,* and interviewed by a French television network. And while traveling with Ed Silvoso, he attended a meeting with high-ranking government officials in another nation and led them one of them (a governor) to the Lord through the gift of word of knowledge in front of a group of other government leaders. Now he has a vision for a global Kingdom banking system. But, in the meantime, he's still learning and growing and serving.

We need more like Chuck Ripka, who are doing the work, and seeing the fruit, without even using or claiming the title. Fortunately, they are out there—some in position and being used of God, and others still searching or waiting or preparing or hiding. A few of their stories have been told in books written by Rich Marshall, Rick Heeren, Morris Ruddick, Ed Silvoso, Bob Fraser, Dr. Gordon Bradshaw, Bob Buford, Os Hillman, John Beckett, Pat Gelsinger, Ken Eldred, Bill McCartney, Paul Cuny, Angus Buchan, Dennis Peacocke, Gunnar Olson, Candace Long, John Garfield, Dr. John Muratori, Dr. Paul Costa, Richard Everett, Dr. Tommi Femrite, Lee Domingue, Dr. Randall Sprague, Jerry Tuma, Ed Turose, Daniel Meylan, Jeff Caliguire, Dr. Tony Dale, Dr. Robert Needham, Wende Jones, Brett Johnson, Graham Power, Steve DeSilva, Lloyd Reeb, Sher Valenzuela, Mark Ritchie, Mike Floyd, Ralph Doudera, Brandon Pope, Larry Julian, Pat Robertson, Laurie Beth Jones, Kris Vallotton, Danny Silk, Tim Redmond, Dr. Ted Baehr, Martin Powell, Dr. Alistair Petrie, Alice Patterson, Tim Taylor, Dr. Nick Castellano, Faytene Kryskow Grassechi, Greg Dalessandri, Bill Hart, Dudley Perio, Ed Delph, Judy Jacobs, Patricia King, Mark Pfeifer, Dr. Kluane Spake, Bill Ebert, Henry Falany, Kay Haugen, Aaron Evans, Norm Miller, Don Ostrom, Bill Swad Sr., Theresa Phillips, Dr. Brian Scott, Dr. A. L. Gill, Margaret (Peggy) Hartshorn, Dr. Berin Gilfillan, Dr. Elizabeth Hairston, Doug Stringer, Dr. Paul Williams, Dr. Sandy Kulkin, Kenn Renner, Ray Landers, Dr. Ron Jenson, Linda Rios Brook, Bart Pierce, Eugene Strite, Dr. Joseph Umidi, Dr. Gayle Rogers, Glenn Henderson, Sam

Soleyn, Dan Stratton, Walt Pilcher, Bob Harrison, Don Wood, Mornay Johnson, Dr. Erik Kudlis, Teri Werner, Dr. Marlene McMillan, Doug Spada, David Van Koevering, Craig Hill, Earl Pitts, Margelee Hylton, Dr. William (Bill) Greenman III, Jack Serra, Buck Stephens, Dennis Wiedrick, John Gagliardi, William (Bill) Thomas, Doug Sheddy, Paul Gazelka, David High, Lynn Scarborough, Michael Pink, Marc Nuttle, Patrick Ondrey, Keith Johnson, Robert Ricciardelli, Dr. Rodney Howard Browne, Dr. Bill Winston, Lt. Gen. William G. ("Jerry") Boykin (U.S. Army, Ret.) Natasha Vermaak Grbich, John Beehner, Chuck Vollmer, Tom Barrett, Woody Young, Ray East, Chinedum Benjamin Anyacho, Hal and Cheryl Sacks, Dr. Cindy Trimm, Dr. Samuel Chand, Bishop Harry R. Jackson Jr., Dr. Joseph Mattera, George Barna, June Hunt, Tamara Lowe, Cindy Jacobs, Robert Henderson, Dr. John Benefiel, Dr. W. Paul ("Buddy") Crum Jr., Dr. Mark Chironna, David Turner and Dr. Raymond Larson, among many others.[2]

This is just a partial listing of a few apostolic authors, and does not even include those who have not written books. The truth is there are millions of others like Chuck who are called by God and either need to be commissioned or need to have someone help equip them, or explain how to respond to a commissioning, or how to begin functioning in it, or how to grow in it. That's where you and I come in.

Jonas Clark offered this description of the growing army of apostolic reformers:

"Today there are thousands across the globe who feel like they just don't fit in. Some have been rejected and resisted for being too fervent, too bold, too zealous, too militant, too everything. Many are discontent, distressed, in debt, and in search of identity and destiny (1 Sam. 22:1-2). Nevertheless there remains in them a cause, a mighty sword that can't be seen. They desire to let God's power be strong in them and see territories, cities and nations impacted by the power of God. 'Who are they?' you ask. They are the coming apostolic reformers."[3]

I would differ with Clark's statement above only slightly, in that there are millions rather than thousands of such apostolic reformers in my opinion, and not all of them are in debt. Some of them are actually quite prosperous and fruitful, and are neither discontented nor distressed. There is a broad spectrum of humanity represented here, and it depends primarily on where such individuals are in the convergence and maturation cycles and processes. Now I will share a little about my own marketplace calling.

MY OWN MARKETPLACE CALLING

It was early in 2008, and I was crying out to the Lord in prayer and feeling a bit frustrated. I had been attending Christian marketplace conferences and apostolic conferences since 2005 and was telling the Lord that business people need to hear more than concepts, theories, principles and rhetoric at these conferences. They need working models, strategies, actual case studies, practical demonstrations of the Spirit and personal testimonies of God at work in scenarios beyond the confines of a church setting. They also need genuine heart transformation if they are to be able to align with the apostolic in practical rather than theoretical terms.

One day, perhaps a month or so later, as I was praying, the Lord spoke to me and said, "Bruce, I want you to convene a World Economic Forum type of gathering for the body of Christ. Most of my marketplace leaders don't know each other, and the ones who do are not cooperating or collaborating with each other. I need for this to change. I also want you to help expose and eliminate the poverty mindset and spirit in the Church, and replace them with biblical prosperity and stewardship. The Scripture I am giving you as a commission is Ezekiel 37: 1-14." I was shocked that the Lord would speak to me this way and I needed to try and grasp what He was saying before I could even wrap my imagination around it. The Lord had called me once before into the financial arena in early 1995,[4] and I knew what that meant. More death. So I had at least learned to count the cost when God speaks to me.

> **Not truly inclined to disavow God's ability, we are often quite willing to resist His action.**

In this well-known passage of scripture, Ezekiel was given a vision of a valley, filled with dry bones. They were disconnected, scattered, and spread about in a widely-disorganized fashion which gave no evidence of order or structure. As the vision spread before him, God asked Ezekiel a very difficult question, "Son of man, can these bones live?" In answer, the prophet responded much as you or I would likely have responded, "O Lord, You know."

Not truly inclined to disavow God's ability, we are often quite willing to resist His action, especially when we are uncertain of our own ability in a given situation. Always confident that God can do anything, we tend to express uncertainty as to whether or not He can, or will do anything with us. As a result, we sometimes miss the most significant opportunities He brings our way in favor of something which requires far more effort and far less faith.

God does know, and in response, He commanded Ezekiel to prophesy to the bones, "O you bones, hear the word of the Lord. Surely I will cause you to rise up and live..." Prophets are sometimes required to speak things which go contrary to conventional experience. **Bleached out, dry, sun-baked, disconnected bones** do not naturally rise up and live. But God commanded, and Ezekiel obeyed. When he did, those bones started moving. They came together, bone to its bone, not in some haphazard, jumbled up, indiscriminate fashion. They aligned themselves and became recognizable skeletons, structures on which flesh could hang, joined together by ligaments, sinew, muscle and skin. As Ezekiel prophesied, the skeletons became corpses, a vast array of identifiable bodies, laid out across the valley, but there was no life in them. They did not have the ability to function, either independently or collectively.

Again, God instructed Ezekiel, "Prophesy to the wind (spirit) and say, come from the four winds and breathe upon these slain, that they may live." So Ezekiel prophesied again, this time to the wind, and the corpses came to life. They stood upon their feet, a vast army—activated, awakened, assembled, armed, aligned, assigned, and accelerated. What an amazing visualization this must have been as Ezekiel's vision unfolded before him. God can indeed make dry bones live, but God had something in mind which was far more significant than giving the prophet a stunning vision.

This was the vision God showed Ezekiel and it was a picture of Israel: dead, dry, cut-off, and without hope. God wanted Ezekiel to be able to preach with utter conviction that God could and would restore the house of Israel. As I reflected on what God had said to me, I realized it contained something more than a prophecy to ancient Israel. God gave this scripture to me as a commission for my assignment in the marketplace and Seven Mountains of Culture. I knew it carried great significance for the mission He was now directing me to accomplish, but what did it mean?

I believe this vision, this passage provides a vivid picture of the marketplace part of the Church today, disjointed, disconnected, dry, separated and cut-off from one another. In many cases, we function without genuine hope that we can effectively influence the world around us. All too often we prophesy with a kind of measured confidence. We speak in faith, addressing the situation that lies before us, a state of affairs which is so far beyond restoration it has lost the stench of decay. The valley, for us, is no longer filled with death and decay. Things have gone far past that stage. The valley is filled with the bleached out, dry, disconnected bones of the past—an army without vitality, in need of a restoration beyond our imagination.

Even the most intrepid of prophets, when looking out on such a scene, recognizes the magnitude of the miracle which must occur if these bones are to live, if this army is to march again in true alignment. It is at this point God again asks the question, "Can these bones live?" Our response is, in all likelihood, the same as Ezekiel's was. "O Lord, You know!"

There was a point to Ezekiel's vision, a life-giving strategy that would impact God's people, and there is a point to God redirecting my attention to it. The bones can live, and they will. The graves of despair, disappointment, disillusionment, and distraction will be opened. God will cause His Spirit to be breathed on a vast army which will rise in apostolic alignment to face the challenges of a world in chaos. But someone must prophesy to the bones and to the wind. Someone must call that army forth to become a cohesive force, an army in alignment for the purpose of bringing order into the disarray that surrounds us. That was the commission He gave me. Create a World Economic Forum-type event which can draw together Kingdom leaders from every corner of the globe and each of the Seven Mountains of Culture.

In addition, He said, "I also want you to create an immersion environment." I understood this to mean such a forum was not a typical conference, where people come to be taught a few new ideas and spend time visiting with old friends. This was to be a setting which plunged leaders into a truly spiritual environment, filled with worship and intercession and angels and God's presence, as well as practical, functional, effectual, applicable strategies and methods which could be put into practice in every circumstance of life. This forum would provide marketplace leaders who are also committed Christians with genuine opportunities to connect—bone to bone—and establish effective, meaningful, useful collaborations, business associations, and alliances to strengthen, encourage, and empower the body of Christ in the marketplace.

To be honest, I was not all that enthusiastic about doing something like this. This was way out of my league, or so I thought, and I protested to the Lord in no uncertain terms: "Lord, you have asked the wrong person. No one knows me and I have never hosted a conference before. I'm not a public speaker, I'm not rich, and I attend a small church." My excuses were as numerous as you can imagine, but the Lord was not impressed with my reluctance. His response to my resistance was simply, "No, I don't have the wrong person, but you have the wrong God." More precisely, you have God wrong. God is not in the habit of choosing the wrong people to accomplish His purposes.

Once I got past my initial shock at what God was requesting, and that He actually wanted me to convene and host this event, I decided I was ready... at least, I was willing to be ready to move forward. Still, I was shaken to the core of my being and I spent the next several days in prayer and fasting, trying to wrap my head and heart around the magnitude of the assignment.

The rise of the apostolic in the marketplace has been painfully overlooked, or worse, has been placed in a subservient role.

I had been acutely aware for some time that the rapidly-expanding apostolic movement was straining to encompass the marketplace. In our universal, headlong rush into the 21st century, the rise and return of the apostolic has been nothing short of remarkable. However, it has been largely proclaimed from pulpits and conference lecterns among ecclesiastical leaders rather than among men and women in the marketplace. As a result, the rise of the apostolic in the marketplace has been painfully overlooked, or worse, has been placed in a subservient role—unrecognized, poorly identified, and hardly distinguishable to the Church as a significant part of God's kingdom order.

My calling has been to the marketplace more than to the ecclesiastical community, though I function both prophetically and apostolically in both. As both a marketplace and ecclesiastical prophet and apostle, I am amazed at the philosophical and emotional separation so often experienced between church and marketplace leaders. While this is largely unintentional, it exists and it has been an ongoing source of frustration for me and for the Lord that this gap has not been diminished or eliminated yet.

I believe it is equally as frustrating for the host of marketplace apostles and apostolic leaders who have never been adequately identified or recognized or commissioned or accepted or honored by the Church. Thus, it really should not have come as a shock to me that God would call me to do something like convene an economic summit. After all, this area remains a pivotal concern, and strategic focus, not only for me, but for many others within the body of Christ.

It is vitally important that a massive assortment of apostles and apostolic leaders around the world become more connected and better identified with one another. God is extending His call to a vast army of disconnected Christians to activate, awaken, arise, arm, assemble, align, assign, acclimate, and accelerate as never before. The time is at hand for the greatest expansion of God's kingdom in human history—an expansion which is already in progress.

Into this rapidly-growing body of believers, millions of apostles have emerged over the past two decades. They are being called by God and sent forth into the world to influence culture through godly persuasion, unflinching integrity, wise and judicious investment, innovation, ethical purity and morally-excellent lifestyles. They are reformers, agents of change, emissaries of transformation who are called to revolutionize the way the Church connects with the world and the way the marketplace responds to the Gospel. They are the communicators of the life of Christ through word and deed, and through attitude and impact. They are the uncommon catalysts in a world of commonality, the salt and light who advance, improve, and bring illumination to a dark world and the savor of righteousness into an atmosphere of moral retreat.

The more connected they are to one another, the more they will collaborate and cooperate together. The more they recognize and identify with each other, the greater their collective impact will be. It is with no small sense of purpose that God asked Ezekiel and I ask you, "Can these bones live?" How you honestly answer that question will be a strong indication of how ready you are to become one of those who is aligned with God's apostolic purpose as it unfolds before us. The answer must no longer be, "O, Lord, you know." It is and must be, "They can and they will." They must!

To the bones in the valley we face, we say, "Hear the word of the Lord." To the wind of the Spirit who we know so well, we say, "Come and breathe upon these slain, that they may live." None of us is able to accomplish this on our own. God is calling forth an army, an apostolic company who will stand on their feet and march together at the command of the Chief Apostle. It is time to align, and to form ranks. His Spirit is breathing new life and purpose and connectivity into His people, and into the vast marketplace army that is roughly 97-98% of the 2.5 billion Christians on the earth today.

I call forth the apostles to come forth and take your place. And as a spiritual father in the body of Christ, I repent in proxy for ignoring you and undervaluing you and seeing you primarily as a financial giver rather than as a king and priest, and for not commissioning you sooner into your sphere of assignment and five-fold or other ministry calling. Please forgive me and give the Church another chance. Give the apostolic another chance also. And teach us and impart to us what you have to share, and your wisdom, not just your resources. There is room for you...for your gifts, your dreams, your passion, your ideas and your energy. Let's join and build together, and align for kingdom purposes.

THE MODERN MARKETPLACE MOVEMENT

We live in a unique time in history which others have longed to see but failed to comprehend and understand. The beginnings of the modern marketplace movement take us back more than half a century. During those decades several influential groups of Christian business leaders were formed and became active in empowering the expansion of God's kingdom into the marketplace. We list some of those here due to the historical parallels, synergies and interrelatedness between the marketplace and apostolic movements.

The Full Gospel Business Men's Fellowship International (FGBMFI) was started in 1952 by Demos Shakarian. At one time, FGBMFI had over one million members, and is still a large, global organization led by the founder's son, Dr. Richard Shakarian. The Fellowship of Companies for Christ, International (FCCI) came later, in 1978. Kent Humphreys expanded this organization into the international arena. The International Christian Chamber of Commerce was started in 1985 by Gunnar Olson and a few others and now is in over 75 nations.

Dr. Bill Bright founded Campus Crusade for Christ in 1951 as a ministry to college students. Since that time, it has expanded its focus to include adult professionals (Priority Associates), families (Familylife), athletes (Athletes in Action), high school students (Student Venture) and numerous other groups. Bill Bright, along with Loren Cunningham of Youth With A Mission (YWAM), are usually credited with the initial vision and advancement of the Seven Mountain Mandate, or seven mind-molders of culture model.

The Christian Business Men's Connection (CBMC), originally the Christian Business Men's Committee, was founded in 1930, and expanded to an international stance (CBMC Intl) in 1938. The Fellowship of Christian Athletes (FCA) was started in 1954, soon after the founding of FGBMFI. The emphasis of FCA was on providing a Christian connection for professional football players, and later expanded to other sports and to college campuses. This, too, was a move toward diminishing the lines between the secular and the spiritual worlds. Dr. Bob Pierce began World Vision to help children orphaned in the Korean War. To provide long-term, ongoing care for children in crisis, World Vision developed its first child sponsorship program in Korea in 1953 and has expanded globally since then.

Opportunity International was founded in 1971 by two visionary leaders who were inspired to take action by their experiences with people living in extreme poverty. Al Whittaker, former president of Bristol Myers International Corporation in America, and Australian entrepreneur David Bussau sought a solution that would transform people's lives without creating dependency. Opportunity was one of the first nonprofit organizations to recognize the benefits of providing small business loans as capital to those working their way out of poverty.

In 1979, Strategic Christian Services was founded by Dennis Peacocke with a specific emphasis on bringing cultural transformation. Then, in 1980, the Christian Men's Network was formed by Dr. Edwin Louis Cole. Far-reaching in its impact, Dr. Cole provided both challenge and encouragement to men, calling them to fully embrace their God-given roles at home and in the marketplace.

Another significant men's ministry came into existence in 1990. Promise Keepers was founded by former University of Colorado head football coach, Bill McCartney. Hundreds of thousands of men were drawn together in large stadium events, and there were inspired to live their daily lives in victory and effectiveness. These ministries along with John Eldredge's *Wild at Heart* book series and boot camps, were, and continue to be a driving force among men, undergirding the integrity and significance of Christian men in every aspect of their lives, not just their spiritual arenas.

Other significant Christian business groups include the Pinnacle Forum, (which became a national organization in 1996), Convene, which draws together CEOs and business leaders in small, effective enclaves, and The C12 Group (1992). All of these groups have chapters in multiple cities and states as well as a national office. Also around the same time period, Os Hillman started Marketplace Leaders, Bob Buford launched Halftime Institute and Leadership Network, Bob Shank founded The Master's Program, Terry and Paula Parker started The National Christian Foundation, and Brett and Lyn Johnson formed The Institute for Innovation, Integration & Impact, Inc. and REP Program. The REP team has re-purposed over 250 businesses in multiple nations as kingdom companies over the last decade.

A few years later, The Barnabas Group was established, by alumni and friends of The Master's Program as a philanthropic outlet to provide executive, technical and financial support to worthy Christian ministries and paraministries. To date, The Barnabas Group has donated collectively and cumulatively through its various city chapters some $50,000,000. Most recently Al Caperna and others have helped launch call2business within the call2all movement. Al is also the Founder and CEO of Affirm

Global Development and is heavily involved in the Business as Mission (BAM) movement with other leaders like Mats Tunehag, Tom Webb, Dr. Steven Rundle, Ken Eldred, Doug Seebeck, Bruce Swanson, Hans Hamoen, and many others.

MODERN HISTORICAL CONTEXT

Beyond meetings and group-related venues for Christians outside of the context of church, a body of literature connecting the marketplace to spiritual life came into being. Between 1994 and 1998, numerous books were written with a faith and marketplace emphasis. These signaled a seismic wave of change, outlining the significant impact the marketplace brought to the church and the culture. That change has become a major movement within the Christian experience, far beyond a men's movement or gatherings for mutual encouragement.

Christians of every era of history have lived out their lives with deeply-held convictions as to how their faith affected their daily lives. However, nothing in Church history indicates the presence of a conscientious and concerted effort to bring the two together in any measure like what is happening at the beginning of the 21st century. Once the initial apostolic thrust of Christianity had dissipated and the Church had become organizationally institutionalized, the separation of the spiritual and the secular was a clear-cut distinction. With the institution of Christian business organizations, that gap began to diminish. Since the 1990s, this has changed substantially. It is, to say the least, revolutionary.

For the first time since the decline of the first century Church, the connection between the Church and the marketplace is being developed as a viable strategy for transforming social structures and influencing culture.

While Christianity has, by and large, maintained an honest awareness of the need to live one's life in the world through the convictions of one's faith, the separation between the spiritual and the sacred, especially in Western civilization, has been the norm. The development of strategic initiatives to extend the influence of the kingdom of God into social order without being controlled by the Church is a relatively new development in historical terms. Thus, the rise of Christian businessmen's organizations, separate from and ungoverned by the Church, was an entirely new development.

The elevation of interest in Christianity, coupled with social structures other than the Church, was bound to see a rise in leadership in those arenas. As the willingness to embrace such strategies grew, inevitably the number of leaders increased with it. This number has grown into an expanding circle of apostolic and prophetic leaders, apart from the Church as an institution or organization. They are destined to be the primary reformers of the marketplace, the voices directly delegated by God and sent from God to bring about true transformation in cities, cultures, regions, and social institutions. For the greater part of history, they were missing, overlooked, or ignored. Today, they are no longer the missing link in transformation; they are the transformers.

A LITERATURE FOR MARKETPLACE CHRISTIANITY

Coupled with the rise of Christian business organizations, the literature related to the church in the marketplace literally exploded. What follows is a partially-complete bibliography of some of the key books in this genre which came into print during the 1990s. Some of the earliest and most popular books included the following:

- *Halftime: Changing Your Game Plan from Success to Significance,* by Bob Buford (1994);

- *Believers in Business,* by Laura Nash (1994);

- *Doing Business God's Way: What Every Christian Called to the Marketplace Should Understand about God's Laws of Prosperity,* by Dennis Peacocke (1995);

- *Jesus, CEO: Using Ancient Wisdom for Visionary Leadership,* by Laurie Beth Jones (1996), followed by her sequel *The Path: Creating Your Mission Statement for Work and for Life* (1998);

- *Sold Out: God's Strategy for the Game of Life* by Bill McCartney (1997);

- *Loving Monday: Succeeding in Business Without Selling Your Soul* by John D. Beckett (1998); and

- *The Call: Finding and Fulfilling the Central Purpose of Your Life,* by Os Guinness (1998).

These books actually helped create a modern movement for the marketplace, building on the momentum which had begun with FGBMFI, FCCI, CBMC and other associations from earlier decades. Then the floodgates opened and a deluge of books appeared starting in 2000 with *God @ Work: Discovering the Anointing for Business,* by Rich Marshall, and have continued unabated to the present, along with a similar proliferation of books on the modern apostolic movement and apostles starting around the mid-1990s.

I want to strongly emphasize that this is not a coincidence, and these are not isolated or independent phenomenon; the modern marketplace movement, and the re-emergence of the apostles to the body of Christ are intricately connected, interrelated and correlated. Both involve a kingship or kingly dimension, among other things. We are beginning to see a fuller integration between these two movements, as education and awareness increase in this critical area, but as Paul Cuny observed in his chapter in Volume Three of this anthology, this integration is still in the early stages, but is poised to expand and explode.[5]

WHAT WORKPLACE APOSTOLIC MINISTRY LOOKS LIKE

The remainder of this chapter draws together strategic observations from some of these authors. Using their words, I have pieced together what I believe to be a reasonably accurate picture of how a workplace apostolic mindset is unfolding and how it will look in the future. It is, to say the least, a cry for a cultural transition which will affect the entire Christian community with an elevated perspective of the kingdom of God in action. According to Dr. Peter Wagner, such a transition is already underway:

"The New Apostolic Reformation is an extraordinary work of God at the close of the twentieth century, which is, to a significant extent, changing the shape of Protestant Christianity around the world. For almost 500 years Christian churches have largely functioned within traditional denominational structures of one kind or another. Particularly in the 1990s, but with roots going back for almost a century, new forms and operational procedures began to emerge in areas such as local church government, interchurch relationships, financing, evangelism, missions, prayer, leadership selection and training, the role of supernatural power, worship and other important aspects of church life."[6]

Such new forms have fostered significant changes within church organization and operation. However, they have not fostered a corresponding adjustment to the social order beyond church dynamics. There is a real and imposing cultural difference between the two worlds, a fundamentally different mindset which affects how the Church interacts with the world around it. Wagner has noted in this regard:

"Speaking of culture, many do not realize how wide the cultural gap is between the nuclear Church and the Church in the workplace...the cultural gap between the two is enormous...these each have different rule books...Obviously, this is a recipe for misunderstanding at best and disaster at worst. For all of us, one of the most urgent tasks at hand is to continue building bridges of recognition, trust and appreciation between the two Church cultures."[7]

Richard Fleming is one who helps to bridge these two cultures. He offered this perspective:

"God is passionately interested in the marketplace. He is moving His people out into the workplace, across the whole community, and He is building His Church in these places. He is raising up workplace apostles, prophets, pastors, teachers and evangelists. These remarkable men and women of God are building the Church out in the world across every element of society. They are claiming the hospitals, businesses, areas of commerce, law enforcement, officers of trade, local and central government, science and technology, education and the court system back from Babylon for the Lord."[8]

This New Apostolic Reformation speaks generally of a Second Apostolic Age, whereby the restoration of the offices listed in Ephesians chapter 4 has become so strategically important to the future. Furthermore, I have come to realize that these offices are not isolated within the organizational structure of the Church. They are, and must be, an integral part of the entire social and cultural landscape in order to be effective. It is largely through the influence and connectivity of these marketplace ministry leaders that cultural transformation will be effected. Called in various circles, the Seven Mountains of Cultural Influence, or the Seven Mind Molders of Culture, seven specific spheres of influence have been identified as having the most significant cultural impact. They are government, education, business, the arts and entertainment, media, religion, and family. Those who have the greatest influence in these areas tend to shape the mindsets of people, thus affecting the culture into which they are injected. Marketplace ministers bring godly influence to their specific spheres of authority, and thus stimulate transformation within those arenas. Wagner elaborated on this point as follows:

"Now that we are in the Second Apostolic Age, we recognize that pastors are not the spiritual gatekeepers of the city, as we once thought. Apostles, more specifically territorial apostles, must be seen as the spiritual gatekeepers of the city. Some of these territorial apostles will emerge from the nuclear Church and most likely will include certain megachurch pastors, but I am convinced that the great majority of them will come from the extended Church. Our workplace apostles have the greatest potential for leading the forces for city transformation. They are the ones most deeply embedded in the six non-church mountains, or molders, of culture. They are winners. They know how to make things happen once they are given the opportunity."[9]

The expansion of the apostolic into the workplace rightly generates some questions and potential concerns as well as expectations, both for ecclesiastical leaders and for marketplace ministers. Unless there is a strategically- and relationally-sound connection and integration between the two, as I advocate here, the potential of conflict, offense, mistrust and misunderstanding looms large. Every age of the Church has been plagued with counterfeit and false leaders, but at no time since the first century have we been more vulnerable than the present.

The contemporary restoration of the apostolic is vitally necessary, and understanding the role of true apostles is of the utmost importance. Dr. Michael Scantlebury stated, "It has become very evident that a new day has dawned in the earth, as the Lord restores the foundational ministry of the Apostle back to the church."[10] He also noted: "There is an awesome, powerful, militant church rising in the earth, as Apostles are being restored to take their place alongside the Prophets, Evangelists, Pastors and Teachers to bring the church into unity and to a place of maturity for function."[11]

Scantlebury further observed:

"We also hear of Apostles now leading the way for the corporate Christ (the saints) to enter a new dynamic and dimension of destiny, with Apostles being recognized in virtually every major stream of the marketplace. From Hollywood to 'The Hood,' Apostles are coming forth in an accelerated thrust, for the reshaping of the Church into the accurate patterns of corporate destiny, transitioning mentalities from Church to Kingdom, into the present administration of Christ's triumphal reign. In such promised order, we affirm that present truth Apostles bring to the table so-to-speak, the very plan of God for the ages, as wise master builders, (Blacksmiths) reconstructing the present position of the Church into the ongoing and progressive rhythm and revelation, that the corporate body is the habitation of God."[12]

Perhaps we are theory rich and practice poor as a people. We have acquired a great deal of insight and information regarding both the substance and the necessity of the extended church. Theory, however, does not implement change; action does. The integration of the nuclear Church with the extended Church must not be passed over. To the degree that God's people are responsible to engage with God's kingdom, we are a covenant people. We hold to the covenant promises of God, both for the future and for the immediate circumstances which are in the world around us. *"The secret of the Lord is for those who fear Him, and He will make them know His covenant"* (Ps. 25:14). In this regard, Scantlebury commented:

> "You can seek to activate and desire to have an operation or manifestation of a spiritual gift without capturing, walking or moving in the relevant move of God that is producing that manifestation or gift...one can receive information about the apostolic, but never embrace and walk in the apostolic. This has been the problem with the church for centuries—we get all this information, but the corresponding walk to match the talk is lacking. In this hour, the Lord is truly releasing the technology for us to walk in what is being released as we tap into His 'apostolic dimension.'"[13]

For a fuller, in-depth explanation, analysis and discussion of this technology to access and appropriate the apostolic dimension, I refer you to Dr. Gordon E. Bradshaw, *The Technology of Apostolic Succession*. This discussion of the Apostolic Industry is a representative sample from this book.

> "There is a powerful sovereign state of being that has arrived in the New Testament Church. It is called *The Apostolic Industry*. During this season, the world is going to begin witnessing the supernatural hand of God in so many different areas of human existence that there will be great waves of conversion. The supernatural *"intelligence"* and the supernatural *"intent"* of God are going to become powerfully evident on a global scale. The restoration of spiritual lineages is going to occur. This will change the church's ability to affect nations and climates because the spirit of continuity will finally be in place. This sovereign event will do for the Kingdom of God what the Industrial Revolution did for the world of technology. It will literally *"re-invent"* the way that God is introduced and shared with the world. All that the Apostolic ministry should evolve into becoming will see fulfillment in this season. This will be the final stage of preparation for the release of sons and daughters into their completed destinies and purposes in the Kingdom of God."[14]

Wagner also noted the importance of workplace apostles to world missions:

> "One of the more promising strategic changes relates to the Church in the workplace. It could well be that apostles of the workplace, if creatively activated, will turn out to be one of the strongest missionary forces

we have ever known. If they see their businesses as Kingdom businesses, they can move through doors that would never be opened to traditional missionaries. Their potential for catalyzing social transformation can be enormous. It is up to the body of Christ as a whole to recognize, affirm, support and encourage apostolic workplace missionaries."[15]

He then added:

"Furthermore, workplace apostles have more experience in dealing with large sums of money than do most nuclear church leaders. They know how to manage. They understand the financial markets. They agree that idle money is a drag on extending the Kingdom. They avoid the pitfalls of fear and greed. They have access to the seven molders of culture (religion, family, arts and entertainment, education, government, media, and business). With them in place, we can expect that God will release the wealth of the wicked that he has been promising to the righteous, large sums of wealth that will be used to bring about significant, measurable social transformation."[16]

While it is tempting to embark on a discussion of biblical stewardship, financial management and wealth transfer here in relation to apostles, that is not the primary focus of this volume, and I will save that discussion for a future book, and defer to my colleagues in Section 10 and Volume Five for the time being. They are eminently qualified to address this topic and have done so in exceptional and exemplary fashion. I will, however, share one quote from Gordon La Du about this as follows:

"Why do we call them Marketplace Apostles? The apostles of the New Testament were people of vision and courage. They saw a need to establish churches, support them and make sure good fruit came from them. They were endued with power from on high to fulfill the vision they were given. In other words, they had an anointing to build something others couldn't see.

"Likewise with Marketplace Apostles they see what others can't. They are endued with power from on high to build a business in the Marketplace, to support it and make sure good fruit comes from it. Also, they walk in an understanding that they are stewards or overseers of God's businesses. The vision, the plans, the businesses, and the fruit all belong to the Lord. MPA's live in the comfort of understanding that they are not their own but rather they are bought with a price and their passion is to do the will of Him who sent them.

"Large dollar amounts don't seem to faze them. Actually, the larger the need or challenge, the better they like it. Don't tell them something can't be done, especially if it is the will of the Lord! Be careful not to make the mistake that you know what a MPA 'looks like.' He or she may be a businessperson in a suit, a lawyer, a plumber, landscaper or realtor. **Whatever one of his/ her endeavors is, they have a heart of an entrepreneur. The heart of a MPA in the marketplace is like a band of marines landing on a beach ready for action."**[17]

Building on La Du's description and list of important attributes of a workplace apostle, Aaron Evans commented:

"This Apostolic Reformation is changing the way apostles and prophets have been used, no longer just emphasizing the ecclesiastical realm. Now the Lord of light is releasing apostles and prophets in economics, technology, science, government, businesses, the military, and the arts. This is not the first time God has done this. Moses, being a prophet, administrated the social, political, economic, and military systems of Israel. Joseph's prophetic anointing was used through his office of prime minister that involved economics, management, and resources. Nehemiah, in rebuilding the wall of Jerusalem, functioned as a master builder. His anointing covered the religious, social, economic, and political arenas. The list goes on as He uses His people to reform and invade."[18]

Similarly, Dr. Jeff Van Wyk commented on this as follows:

"Throughout history God has always used people to build His kingdom and He has always raised up the right leaders for each generation to fulfill His purposes for that particular season. These leaders represent God and were sent by Him to advance His plans. Depending on the mission, God would send a person who had the unique characteristics needed to perform the task. They functioned in an apostolic anointing that empowered them to overcome any obstacles placed by the enemy to hinder God's work which generally involved the nations."

"After Pentecost, the apostolic ministry was birthed and the apostles were sent by God to preach the gospel everywhere and to establish churches."[19]

Van Wyk also added: "The restoration of the apostles will bring the necessary stability to the family of God that fathers and mothers bring to natural families."[20] He continued, "When the apostles are restored to the church, the five-fold ministry will be complete and the apostolic anointing will flow and bring divine order to the house of God. The church will come into the fulness of God's power and anointing that will be needed to meet any challenge and bring in the harvest at the end of the age."[21]

As Bill Vincent has noted, even churches will look and function differently as apostles and the apostolic are restored and embraced:

> "A whole new government is coming to the church. It's apostolic.
>
> "This new structure will encompass apostles, prophets, pastors, teachers, evangelists and team ministries running churches. They will yield to one another and recognize each other after the spirit and have freedom to operate in their different anointing. Competition will not exist; friendship, relationship and a team spirit will be the order of the day. Senior pastors will trust their senior prophet, senior teacher and apostolic authority, based on their solid relationship. There will be camaraderie in what God is doing. Local churches will exist, but the face and the government of the local church will change. I see this new face or structure being established in apostolic centers."[22]

Finally, Dr. Bill Hamon has identified the current era as a Third Reformation, which he calls the Saint's Movement:

> "In April of 2007 the Saints Movement was birthed and witnessed by several major national and international prophets who were present at the meeting. The full explanation of the ministry and purpose of the Saints Movement is presented in The Day of the Saints. The revelation and teaching of the Saints Movement was essential in preparation for the Third Reformation. Some of the key revelations included the following: every saint is a minister and Kingdom demonstrator

in the marketplace as well as in the local church; the saints need to be activated in their divine gifts and ministries; saints possess and demonstrate the Kingdom of God; every saint has the power and privilege of demonstrating the supernatural works of God and taking that power outside the wall of the local church and meeting the practical needs of mankind, plus many more truths and ministries."[23]

CONCLUSION

An alliance between the ecclesiastical community and the marketplace is now being manifested across the globe and this will increase and accelerate with each passing year as the end times unfold. The rise of apostolic and prophetic men and women within the various spheres of influence throughout the world is not to be taken lightly. We have seen again and again how effective a vital Christian presence is within each of the seven cultural spheres. These spheres, known both as the Seven Mountains of Cultural Influence, and the Seven Mind-Molders of Society, cannot be transformed solely through the sphere of Religion. Even if they were to be challenged from the very pinnacle of that mountain, as has occurred periodically, they would each still need to be influenced from within.

In that regard, Tommi Femrite commented that "...the church has for the most part applied the Seven Mountain strategy strictly to evangelistic efforts at the cost of excluding all other avenues in which the church should operate... Clearly, the Religion Mountain alone has not been able to transform the world. Every mountain must be inhabited and ruled by the church for it to rise to the position God intends."[24] It is important to clarify that the term "church" as used here means a living organism and not a static institution, and that the term "ruled" means influenced.

As I have tried to demonstrate, a wide-ranging company of apostolic and prophetic leaders globally understand and encourage the marriage which must now occur. Without strategic determination and committed action on the part of the Church community, progress will continue to be slow—much slower than necessary or desirable. The night is far spent and the day soon approaches. Culture will not transition for the better unless the influences which direct its change are better. Marketplace apostolic and prophetic leaders have the most significant platforms from which to address the cultural and fast deterioration around us.

Pulpits must become aflame with passion to implement marketplace and kingdom strategies, but rhetoric alone will not get the job done. Ecclesiastical five-fold leaders must be prepared to recognize, receive, honor and embrace their increasingly effective marketplace counterparts, and vice versa. The Church is not under attack from the marketplace per se—not really. It is under assault from the enemy, however, and those indiviudals and organizations which the enemy is able to influence or control, but few if any of those whom God has positioned in marketplace ministry have any real desire to supplant ecclesiastical leaders.

They know that the Church—along with a vast array of parachurch ministries—is a vital link in the development and deployment of effective Christians throughout culture. We cannot survive without it. We must, however, not be seduced into thinking the Church is the whole answer. We must broaden our focus and our efforts to include the kingdom of God and the Seven Mountains of Culture.

Hirsch and Catchim effectively summarize the decision at hand facing Church leaders:

> "We are designed for continuous movement, and **apostles are the permanent revolutionaries given to the church to catalyze the permanent revolution.** If we can receive them yet again, we not only open ourselves up to a permanent revolution, we also open ourselves up more fully to the One who has given them to us. **It is not too much to say that in the vocation and person of Jesus, apostles stand at the door and knock. If we let them in, we will, once again, God willing, experience the permanent revolution that we were intended to be in the first place."**[25]

Apostles are indeed knocking, not just on the doors of traditional churches, but also on the doors and gates of the kingdom of God and the Seven Mountains of Culture, where the Holy Spirit is moving. That is one reason we have not heard them, or been as responsive as they deserve and as the times require. It is time to reembrace our apostolic brothers and sisters, welcome them back into the Church, and receive them as God's Ambassadors once again.

The remainder of this book, and the volumes which will follow, are presented with a wide variety of viewpoints and perspectives from seasoned apostolic leaders around the world and across the Seven Mountains. They may not agree on every point of theology, but they all agree, however, that the Church must embrace its responsibility to equip, empower, and release a vast army of Christian warriors in the Seven Mountains of Culture and the workplace who are intent on advancing God's kingdom.

Victoria Boyson has described a recent vision she had of what that army looks like--an army of glory:

"The Lord showed me a glimpse of His incredible last day army of glory; I saw God's children filled with Him. I saw Him literally impart Himself into each individual, and as He did, they were transformed. They were not only radiant in the darkness, but also seemed alien to the rest of the world around them in their countenance and behavior. They were indifferent to the things that seemed to compel the world. **Not driven by selfish desires, their only thoughts were for God's purposes to be executed on earth, and this empowered them with incredible joy.**

"In the vision, the earth was indeed in a truly darkened condition, yet God had established His people all over the world. **Standing firm with quiet peace, they emitted incredible strength and confidence.** They radiated immense peace when all around them was chaos and fear. **The peace they carried was a glorious beacon of hope to the world, and it gave them great influence and authority.**

"I felt they easily represented the Scripture, *'Each one of you will put to flight a thousand of the enemy, for the Lord your God fights for you...'* (Joshua 23:10, NLT).

"**They were truly an army of great strength. Their strength lay in purposing to live only for the Lord's Kingdom. They were filled with Him and purposed for God to be glorified in and through their lives, no matter the personal sacrifice required.**"[26]

God is raising up a new generation of apostles and apostolic teams to mobilize and lead His apostolic movement, apostolic networks, and apostolic army. It is indeed an army of glory, strategically positioned and connected in the Seven Mountains of Culture, armed with spiritual weapons, filled with the Holy Spirit, clothed in robes of righteousness, and led by the King of Glory.

This concludes my introductory section and I now invite you to continue reading the chapters that follow from other apostles and apostolic leaders (contributing authors) in the subsequent sections and volumes of this anthology.

ENDNOTES

1. Chuck Ripka, *God Out of The Box*, pp. 184-85, author's emphasis. Lake Mary, FL: Charisma House, 2007.

2. For other examples of modern workplace apostles, see among others: Rich Marshall, *God @ Work, Vols. I & II*; Rick Heeren, *Marketplace Miracles*; Ed Silvoso, *Anointed for Business, Women: God's Secret Weapon,* and *Transformation*; Morris Ruddick, *The Joseph-Daniel Calling, The Heart of a King, Something More* and *God's Economy, Israel and the Nations*; Bob Fraser, *Marketplace Christianity*; Paul Cuny, *Secrets of the Kingdom Economy*; Laurie Beth Jones, *The Path, Jesus CEO,* and *Jesus in Blue Jeans*; Bob Buford, *Half Time: Changing Your Game Plan from Success to Significance*; John Beckett, *Loving Monday: Succeeding in Business Without Selling Your Soul,* and *Mastering Monday: A Practical Guide to Integrating Faith and Work*; Pat Gelsinger, *The Juggling Act: Bringing Balance to Your Faith, Family, and Work*; Bill McCartney, *4th and Goal, Two Minute Warning,* and *Sold Out*; Os Hillman, *The Upside of Adversity: Rising from the Pit to Greatness, Change Agent: Engaging your Passion to be the One who Makes a Difference,* and *The 9 to 5 Window: How Faith Can Transform the Workplace*; Linda Rios Brook, *Wake Me When It's Over,* and *Frontline Christians in a Bottom Line World*; Kent Humphreys, *Shepherding Horses, Vols. I & II*; Ken Eldred, *God Is at Work: Transforming People and Nations Through Business,* and *The Integrated Life: Experience the Powerful Advantage of Integrating Your Faith and Work*; Dennis Peacocke, *Doing Business God's Way,* and *The Emperor Has No Clothes*; Angus Buchan, *Faith Like Potatoes*; John Garfield and Harold Eberle, *Releasing Kings*; Dr.

John Muratori, *Money By Design;* Richard Everett, *Whatever Happened to the Promised Land?;* Lee Domingue, *Pearls of the King;* Dr. Nick Castellano, *Awaken the Sleeper;* Ed Turose, *The Focus Fulfilled Life;* Lloyd Reeb and Bill Wellons, *Unlimited Partnership;* Mark Ritchie, *God In The Pits;* Sher Valenzuela, *The World's Best Customer;* Dr. Robert Needham and Mark Schrade, *Why Divide When You Can Multiply?;* Mike Floyd, *Supernatural Business;* Wende Jones: *The God Port: Accessing God in Real Time;* Brandon Pope, *Spiritual Lessons from Wall Street;* Ralph Doudera, *Wealth Conundrum;* Larry Julian, *God Is My CEO,* and *God Is My Success;* Stephen DeSilva, *Money and the Prosperous Soul;* Graham Power and Dion Forster, *Transform Your Work Life;* Jeff Caliguire, *The Convergence: Seven Resolves to Release What You Were Born to Do;* Daniel Meylan, *The Compound Effect: The Transformational Power of Business Competency & Spiritual Maturity;* Dr. Pat Robertson, *The Secret Kingdom;* Jerry Tuma, *From Boom to Bust and Beyond;* Drs. Tony and Felicity Dale, *Small is Big, Simply Church,* and *The Rabbit and the Elephant;* Brett Johnson, *Convergence, Lemon Leadership, Repurposing Capital,* and *Transforming Society;* Kris Vallotton, *Supernatural Ways of Royalty;* Danny Silk, *Culture of Honor;* Dr. Paul Costa and John Kelly, *Power to Get Wealth;* Tim Redmond, *Power to Create;* Martin Powell, *Money Matters: In My Kingdom;* Dr. Alistair Petrie, *Releasing Heaven on Earth, A Sacred Trust,* and *Transformed!: 10 Principles for Sustaining Genuine Revival;* Candace Long, *Wired for Creativity;* Dr. Gordon E. Bradshaw, *Authority for Assignment: Releasing the Mantle of God's Government in the Marketplace;* Dr. Tommi Femrite, *Invading the Seven Mountains with Intercession;* Dr. Ted Baehr, *Faith in God and Generals, The Media-Wise Family, The Culture-Wise Family, Amazing Grace of Freedom, So You Want to Be in Pictures?,* and *How to Succeed in Hollywood (Without Losing Your Soul);* Alice Patterson, *Bridging the Racial & Political Divide;* Aaron Evans, *The Emerging Daniel Company;* Bill Swad Sr., *Wealth Building Strategies;* Dr. Randall Sprague, *The Cyrus Anointing, The Money is in the Mantle* and *Women With Wealth;* Henry Falany, *God, Gold & Glory!;* Dr. Theresa Phillips, *The Monarchy of Heaven;* Kay Haugen, *From the Poorhouse to the Penthouse;* Norm Miller, *Beyond The Norm;* Don Ostrom, *Millionaire in the Pew;* Bill Hart, *Show Me Your Glory;* Greg Dalessandri, *God's Rhythm: The Key to God's Prosperity for This Age;* Dr. Berin Gilfillan, *Unlocking the Abraham Promise;* Tim Taylor, *Developing Apostolic Strategy;* Bill Ebert, *Power of an Endless Life;* Dr. A. L. Gill, *Destined for Dominion;* Judy Jacobs, *Take It By Force!,* and *Stand Strong;* Dr. Brian Scott, *God's Pattern for Business Success;* Mark Gorman, *God's Plan for Prosperity;* Dr. Nasir Siddiki, *Kingdom Principles of Financial Increase;* Mark Pfeifer, *Change Agents, Breaking the Spirit of Poverty,* and *Alignment: Blueprint for the 21st Century Church;* Patricia King, *Help, God! I'm Broke;* Ed Delph, *Nation Strategy,* and *The 5-Minute Miracle;* Dr. Kluane Spake, *40 Day Focus on Prosperity;* Faytene Kryskow Grassechi, *Stand On Guard,* and *Marked;* Dr. Margaret H. (Peggy) Hartshorn, *Foot Soldiers: Armed with Love;* Sam Soleyn, *My Father, My Father;* Bart Pierce, *The Bribe of Great Price, Cover Me in the Day of Battle,* and *Seeking Our Brothers, Prayer Works;* Dr. Gayle Rogers, *Healing the Traumatized Soul;* Eugene Strite, *God's Principles of Financial Success;* Glenn Henderson, *Treasures of Darkness:* Dr. Joseph Umidi, *Transformational Coaching;* Dan Stratton, *Divine Provision: Positioning God's Kings for Financial Conquest;* Dudley Perio, *Living in God's Glory;* Walt Pilcher, *The Five-fold Effect: Unlocking Power Leadership and Results for Your Organization;* Mornay Johnson and Dr. Mark Chironna, *Godly Success: God's Blueprint for Success and Prosperity in Your Life;* Lynn Scarborough, *Spiritual Moms* and *Talk Like Jesus;* Bob Harrison, *Power Points for Success,* and *Power Points for Increase;* Don Wood, *Father Power: Generational Leadership, Secret of a Three Generation Vision,* and *The Arena of Truth;* Doug Spada, *Monday Morning Atheist;* Dr. Erik Kudlis, *The Omnipotent God: And the Impotent Church?;* Dr. Marlene McMillan, *Declaration of Dependence;* Teri Werner, *From Train Wreck to Transformation;* Gunnar Olson, *Business Unlimited;* Dr. Elizabeth Hairston, *Apostolic Intervention, Gates of Freedom, The Wonder of Worship;* Margelee Hylton, *Glory Explosion The Heart of a True Worshiper;* Doug Stringer, *Who's Your Daddy Now?: The Cry of a Generation in Pursuit of Fathers;* Dr. Paul Williams, *When All Plans Fail: Be Ready for Disasters;* Dr. Sandy Kulkin, *The DISC Personality System - Enhance Communication and Relationships;* Kenn Renner, *First Time Home Buying Secrets;* Ray

Landers, *Wealth or Mammon?*; Dr. Ron Jenson, *Taking the Lead, Life Maximizers, Fathers and Sons,* and *Make a Life Not Just a Living*; David Van Koevering, *Elsewhen, Keys to Taking Your Quantum Leap, Quantum Healing, Quantum Prayers,* and *Quantum Entrepreneurism*; Craig Hill and Earl Pitts, *Wealth, Riches & Money*; Dr. William (Bill) Greenman III, *How to Find Your Purpose in Life*; Dr. Candice Smithyman, *His Sufficiency for My Authenticity: Eight Keys to Authentic Relationship with God and Others*; Jack Serra, *Marketplace Marriage & Revival: The Spiritual Connection*; Buck Stephens, *The Coming Financial Revolution,* and *Secrets of a Supernatural World*; Doug Sheddy, *My Experience in the Glory*; William (Bill) Thomas, *Kingdom Holdings, Inc.: Rise of the Sons of God*; Dennis Wiedrick, *A Royal Priesthood*; John Gagliardi, *The Marketplace: Our Mission*; Paul Gazelka, *Marketplace Ministers*; David High, *Kings and Priests*; Tom Barrett, *Building & Protecting Kingdom Wealth*; Michael Pink, *Selling Among Wolves*; Marc Nuttle, *Moment Of Truth: How our Government's Addiction to Spending* and *Power Will Destroy Everything that Makes America Great*; Patrick Ondrey, *You're More Than You Think You Are,* and *The Force of Vision*; Dr. Keith Johnson, *The Confidence Makeover, Leading in Crisis Times,* and *The Confidence Solution: Reinvent Yourself, Explode Your Business, Skyrocket Your Income*; Robert Ricciardelli, *Refining Your L.I.F.E.—Principles of Love, Identity, Formation, and Excellence*; Dr. Rodney Howard-Browne, *The Touch of God, Flowing in the Holy Spirit,* and *Seeing Jesus as He Really Is*; Dr. Bill Winston, *Seeding for the Billion Flow, The Kingdom of God in You: Discover the Greatness of God's Power Within,* and *Transform Your Thinking, Transform Your Life: Radically Change Your Thoughts, Your World, and Your Destiny*; Lt. Gen. William G. ("Jerry") Boykin (US Army, Ret.), *Never Surrender: A Soldier's Journey to the Crossroads of Faith and Freedom,* and *Danger Close*; Natasha Vermaak Grbich, *The Protocol of the Kingdom*; John Beehner, *The Freedom Revolution…Rocking Our World,* and *True Wealth by the Book: How 100 Inspirational Americans Encountered Character, Moral, and Spiritual Truths*; Chuck Vollmer, *Jobenomics: A Plan for America: 20 Million New Jobs by 2020*; Hal Sacks, *Two Nations One Prayer*; Cheryl Sacks, *The Prayer Saturated Church* and *Prayer Saturated Kids*; Dr. Raymond Larson and

Deborah Larson, *SHIFT: The Transfer of Wealth;* Ray East, *The Life of Manny: Discovering Why People Follow a Leader;* Chinedum Benjamin Anyacho, *Bold, Fresh Wine;* Dr. Cindy Trimm, *Commanding Your Morning, Rules of Engagement,* and *The Art of War for Spiritual Battle;* Dr. Joseph Mattera, *Kingdom Awakening, Kingdom Revolution, Ruling In The Gates: Preparing the Church to Transform Cities,* and *Walk in Generational Blessings: Leaving a Legacy of Transformation through your Family;* Dr. Samuel Chand, *Failure: The Womb of Success, Who Moved Your Ladder?, Cracking Your Church's Culture Code: Seven Keys to Unleashing Vision and Inspiration, Who's Holding Your Ladder?, What's Shakin' Your Ladder?: 15 Challenges All Leaders Face, Seven Keys to Unleashing Vision* and *Inspiration, Ladder Shifts: New Realities, Rapid Change, Your Destiny;* Bishop Harry R. Jackson Jr., *The Warrior's Heart: Rules of Engagement for the Spiritual War Zone,* and *Personal Faith, Public Policy* (with Tony Perkins); George Barna, *Revolution, Maximum Faith, Think Like Jesus,* and *Futurecast: What Today's Trends Mean for Tomorrow's World;* Tamara Lowe, *Get Motivated!: Overcome Any Obstacle, Achieve Any Goal, and Accelerate Your Success with Motivational DNA;* June Hunt, *Bonding with Your Teen through Boundaries, How to Handle Your Emotions, How to Forgive...When You Don't Feel Like It, Seeing Yourself Through God's Eyes,* and *How to Rise Above Abuse;* Dr. John Benefiel, *Binding the Strongman Over America: Healing the Land, Transferring Wealth,* and *Advancing the Kingdom;* Dr. W. Paul ("Buddy") Crum Jr., *Much More Than a Job: Your 24:7 Mission;* Cindy Jacobs, *Possessing the Gates of the Enemy: A Training Manual for Militant Intercession, Women of Destiny: Releasing You to Fulfill God's Call in Your Life, The Supernatural Life: Experience the Power of God in Your Everyday Life, Reformation Manifesto: Your Part in God's Plan to Change Nations Today, The Voice of God: How God Speaks Personally and Corporately to His Children Today,* and *Deliver Us From Evil: Putting A Stop To The Occultic Influence Invading Your Home and Community;* Robert Henderson, *The Caused Blessing: Connecting to Apostolic Power Through Strategic Giving, Consecrated Business: Apostolically Aligning the Marketplace, Apostolic Dominion Through Signs and Wonders,* and *A Voice of Reformation: An Apostolic and Prophetic View of Each of the Seven*

Mountains in a Reformed State; Dr. Mark Chironna, *The Power of Passionate Intention: The Elisha Principle, Live Your Dream: Planning for Success, Seven Secrets to Unfolding Destiny, Breaking the Boundaries of the Possible,* and *Beyond The Shadow Of Doubt: Overcoming Hidden Doubts that Sabotage Your Faith;* David Turner, *Seeds of Faith* and Woody Young, *Business Guide to Copyright Law: What You Don't Know Can Co$t You!, Uncommon Wisdom, Countdown to Eternity, Christian Book Writers' Marketing Guide.* See also books by or biographies of such individuals as R. G. LeTourneau, J. C. Penney, Mary Kay Ash, Demos Shakarian, George Washington Carver, etc. Three such sources are *Christian Business Legends* by Rick Williams, *True Wealth by the Book* by John Beehner, and *Think and Grow Rich* by Napoleon Hill. To my knowledge, there is no extant list of workplace apostles, nor a comprehensive list of ecclesiastical apostles historically, except in heaven. I apologize in advance to any apostles that I have inadvertently omitted or overlooked from this partial listing, which barely scratches the surface, or for anyone listed who believes they are not an apostle, and ask for your forgiveness and grace.

3. Jonas Clark, *Governing Churches & Antioch Apostles: Discovering the New Apostolic Reformation,* p. 252. Hallandale, FL: Spirit of Life Publishing, 2000.

4. That story is told in one of my earlier books, *Partnering with the Prophetic.* Leander, TX: Kingdom House Publishing, 2011.

5. Paul Cuny, "The Apostolic Release," in *Aligning with the Apostolic, Vol. III.* Leander, TX: Kingdom House Publishing, 2013.

6. Dr. C. Peter Wagner, *Churchquake! How the New Apostolic Reformation is Shaking Up the Church As We Know It,* p. 1. Ventura, CA: Regal Books, 1999.

7. Dr. C. Peter Wagner, *Dominion! How Kingdom Action Can Change The World,* pp. 144-145. Grand Rapids, MI: Chosen Books, 2008.

8. Richard Fleming, *The Glory Returns to the Workplace,* pp. 1-2. Pessaca, Italy: Destiny Image Europe, 2004.

9. Wagner, *Dominion! How Kingdom Action Can Change The World,* pp. 154-155.

10. Dr. Michael Scantlebury, *Five Pillars of the Apostolic: Towards a Mature Church*, p. 13. Winnipeg, MB: Word Alive Press, 2000.

11. Ibid, p. 14.

12. Dr. Michael Scantlebury, *Apostolic Reformation: The Equipping Dimension of the Apostolic*, pp. 69-70. Winnipeg, MB: Word Alive Press, 2005.

13. Ibid, p. 191.

14. Dr. Gordon E. Bradshaw, *The Technology of Apostolic Succession: Transferring the Purposes of God to the Next Generation of Kingdom Citizens*, p. 217. Leander, TX: Kingdom House Publishing, 2010.

15. Wagner, *Dominion! How Kingdom Action Can Change The World*, p. 208.

16. Ibid, pp. 208-209.

17. Gordon La Du, *Marketplace Apostle*, pp. 8-9. Portland, OR: JCF Ministry, 2006, 2011.

18. Aaron Evans, *The Emerging Daniel Company*, p. 167. Boxford, MA: The Emerging Daniel Company Intl., 2010.

19. 19. Dr. Jeff Van Wyck, *The Apostolic Anointing: Preparing the Church for the Coming Glory*, Kindle 57% -- 1933 of 3413. Baton Rouge, LA: Team Impact Publishing Group, 2012.

20. Ibid, Kindle 9% -- 303 of 3443.

21. Ibid, Kindle 10% -- 349 of 3443.

22. Bill Vincent, *Apostolic Breakthrough: Birthing God's Purpose*, Kindle 78% -- 2030 of 2617. Litchfield, IL: Revival Waves of Glory Books & Publishing, 2012.

23. Dr. Bill Hamon, *Prophetic Scriptures Yet to Be Fulfilled*, p. 167. Shippensburg, PA: Destiny Image Publishers, 2010.

24. Dr. Tommi Femrite, *Invading the Seven Mountains with Intercession: How to Reclaim Society Through Prayer*, pp. 13, 19. Lake Mary, FL: Creation House, 2011.

25. Alan Hirsch and Tim Catchim, *The Permanent Revolution: Apostolic Imagingation and Practice for the 21st Century Church*, p. 249, author's emphasis. San Francisco, CA: Jossey-Bass, 2012.

26. Victoria Boyson, *His Passionate Pursuit*, from Chapter 6, "An Army of Glory," as reported on *The Elijah List*, 9/17/12, author's emphasis. Maricopa, AZ: XP Publishing, 2012.

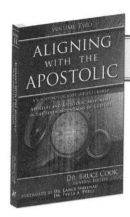

VOLUME TWO

ALIGNING WITH THE APOSTOLIC
A FIVE VOLUME ANTHOLOGY OF
APOSTLESHIP & THE APOSTOLIC MOVEMENT
DR. BRUCE COOK, GENERAL EDITOR

Foreword by Dr. Lance Wallnau
Foreword by Dr. Paula A. Price

VOLUME TWO

SECTION 2:
Apostolic Government

SECTION 3:
Apostolic Foundations

www.KingdomHouse.net

KINGDOM HOUSE
PUBLISHING

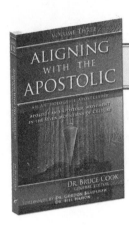

VOLUME THREE

ALIGNING WITH THE APOSTOLIC
A FIVE VOLUME ANTHOLOGY OF APOSTLESHIP & THE APOSTOLIC MOVEMENT
DR. BRUCE COOK, GENERAL EDITOR

Foreword by Dr. Gordon Bradshaw
Foreword by Dr. Bill Hamon

VOLUME THREE

SECTION 4:
Apostolic Intercession

SECTION 5:
Apostolic Character & Maturity

SECTION 6:
Apostolic Education

www.KingdomHouse.net

KINGDOM HOUSE
PUBLISHING

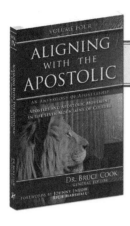

VOLUME FOUR

ALIGNING WITH THE APOSTOLIC
A FIVE VOLUME ANTHOLOGY OF
APOSTLESHIP & THE APOSTOLIC MOVEMENT
DR. BRUCE COOK, GENERAL EDITOR

Foreword by Johnny Enlow
Foreword by Rich Marshall

VOLUME FOUR

SECTION 7:
Apostolic Fathers & Mothers

SECTION 8:
Apostolic Leadership & Teams

SECTION 9:
Apostolic Creativity
& Innovation

www.KingdomHouse.net

KINGDOM HOUSE PUBLISHING

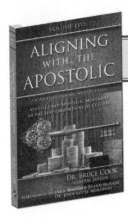

VOLUME FIVE

ALIGNING WITH THE APOSTOLIC
A FIVE VOLUME ANTHOLOGY OF
APOSTLESHIP & THE APOSTOLIC MOVEMENT
DR. BRUCE COOK, GENERAL EDITOR

Foreword by Lynn Wilford Scarborough
Foreword by Dr. John Louis Muratori

VOLUME FIVE

SECTION 10:
Apostolic Multiplication & Wealth

SECTION 11:
Apostolic Culture

SECTION 12:
Summary & Conclusion

www.KingdomHouse.net

KINGDOM HOUSE
PUBLISHING

Made in the USA
San Bernardino, CA
15 November 2019